Why Suyá Sing

A Musical Anthropology of an Amazonian People

Anthony Seeger

University of Illinois Press
Urbana and Chicago

∞ This book is printed on acid-free paper.

P 6 5 4 3 2

Library of Congress Cataloging-in-Publication Data

Seeger, Anthony.
Why Suyá sing: a musical anthropology of an Amazonian
people / Anthony Seeger.
p.   cm.
Originally published: Cambridge : Cambridge University
Press, 1987.
Includes bibliographical references and index.
ISBN 10: 0-252-07202-2 (pbk.: alk. paper)
ISBN 13: 978-0-252-07202-4
1. Suya Indians—Music—History and criticism. I. Title.
ML3575.B7S36   2004
780'.89'984—dc22   2004007220

TO

my family and friends: without the
one there would be no life; without
the other life is not worth living
and

FOR

Judy and the Suyá, companions of
many days and nights, in memory
of the songs we sang, the stories
we told, and the difficulties and
pleasures we shared.

Contents

Illustrations

viii

Figures

Tables

Audio examples on the CD

The accompanying CD includes the twenty-two audio tracks originally released on cassette in 1987 with the exception of example 1.2 (track 2), which was replaced with another example and a bonus track (23), "The Anthropologist Song," recorded in 2004. The 1987 master was digitized by Pete Reiniger of the Smithsonian Institution Center for Folklife and Cultural Heritage. The author's announcements (necessary on a cassette but not a CD) were removed and some digital editing improved the examples. He also recorded the bonus track.

The Suyá music recordings were made on Uher reel-to-reel tape recorders (mono and stereo) using Uher microphones with the tape moving at 7.5 inches per second. Darkness, dust, wind, fatigue, and the challenges of portable equipment already old in the 1970s affected their quality. The Suyá sometimes made mistakes too. But, in the compensation, this is the essence of musical performance: these pieces are sung and danced in euphoria of the moment with the inevitable slip-ups of life itself. In the coming years I plan to make some of the video recordings of the 1996 performance available, which I believe will further enhance readers' understanding of Suyá music and this book.

Ethical Advisory

These recordings were made with the knowledge and approval of the Suyá and have been published with their permission. In 2001 they specifically requested that their music not be posted on the Internet. All rights of composition (where applicable) and performance are reserved by the members of the Suyá community. Permission must be obtained and royalties paid to the community for any further use, as required by U.S. copyright legislation. The unauthorized use of these recordings is prohibited not only by law, but also by the moral obligation to prevent the exploitation of these artists. Interested licensees should contact the author.

Track No.	Chapter Ref.	Title (Time)
1	1.1	Hwinkradi's shout song opens the Mouse Ceremony (0:46)
2	1.2	Informal speech in the men's house (0:52)
3	1.3	Rainy season unison song (7:23)
4	1.4	Boys and young men sing shout songs (11:04)
5	1.4	Author and his wife sing Abiyoyo (1:09) (Melody Traditional)
6	2.1	A myth told by Iawekidi (3:13)
7	2.2	Instruction by Takuti (0:50)
8	2.3	Invocation by Takuti (1:10)

Preface

This is a book about singing in a native South American community; it is also a book about the study of music and the role of music in social processes. It addresses a number of deceptively simple questions about musical events in a small Brazilian Indian community, such as Why do members of a particular group value song so much? Why do performances of songs have certain structures, timbres, and styles? Why do certain members of the community sing those particular things in those particular ways for that particular audience in that particular place and time? The answers are to be found both in the people's ideas about sound and song, and also in the relationship of singing with other verbal forms and social processes in their society. The ways the questions are answered will suggest a methodology for ethnomusicological study. This book is a kind of musical anthropology as distinct from an anthropology of music – a study of society from the perspective of musical performance, rather than simply the application of anthropological methods and concerns to music.

A great deal of writing in musicology and ethnomusicology has been about products: Beethoven's Ninth, Plains Indian song, and fiddle tunes, for example. These studies usually begin with the question 'What is it?' and use musical transcriptions and other analytic methods to arrive at a description of the structure and performance of a certain genre or period. Detailed analysis of musical products can produce highly competent descriptions of musical forms from around the world, but rarely relate their musical analysis to other aspects of the social and cultural environment of which music is always a part. Very few studies ask 'Why is the music performed in that way rather than another?' and 'Why perform music at all in a given situation in a society?' These are central preoccupations of this book.

The anthropology of music and musical anthropology

The difference between an anthropology of music and a musical anthropology is largely one of emphasis and perspective, but it has important implications for ideas about what music and society are all about. An anthropology of music brings to the study of music the concepts, methods, and concerns of anthropology. These have largely been developed through attempts to come to grips with the social and ideational structures and processes of transformation in human groups. Although it has a strong tradition of analyzing artistic productions, anthropology shares with the other social sciences an emphasis on social and economic formations rather than on music and other arts, and has tended to isolate economic processes from those that employ language, music, or other non-tangible concepts and items.

An anthropology of music looks at the way music is a part of culture and social life. By way of contrast a musical anthropology looks at the way musical performances create many aspects of culture and social life. Rather than studying music *in* culture (as proposed by Alan Merriam 1960), a musical anthropology studies social life as a performance. Rather than

xiii

assuming that there is a pre-existing and logically prior social and cultural matrix within which music is performed, it examines the way music is part of the very construction and interpretation of social and conceptual relationships and processes. Through its emphasis on performance and the enactment of social processes rather than social laws, this musical anthropology shares an emphasis on process and performativity common to much of contemporary anthropology (Bourdieu 1977; Herzfeld 1985; Sahlins 1981; each in a different way). Yet because of the nature of music, it presents a slightly different perspective on social processes that complements, but does not replace, the others.

The community taken as a reference for this study is the Suyá Indians, a Gê-speaking community in the state of Northern Mato Grosso, Brazil. The Suyá lend themselves to a musical anthropology because central parts of their social life are constituted through ceremonies and musical performances, and because they often define themselves as a group by certain song genres and by body ornaments they associate with the production of and attention to sounds. The sonic transparency of their community makes of their village a concert hall, the seasonal organization of songs makes of their year a concert series (or a single piece of music), and the rites of passage make of their lives a process punctuated with transformations achieved through long periods of song.

My experience with the Suyá was musical from the start – in the exchange of songs that was part of this fieldwork, in the discovery of their social forms as they appeared in ceremonies, and in subsequent collaboration on a record. The Suyá have been described in *Nature and Society in Central Brazil* (Seeger 1981), as well as in a number of articles. In order to avoid burdening the reader with detail, this text sometimes refers to the earlier works, to which specialists can turn for further documentation. This book provides a dynamic perspective that is missing in the earlier works: the musical, performance-centered, and creative features of Suyá life. While the earlier publications discussed structures, this book presents the creation, re-establishment, maintenance and alteration of structures and processes.

If the anthropology of music and Alan Merriam's book by that title (Merriam 1964) firmly establish music as part of social life, this foray into musical anthropology is meant to establish aspects of social life as musical and as created and re-created through performance. Music making is an important endeavor in many native South American societies. It is quite possible that there are places and times when music is the chosen mode for many social processes.

Music

Music is much more than just the sounds captured on a tape recorder. Music is an intention to make something called music (or structured similarly to what *we* call music) as opposed to other kinds of sounds. It is an ability to formulate strings of sounds accepted by members of a given society as music (or whatever they call it). Music is the construction and use of sound-producing instruments. It is the use of the body to produce and accompany the sounds. Music is an emotion that accompanies the production of, the appreciation of, and the participation in a performance. Music is also, of course, the sounds themselves after they are produced. Yet it is intention as well as realization; it is emotion and value as well as structure and form.

A parallel can be drawn with speech, which is also much more than a collection of sounds. With a limited number of phonetic possibilities, people around the world say many different things; with acoustical resources limited by the physics of sound production and perception, people around the world make many kinds of music for many different reasons.

Some authors have sought to describe the values and emotions of non-Western musical traditions, rather than limit themselves to their structure and form. David McAllester prefigured many more recent studies with his *Enemy Way Music* (1954). Alan Merriam's *Anthropology of Music* (1964) advocated the study of all aspects of musical production. John Blacking, in *Venda Children's Song* (1967), reveals some of the non-musical sources of the sounds of the songs of Venda children, and in his later works he has given considerable importance to bodily movement, emotions, and the social and cultural context in which music is performed (see, for example, Blacking 1973). Steve Feld's *Sound and Sentiment: Birds, Weeping, Poetics, and Song in Kaluli Expression* (1982) brilliantly argues that emotion, metaphor, and social context have a central role in the music of a New Guinea people (see also Feld 1984). Ruth Stone's *Let the Inside Be Sweet* (1982) is a methodical endeavor to bring together the study sounds of performance and the behavior of performers and audience through a careful study of Kpelle music events in Liberia. Ellen B. Basso's *A Musical View of the Universe* (1985) argues for a unified approach to performance genres through the symbolism of sound production.

One of the reasons people rarely write about why members of a group perform the music they do is that there is considerable disagreement about what would be a good answer to the question. This is a problem ethnomusicology and anthropology share with philosophy and theology, so it is worth being quite specific about the kinds of answers to be found in the following chapters. The 'because' answers to 'Why do Suyá sing?' are not final causes. No genetic imperative for singing has been discovered in human beings, although highly structured sounds are produced by members of every society. Nor does this study attempt to construct a natural history of human song, as in C. M. Bowra (1962) or the more sophisticated work of Alan Lomax (1968), which associates the social complexity of the society with certain musical features. At the analytic level proposed by Lomax, the Suyá sing the way they do because they are native South Americans who live in an isolated region, possess neither industry nor social classes, and therefore have few musical instruments and have never thought of writing music. Generalizations of this sort tend to characterize native South Americans through negatives: lacking certain instruments, lacking orchestras, lacking certain musical forms, little attention is paid to what they do with what they have.

Instead of approaching Suyá musical products through the features they share with those of other groups, this book addresses a more specific issue. Given that all native South American music shares certain features of form and performance style, why is it that the Suyá sing when they do? Why do people of different ages sing differently? Why does the pitch of a unison song rise the way it does? The answers are sought in Suyá social processes and values, not in ultimate biological or material causes, or in comparative generalizations.

The answers to the questions posed in this book are tentative, working hypotheses. They are a point from which to begin comparisons that are based not simply on our own ideas about music, but on what we can learn of other people's ideas about music. As Steve Feld has argued, the meaningful comparisons are only going to be made from carefully presented examples in their full social context (Feld 1984: 385) of which this is meant as an example.

By addressing musical production rather than musical product, this book suggests some parameters for comparison of the Suyá with other musical traditions, and is written to establish firmly the interrelationship of musical, social, and symbolic forms and processes. *Why Suyá Sing* shares with earlier books the desire to clarify the relationship of music and the broad social and cultural contexts of its performance. It differs from them in the way it proceeds, and the extent to which it documents its assertions with concrete examples.

Ethnographic grounding in a performance event

Few readers ever have visited, or ever will visit, the Suyá Indians in Mato Grosso, Brazil. As a device to present both music and its performance context, this book is written around the performance of a single ceremony in 1972, in which I participated as well as researched. It was performed a second time in 1976 and I was able to obtain tape recordings of a performance in 1963. The richness provided by three performances and the central institutions mobilized in this particular ceremony make it the best choice for an ethnographic treatment. The course of the ceremony provides a framework through which more general issues are raised.

Chapter 1 opens with the first day of the Mouse Ceremony, 24 January 1972. It describes many features of Suyá musical performance and social life that are taken up separately in the following chapters, and inserts both the ethnographer and the reader in an ongoing, unfolding, event. The ensuing chapters address the relationship of Suyá vocal art forms used during the ceremony to each other, the origin of music, the creative role music plays in social processes, and the reasons for a regular pitch rise in unison songs. Each chapter analyzes Suyá materials and also addresses one or more more general issues in ethnomusicology or the anthropological study of music. Chapter 6 returns to the Mouse Ceremony to describe its elaborate conclusion on 6 and 7 February 1972. The final chapter, building on the previous discussions, returns to the question of why Suyá sing.

The general issues raised include the nature of field research and its personal, social, and ethical facets (Chapter 1), the necessity of treating music as part of a larger body of aesthetic forms that may be interrelated in systematic ways (Chapter 2), the importance of understanding the native musicology in order to discover what music is all about (Chapter 3), the creative, constitutive role music plays in many social processes (Chapter 4), the usefulness of using multiple approaches in investigating any particular musical feature (Chapter 5), and the often conscious use of musical performances as part of political struggle (Chapter 7).

Finally, a word must be said about the writing style employed in the book. The use of the present tense to describe events that were witnessed in the past, often called the 'ethnographic present,' has been roundly criticized by Johannes Fabian (1983) and a number of other authors. Fabian argues that the ethnographic present removes the events from their historical (and often colonial) context, and places them in a kind of 'never-never-land' of time and space. It also tends to create a normative description out of an event that may not have been the norm at all. His criticism is quite appropriate: anthropologists only reside with a group for a few years, and of necessity see events occurring at a certain moment in history. Anthropologists themselves change during their lives; the events described are thus those of a particular group at a given moment in their history, as witnessed and investigated by an anthropologist at a certain moment in his or her life and theoretical development. The use of the present tense to describe what was in fact a very particular occurrence can result in considerable distortion and misunderstanding. I would argue the problem is not with the tense employed, but with the assumptions the use of the present tense is meant to convey.

I employ the present tense in the chapters that describe the Mouse Ceremony (Chapters 1 and 6). The reason I do so is exactly the opposite of the reason criticized by Fabian. By using the present tense in those chapters I mean to emphasize the particularity of the events, not their normativity. Each part of the description is given a date, and the use of the present is meant to convey the unfolding of the events. The present tense here is not employed to remove the events from their contexts, but to emphasize their insertion in them. It emphasizes that what I describe was a particular occasion, not a normative one. When Hwinkradi chose to sing over his name receiver, or an old man began to shout, they were making a number of decisions that increased the intensity and interest of the occasion. Each person sang a new song and some of them did so in new ways. Since it is difficult for any anthropologist to know what is especially new and interesting and what is repeated (even though I saw the ceremony twice and have recordings of a third performance), my use of the present tense is partly a device to express a commitment to a theoretical postulate: societies are always creating and re-creating themselves, singing is an important part of the process, and we should avoid thinking of an event as static and continuous. In the rest of the chapters I use the past tense, since my observations represent observations and discussions that occurred between 1971 and 1982. Over the years many things will undoubtedly change, and this book should be read as a document of what music was for the Suyá during the years of our field research. The Suyá sang because they were happy; singing made them happy. It was creative, innovative, and interesting because it was never exactly the same, but no one was there to write about it before or after our visits.

Acknowledgements

This book has grown out of more than fifteen years of research, thought, and conversation. During that time I was supported by many different agencies, stimulated by generations of students and by colleagues, and encouraged by my wife who participated in all stages of the research and write-up, by my friends, and by my family.

It is a pleasure to acknowledge the financial support that made the research possible in chronological order: The National Institute of General Medical Science (USPHS GM 1059), the Financiadora de Estudos e Projetos (FINEP), the Ford Foundation of Brazil, the Wenner-Gren Foundation, the Federal University of Rio de Janeiro, and the Social Science Research Council (U.S.A.). The research was carried out in what was then a remote part of Brazil; without the funds these institutions provided it would have been impossible to write this book.

Money alone would not have made the fieldwork possible. It required authorization and logistical support. The Conselho Nacional de Desenvolvimento Científico e Tecnológico (CNPq) and the Fundação Nacional do Índio (FUNAI) authorized the research. Successive directors of the National Museum in Rio de Janeiro authorized my research leaves and provided me with the necessary letters and documents. Some of the FUNAI employees were extremely helpful. Notable among these were Orlando and Claudio Villas Boas, directors of the Xingu National Park until 1976, and Olympio Serra, who succeeded them. Mairawé Kayabi, head of the Indian Post called Diauarum, was unstintingly hospitable and supportive, and often provided river transportation to help us reach and leave the Suyá village. The Brazilian Air Force (FAB) provided transportation to the Xingu on several occasions. Several nurses helped us and the Suyá through periods of ill-health, and we are especially grateful to Dona Cida, who for many years worked in the Xingu.

The Suyá were gracious hosts; we have reciprocated in as many ways as we could. In some senses this book barely goes beyond some things they told me in a few phrases, but which take chapters to present in another framework. 'Children, listen to my speech and behave correctly.' 'When we sing, we are euphoric.' 'When we sing we eat a lot.' 'Yes, the dancers are mice. Yes, the dancers are Suyá.' 'It is beautiful when everyone sings. When there are only a few people it is ugly.' 'A village that performs ceremonies is a good village. One that does not is ugly, and witches are very active.' 'When we stop singing, we will really be finished.' 'I am going to speak. Write it down; you do not remember anything.' 'Tony, a Brazilian showed us your book. He read us part of it [the dedication, in *Os Índios e Nós*] and it was beautiful.' These, and many other observations, conversations, and shared musical performances, are distilled in this book. I am grateful for the intense interest the members of the Suyá community showed in this project, and for their constant attempts to teach me what they knew. Where I have failed, the fault is not theirs but my own. Where I have succeeded it attests to their dedication as teachers and companions and to their generosity. The men who taught me so much, Petí, Robndó, Kuiussí, Temuensotí, Kogrére, Uetágü, Bentugarürü, and Kuni, and the women who instructed me and my wife so carefully, Mbéni, Gaisó, and Gaisári, deserve to be mentioned by their real names – their names have been changed in the text. To my companions of many hunting and fishing expeditions, Botkó, Ianarú, Kokombá, and the others whose patience was so great, I am grateful and acknowledge my ignorance and slow progress. With our daughter's name givers and my 'sister for ceremonies', Mapálu, and with the boy who shared my name before we ever knew of each other, Tonwutí, I share fond memories of the Mouse Ceremony.

A book does not write itself even after productive field research has been financed, logistically suported, and encouraged by those being studied. Many colleagues and students contributed to this one. Above all, I am indebted to the faculty and students of the Graduate Program in Social Anthropology of the Department of Anthropology of the Museu Nacional, in Rio de Janeiro, where I taught from 1975 to 1982. In that intense atmosphere of collegiality and professional effervescence, I learned from them all, especially Roberto Da Matta, Eduardo Viveiros de Castro, and Gilberto Velho. From my students at the Museu Nacional, Bruna Franchetto, Vanessa Rosemary Lea, Edwin Reesink, Elizabeth Travassos, Maria Laura Viveiros de Castro, and many others I received constant challenge, encouragement, and energy. From my students at other institutions, especially Marina Roseman and Victor Fuks, I have received many excellent suggestions. Marina Roseman has kindly given me permission to publish parts of an unpublished manuscript of hers. Eduardo Viveiros de Castro and Michael Herzfeld kindly read parts of this manuscript and made many valuable suggestions, as did John Blacking, editor of this series. Judy Seeger has not only accompanied me on nearly all fieldtrips, but has made substantive contributions to my thinking about the issues.

The delight of the past fifteen years has been enjoying the friends we made in Brazil and the new views of them provided by the challenges we met together, in the jungles and on the beaches, at bureaucratic meetings and at effervescent parties where cold beer punctuated heated conversations, song, and dance. We have been fortunate in our friends; my chest and thoughts are full as they are remembered now, in this instant of dedication, as if they were all with us again.

Notes on Suyá orthography

In transcribing the Suyá language in this book I have endeavored to simplify the orthography so as not to interfere with the reading, and yet to provide enough information to be of help to specialists in the Gê languages. Should a reader ever have the opportunity to discuss the concepts with a Suyá, I believe he or she would be understood using a rough pronunciation given here.

In the pronunciation of Suyá words and phrases used in the text, consonants should be pronounced as they are in English, except the r, which is flapped. Unaltered vowels are similar to those in Spanish or Portuguese.

a is pronounced as the a in father
à is pronounced as the u in up
e is pronounced as the e in men
i is pronounced as the ee in feet
ï is pronounced as the i in hit
o is pronounced as the o in open
u is pronounced as the oo in shoot
ü is pronounced as the oeu in boeuf
 ˜ indicates that a vowel is nazalized
 ' indicates emphasis on a syllable within a word

1 *The Mouse Ceremony begins*

24 January 1972

'Sister, I am going to sing over my name receiver.'

By the last light of the western sky, Hwinkradi (pronounced 'wheenkrádee') speaks with his sister. A solidly built man of about thirty, he stands in front of her house and speaks loudly enough to be heard in the center of the village plaza by the group of men gathered there for the evening session of talk and decision-making. They are ready to begin the ceremony they have decided to perform, but they require the approval of the mother of a young boy named Kogrere.

'You may. Start singing your shout song,' she replies.

Hwinkradi returns to his seat in the center of the village plaza – a large clearing of dust and packed earth formed by a circle of seven thatched houses. About twenty men and boys, wearing only shorts, sit on low stools or logs, their talk punctuated by slaps at mosquitoes in the deepening dusk. Hwinkradi picks up his low wooden stool and sits next to Kaikwati, a man of about fifty who has been silently looking into the coals of a small fire at his feet, paying no attention to his companions' words. Ignoring discussions of the day's hunting and boisterous requests for tobacco to roll a smoke, the two sit side by side. The older man begins to sing under his breath, and the younger one looks at the ground and listens carefully. The song is so quiet it can only be heard by those seated closest to them, and a couple of those turn their heads to listen as well. The conversation eddies around them.

'Huaaaaaaaa! There goes a shooting star!'

'. . . and then she . . .'

'I am sure you have been screwing too much, look at you . . .'

'My mother's brother . . .'

'Zip! Tuk! I killed three of them when the palm nuts were falling. One screamed like this "hīīīīī" I shot until I ran out of arrows . . .'

After a few minutes the old man finishes, sucks on his lip disc and pushes more of the sticks into the fire. Hwinkradi picks up a rattle, rises, walks toward a shelter to the east of the plaza and begins to step back and forth facing his sister's house. At each step he shakes a rattle he holds in his right hand. Slightly more emphasis marks the forward step, a lesser one marks the backward one. The men are quieter now, the women are darker shadows in front of the houses in the evening light.

After a minute of stamping and shaking his rattle Hwinkradi begins to sing. He shouts. His strained voice peals above the quiet talk of the men, easily reaching all of the houses where the women sit. It reaches people who are finishing an evening meal in back of the houses. His song rings out over the surrounding manioc gardens, sails across the hundred-foot expanse of the rain-swollen Suiá-missu river, and bounces back from the flooded trees on the opposite bank. The echo emphasizes the final note of each phrase. No motors, sirens, or generators disturb the sound. There is nothing else to be heard but the calls of night birds, frogs, and swarms of mosquitoes. Lightning flashes illuminate distant spots in the sky, silhouetting towering clouds for an instant. Somewhere it is raining; in this isolated part of Mato Grosso it is always raining somewhere nearby in January.

Example 1.1 on the cassette gives part of Hwinkradi's opening song, which can be translated as 'Black mouse, we go to our name receivers and leap and sing. I leap and sing the Mouse Ceremony. We go to our name receivers and leap and sing.'

Amto	*tukchi,*	*wa*	*krãnduwe*	*sülü*	*iarī*
mouse	black,	we	our name receivers	go to	and leap and sing

Amto		*iarī*	*ne,*
Mouse Ceremony		I leap and sing	thus

Wa	*krãnduwe*	*sülü*	*iarī ne* (3 times)
We	name receiver	go to	leap and sing

Hwinkradi sings for almost an hour. Occasionally an old man shouts a falsetto accompaniment. The men continue to talk; the women sit in front of the houses with their young children. The Mouse Ceremony has begun.

The Mouse Ceremony is a rite of passage in which a young boy begins his initiation into the male-oriented activities of the village plaza. It is one of a number of initiation rituals that punctuate a Suyá male's life from birth through old age, with their greatest concentration around puberty. The Mouse Ceremony is one that focuses on the relationship between an adult man and the boy to whom he has transmitted his own names, and it highlights their relationships to other kinsmen (especially the man's sister and boy's mother) and to certain age groups within the society as a whole. Although one boy is the focus of the ceremony, each performance of it also reaffirms the relationships of all men with their name receivers, their sisters, their joking relatives, formal friends, and affines. Every performance also reestablishes certain relationships between human beings and animals, between the village and its surroundings, and between the Suyá and the cosmos they have created and within which they live.

In 1972, the Suyá Indians lived in a single circular village with a population of about 120, on the Suiá-missu River in the Xingu National Park, in the state of Mato Grosso, Brazil (see Figure 4.1, p. 66). The Xingu National Park is a reservation containing approximately fifteen different native groups (see Illustration 1 for the village, and Figure 1.1 for a map of the region). The Indian communities in the Xingu National Park may be divided into two sets: those that share a common style of body ornamentation, material culture, and many features of ritual life but with different languages, known as the Upper Xingu Indians, and those that do not. The Upper Xingu Indians live in the southern part of the Xingu Park, while the others live in the middle and northern part. The Suyá belong to both groups: they share some material culture with the Upper Xingu Indians. They have learned some Upper Xingu ceremonies, but maintain themselves separate from the groups there. Their ceremonies are largely internal affairs revolving around kinship and naming relationships within the group. Their interactions with their neighbors in the northern part of the reservation are guarded;

1. Aerial photograph of the Suyá village, 1980

most of them were enemies in the past and intertribal witchcraft accusations and assassinations are not uncommon. Unlike most of the groups in the north, the Suyá have been living in the area since the mid-nineteenth century. They met their first non-Indian only a few miles from their present village, in 1884 (Steinen 1942).

The Mouse Ceremony described here begins on the evening of 24 January 1972, and will end at dawn on 7 February. With it begins a period of heightened euphoria and ritual activity that will last throughout the entire two-week period, created and accompanied by extended periods of singing, dancing, and collective activities. During the opening days more and more men and boys will learn new shout songs and begin to sing them. Almost every day will be punctuated by the pre-dawn and late afternoon unison singing of seasonal songs. Simultaneously, collective hunting expeditions will bring fish and game to the village that will be distributed to everyone, in marked contrast to the non-ceremonial distributions of food within domestic groups. Relatives of the woman who told Hwinkradi he could begin singing will prepare vast amounts of garden food, and distribute them to the entire village. Men will search for burity palm buds that are essential for the central ritual object, the mouse capes. These buds will be split and the new fronds dried by women. Capes will be woven from these by certain skilled men, and on the last afternoon these will be cut and painted by certain ritual relatives and worn by each man during the final night of leaping, dancing, and singing. With a

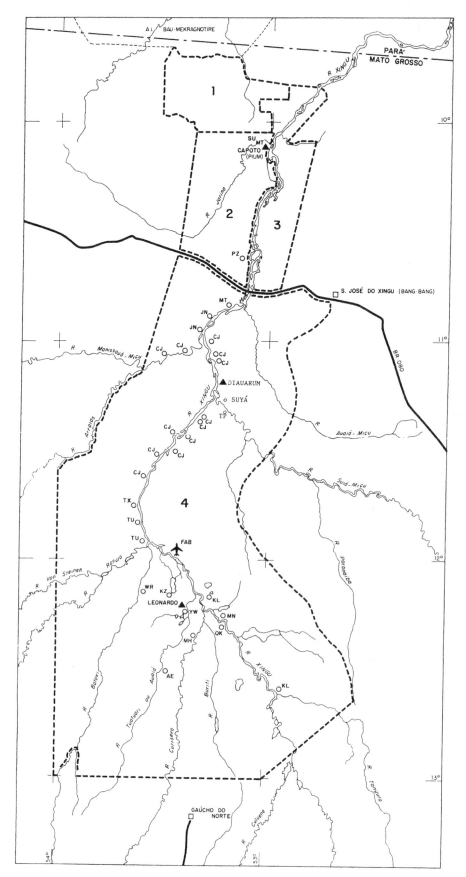

Figure 1.1   Map of Xingu region

1. Capoto Indian Area
2. Jarina Indian Reserve
3. Jarina Indian Area/Right Bank
4. Xingu National Park (later renamed Xingu Indian Park)

AE = Aweti
CJ = Kayabi
JN = Juruna
KL = Kalapalo

KZ = Kamayurá
MH = Mehinaku
MN = Matipu-Nahukwa
MT = Kaiapó-Metuktire (Txukahamae)
PZ = Panará
QK = Kuikuru
SUYÁ = Suyá (period 1970–1983)
TP = Tapayuna (after 1980)
TU = Trumai

TX = Txikão
WR = Waurá
YW = Yawalapiti

- - - - - - - = Boundaries of Indian area
O = Indian village
▲ = FUNAI administration post

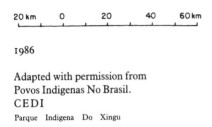

20 km   0   20   40   60 km

1986

Adapted with permission from
Povos Indigenas No Brasil.
C E D I
Parque   Indigena   Do   Xingu

couple of desultory phases, the ceremony will build up to a grand finale to which a few members of other Indian groups will be invited, and in which the singers will undergo a metamorphosis into beings that are at once human and animal. The power of this transformation will provide the ceremony, and the initiation of the boy into his name set, with much of its efficacy.

The course of the ceremony is graphically represented in Table 1.1. It has a clear beginning, then a long stage in which slow preparations are made for a dramatic final night in which the songs, ritual objects, and social relationships that have been learned, manufactured, and reactivated during the preceding weeks are finally brought together. In this and

Table 1.1. *Overall structure of the Mouse Ceremony*

EVENTS	JANUARY								FEBRUARY					
	24	25	26	27	28	29	30	31	1	2	3	4	5	6 7
Days described in the narrative text	xxxxxxxxxxxx					xxxxxxxx					xxxx			xxxxxxxx
Mouse Ceremony began	xxxx													
Mouse Ceremony ended														xxxx
Sang shout songs	xxxxxxxxxxxxxxxxxxxxxxxxxxxxxxxxxxxxxxxxxxxxxxxxxxxxxx**XXXXXXXX**													
Sang seasonal unison songs			xxxxxxxxxxxxxxxxxxxxxxxxxxxxxxxxxxxxxxxxxxxxxxxxxxxxxxx											
Collective food distribution	xxxxxxxxxxxxxxxxxxxxxxxxxxxxxxxxxxxxxxxxxxxxxxxx**XXXXXXXX**													
Preparation of capes & other artifacts			xxxxxxxxxxxxxxxxxxxxxxxxxxx**XXXXXXXXXXXXXXXX**											

Note: xxxx = activity occurred on that day
      XXXX = intensification of the activity

the ensuing chapters I describe parts of the ceremony indicated by the shaded area of the table.

During the Mouse Ceremony the Suyá perform a number of song styles and speech forms that also occur in many other ceremonies, and which are the subject of this book. These speeches and songs are central to the ceremony, and part of its efficacy. The major genres of Suyá vocal art are described in the following chapter. They include individually owned and performed shout songs – such as the one with which Hwinkradi opened the ceremony, seasonal unison songs that may be sung any time during the rainy season, specific Mouse Ceremony unison songs that are only performed on the final night of the ceremony, myths, plaza speeches, and invocations.

The Mouse Ceremony also shares many structural features with other major Suyá ceremonies. All of the ones I witnessed began with a clear opening, continued with a long period of learning and preparation that gradually built up to a dramatic final day or night. Within these larger structures, the Suyá inserted optional short ceremonies, usually within the long build-up period between the opening and the final night. These shorter units gave the longer ceremonies some of their variety, and also permitted considerable overall creativity. The 1972 Mouse Ceremony was performed by itself and largely for itself. The 1976 Mouse Ceremony was structurally the same, but was performed as a prelude to another ceremony (the Savannah Deer Ceremony) which was followed by the Small Bow Ceremony. After the opening of the 1976 Mouse Ceremony the Suyá performed a string of smaller ceremonies, each of which was considered a separate unit, and none of which had occurred in 1972. All of them involved the same ceremonial groups, and used time, space, and song in similar manner. Because of the interchangeability of many of the musical features of Suyá ceremonies and because of the general similarity in structure, performance, and efficacy of the Suyá ceremonies I witnessed, it is possible to generalize from the Mouse Ceremony to talk about Suyá verbal performance as a whole.

Suyá social life may be thought of as operating on a kind of alternating current. Either the Suyá are in a ritual mode or they are in a non-ritual mode. Every formal ceremonial beginning has a similar formal conclusion, every ceremony is eventually followed by another. The ritual mode is associated with euphoria, with collective public activities including song as well as collective hunting and village-wide food distribution. It involves the intensification of relations between men and their mothers, sisters, and sisters' children, and with their name givers, name receivers, and the members of their ceremonial groups (or, from the woman's point of view, the intensification of relations between herself and her brothers, and with members of certain ceremonial groups). The non-ritual mode is associated with everyday life, a predominance of individual or nuclear family activities including more restricted groups for food gathering and distribution, and everyday speech. Predominant relations are those between a man and his wife (or wives) and children, and more generally with his kinsmen; from a woman's point of view, it stresses kinship relations and relations between herself and her husband. The alternation of these two essentially complementary modes of existence creates the interlocking whole of Suyá social life, which includes consanguinity as well as affinity, collective activities as well as domestic ones, public forms of verbal art as well as private forms. The alternation between ritual and non-ritual periods, and between the activities, relationships, and feelings associated with each, creates the fabric of social life.

Music and some speech forms are one of the ways the ceremonial periods are set apart from the non-ceremonial ones. Suyá speech and song are central to the establishment of relationships and emotions that are said to characterize all their ceremonies. In this the Suyá resemble other native South American societies.

Although we know relatively little about musical traditions in the lowland regions of South America, it appears that whenever music is heard, something important is happening. Usually some connection is being created or recreated between different domains of life, the universe, or the human body and its spirits. Music transcends time, space, and existential levels of reality. It affects humans, spirits, animals, and those hard-to-imagine beings in between. In the Northwest Amazon region (the frontiers of Brazil, Venezuela and Colombia) sacred flutes may recall and reenact scenes from the travels of the primeval anaconda canoe that brought the ancestors and left them at their settlements (Hugh-Jones, C. and Hugh-Jones, S. 1980). In other parts of the Amazon region, songs may inspire, or control, the effects of hallucinogens (Kensinger 1973; Dobkin de Rios and Katz 1975). In the Upper Xingu region, in the state of Mato Grosso, singing is associated with ceremonies taught to men by spirit ancestors when they walked on earth, and music makes possible a return to and renewal from the sacred past (Bastos 1978; Basso 1985). For the Gê-speaking societies that occupied a large expanse of the Brazilian interior, music communicates among human beings and creates a feeling of euphoria. For the Gê-speaking Suyá who live near the Xingu river which flows north into the Amazon river, certain song styles identify them as uniquely Suyá, different from all other groups. As far as we know, throughout lowland South America music is used to represent and create a transcendence of time and substance: past and present are linked and humans and non-humans communicate and become comingled. The time and potentiality of myth is to some degree reestablished in the present through the sound of flutes, rattles, and voice.

In spite of broad similarities in the importance of music, the musical performances of Amazonian native communities are so different they can only be discussed as a group in a general way. Musical instruments can be described for the region (Izikowitz 1935, Seeger 1986). Some general statements can be made about musical structures, but great care must be taken not to place too much faith in them, since very few people have had access to extensive recordings. There is still no published detailed analysis of the use of music for any native South American group. Because of the small size and isolation of the communities, and the unfamiliar musical styles, the music of native South America is probably the least known of all the major regions in the world. Some descriptions and preliminary analyses do exist, among them Cameu (1977), Bastos (1978), and Aytai (1985). Although recordings from this region are not easy to encounter, Beaudet (1982) has published an excellent discography of those that have appeared.

The lack of scholarly attention to lowland South American Indian music masks the real importance of music in the lives of those communities. They often devote considerable time to making music. Hours of each day may be spent playing flutes or singing. During ceremonial periods it is common to hear singing all day for days or weeks on end. A large amount of time and resources is devoted to music and ceremony. Studies of the work habits in this region indicate that subsistence can be assured with between three and four hours of work per day under traditional conditions (Carneiro 1961; Bergman 1980). Members of many lowland Indian societies play flutes or sing for that number of hours for long periods. Yet we know much more about the socio-economic features of these communities than about the musical ones. Anthropological research priorities rarely start from the natives' views of what is important about their own lives.

While musical performances may occupy many hours of the day, the kinds of music found in lowland South American societies do not include many of those prominent elsewhere. The Suyá, for example, sing no love songs, work songs, songs of protest, or lullabies. Instead, there are ceremonial songs, individual shout songs, unison songs, curing songs, and many songs learned from members of other societies. Music is part of dance and ceremonial activity, either their own or those the Suyá have learned from other communities. This does not mean that all Suyá music is serious. Ceremonies are fun as well, and the songs and dances of other societies are especially fun since their performance is not as constrained by Suyá cosmology. But even songs that make their listeners weak with laughter are sung at a certain time of day by people of a certain age and sex, in certain places, often at certain seasons. From the very start, in the relationship of ceremony and subsistence, of fun and seriousness, these South American societies are as difficult to understand as their music is difficult to comprehend. Music is at once serious and funny, secular and sacred, good to think and good to eat (as Lévi-Strauss [1963a] suggested of totems), good to sing and important to listen to.

The performance of any ceremony, such as the Mouse Ceremony, involves the apparently timeless relationships of men, women, animals, parents, name-givers, and name-receivers, which are all expressed through song, dance, silence, feeding, and eating during the ceremonial period. But every performance also involves specific actors who make particular choices about who will sing, who will be sung to, who will hunt, who will eat what, and the specifics of a myriad of decisions and potential relationships only abstractly involved in the ceremony.

The main actors in the ceremony are Hwinkradi, his brothers, his half-sister, and her son, and the other members of his half-sister's family. A reduced kinship diagram shows how they are linked, and also includes some other Suyá who play a prominent role in the tape-recorded performances analyzed in future chapters (Figure 1.2). Hwinkradi is a member of a large family and a strong faction. His full brothers include an hereditary leader and Kaikwati, the ritual specialist. His full sister is married to Niokombedi, leader of the strongest faction and 'chief' of the village in the eyes of the Brazilians and other Indian groups. Respected for his knowledge, possessed of many young male relatives who will sing strongly during the

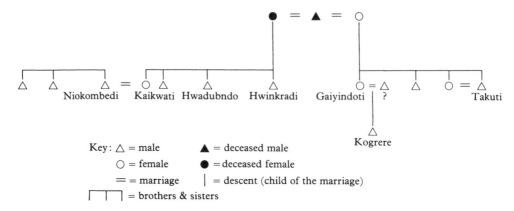

Figure 1.2 Genealogy indicating relationships among principal participants

ceremony, and with a young son whom he wants to learn to participate in ceremonies, Hwinkradi is an appropriate person to begin the ceremony and play an active role in its realization.

The woman who told Hwinkradi he could start singing his shout song is Gaiyindoti, his half-sister. She is the daughter of a Waura Indian captive who was the second wife of Hwinkradi's father. Gaiyindoti's hands have been crippled by a bone disease, and she is unmarried. Her three-year-old son has no socially accepted father, although he is widely believed to have been a Kayabi Indian living at the Indian post. The women called the boy 'somebody's child.' Although it is not a scandal to have a child and not live with a man, it is a social handicap. The crippled woman is assisted in everyday tasks by her mother, and by her full brothers and sister who live with her.

Hwinkradi had held the boy briefly when he was only a few days old, and transferred his names to it. Although the boy has no father, he does have many maternal relatives. These sponsored the Mouse Ceremony. By doing so, they reaffirm the boy's name-based social identity.

When the boy's mother told Hwinkradi to go ahead and sing his shout song, she also committed herself, her mother, and her full brothers and sister to providing food for the entire village at regular intervals. It is both an honor for her son to be sung over, and a lot of work for his relatives. The ceremony confers some prestige to the boy – all the more important because he is without a father.

Every ceremony involves a fairly constant general pattern of relationships and actions as well as a plethora of decisions and strategies. Many decisions about who would do what were doubtless made before Hwinkradi spoke to his sister on 24 January 1972. Many decisions will still be made during the ceremonial period. But once she told him to sing his shout song, and he began to sing 'we go to our name receivers and leap and sing' a process was set in motion that will culminate in a grand final night of singing, eating, metamorphosis, and collective euphoria. The particularities of this performance endow the ceremony with its immediacy and some of its importance for the performers, while its regular features ensure the reality of those parts of it that transcend individuals and everyday social processes.

The way in which a Suyá receives his or her name is central to an understanding of Suyá music and ceremony. When a child is born, its parents decide which member of a certain group of relatives will be its name giver, or *krã tumu*. If it is a boy, that group is composed of his mother's brothers – both actual brothers and more distant relatives called by that term. If it is a girl, the parents decide among a group composed of her father's sisters, both close and more distant. Whoever is chosen comes to the house, holds the newborn child for an instant, then leaves the house. All the other members of the village who share the same name also come to the house, hold the infant, and leave, even though they are unrelated to it. The child begins to be called by one of the names it has been given only after around the time it can walk – about the time the Mouse Ceremony might be performed for it. Before that it is simply known as 'baby.'

There is more in a Suyá name than a label. Each male name is part of a fixed set with between four and forty linguistically distinct parts, each of which can be used as an individual's name. For example, one name set has eight male names, Dombeti – Hwatkadnto – Iõkrekatumu – Kodngoti – Sokiniti – Kokoiatenti – Ikwaniari – Kogata, and three female names, Gaindawhraw – Gaihwuti – Gaikrãmbeti. Any person called by one of those names is a member of a ceremonial group made up of all those that share the set. A name set bestows a complete social identity. Name set membership determines which log-racing team a boy races in, how he paints his body in a number of ceremonies, where in the line of men he will dance, with whom he will sing, what special songs or actions he will perform in certain ceremonies, and a myriad things that are not commonly associated with names in the United States and Europe. A boy who receives names from his maternal uncle participates in rituals as a small double of his maternal uncle. The Suyá compare a man and the child who receives his names to a double rainbow: identical but different in size. The members of the name set above are members of the *Ambàn* moiety, associated with the east. They are also in the *Soikodnto* moiety (associated with the west and appearing at different times from the *Ambàn/Kren* pair) and thus dance near the end of the line of dancers in the Mouse Ceremony. Women with the names in the set appear with the male members of their name set in a number of ceremonies, though they do not sing. There are a total of twenty-two male name sets in circulation, fairly evenly divided according to moiety memberships.

Female names may be members of a larger set of male and female names, or may be single names unaffiliated with sets. The relationship between name givers and name receivers is much the same, but there are many more different name groups, and they less frequently appear in ceremonies. When women have names that are part of male name sets, they accompany the men of their name set in certain ritual activities – such as leaving the house in the final day of the Mouse Ceremony.

All Suyá names in the book have been systematically altered. I have given each individual a different name from his or her own name set, and therefore associated with the same moiety and ceremonial groups. This maintains ethnographic accuracy but reduces the public attention they might receive were I to use their actual names.

25 January

'Let's go! Tony! Ianaru! Botkaw! Let's go!' someone on the other side of the thatch wall is calling in a low voice.

At 4:30 in the morning it is still dark. Fumbling for my clothes and possessions, as always I am the last one to leave the house. I carry my bow, arrows, wooden paddle, .22 rifle, and a bag with fish line, hooks, weights, knife, and bullets in a plastic pillbox. The others are already standing outside. When I arrive we make our way single file along a path that cuts a large curve of the river and leads to a canoe-beaching spot some 3 kilometers from the village on foot and some 10 kilometers by river.

It is so dark I can only follow my companion by looking sideways and catching the faint glow of his back with my peripheral vision. His bare feet find the path without difficulty. 'Look out for the log' he advises me. A dog trots along behind us. I am careful to keep my distance so as not to impale myself on the arrows he carries over his shoulder, should he stop suddenly. In spite of my fatigue it is pleasant to walk along this path in the pre-dawn, listening to the sounds of the birds waking up, the thrashing of fish in the shallows as we pass near the river's edge before the bend, and the thud of bare feet on the packed ground. The air is cool. It is even darker when we enter the woods.

I do not go hunting and fishing because I want to. I go because I have to. During our first month with the Suyá I discovered that in order to get food enough for my wife, Judy, and me to eat I have to go hunting or fishing every other day or every third day during most of my stay. Although I am not particularly adept at it, the Suyá accept my efforts as sufficient, and we get a share of the house's kill regardless of my individual success. Or rather, we do so long as I keep trying. It never occurred to me that we would be forced to participate so fully in their economic lives; it never occurred to them that they would have to feed visitors for over a year. Since there are no stores for hundreds of miles, no markets, and no money, all we have is our arms, legs, and our slowly improving skills. Anthropologists do not choose many aspects of our relations with people in the field. They are chosen for us. Flexibility, imagination, and humility are essential.

When we arrive at the end of the path, emerging from the forest onto a high bank where the river begins its long oxbow curve, there is light enough to see. I take my small notebook from my pocket and write down some impressions and ideas.

> 'Look, he writes on leaves again.'
>
> 'His ears are swollen; he cannot remember anything. Isn't that right, Tony?'
>
> 'Uh-huh' I reply, used to the banter.

I climb into the bow of one of the three canoes and we push off up river. The sides of the canoe are only two inches above the rippling water. We sit on small sticks across the bottom of the canoe and use short paddles. We paddle against the current for about an hour and a half, hugging the banks where the current is slowed by the shallow bottom and trees whose boughs drag in the water. It is hard work to push the heavy dug-out canoes along. Paddling is done with short, hard, strokes. As soon as we rest for a moment the canoe slows down and begins to drift downstream. A man in the front canoe stands and shoots a fish among the branches of a fallen tree. The fish splashes as it leaves the water, shakes itself off the arrow, and leaps around the canoe until the fisherman silences it with a few quick blows of the stick he has been sitting on.

> 'Tony, what is the name of that lake?' Hwinkradi calls from through the mist from another canoe. Most of the men on this trip are relatives of his and of the mother of his name receiver. It dawns on me that this collective hunt is part of the Mouse Ceremony that opened last night. The relatives of the boy will provide food for the ceremony participants.
>
> 'It is "the place where the moon died",' I respond, 'where many years ago Suyá men were beating fish poison by the light of the full moon and it suddenly began to disappear in an eclipse.'
>
> 'That's right. Further upstream we will come to "Iamuricumã's water," a lagoon on the edge of which perched the Suyá village called Iamuricumã.'

We do not just paddle up a stream, but through a personalized environment whose physical details are known by what has happened there. Every trip up river is a history lesson. I am often quizzed about the places we pass, as are young boys making their second and third trips.

We stop a moment while Hwinkradi and a dog leave the canoes and disappear into the forest after game. Then we enter 'Iamuricumã's water' and start to fish, using fish line baited with pieces of the fish that was shot. We are quiet; this is no time for interviewing or even directed conversation about village matters. Fishing is serious business, but the river is high and the fish are dispersed. By ten o'clock I have caught only a piranha. My companion, Hwinkradi's older brother, has only a small catfish. The bright colors of the fish fade, and they stiffen in bottom of the canoe between us. I am hungry. None of us has eaten anything since the night before. When the Suyá say they are hungry, they mean they are weak and a little dizzy from lack of food. It is not a desire but a physical demand.

A high yelp signals the dog has flushed some game. In a few minutes we see a v-shaped wedge in the water with a dot at the point. It is a deer swimming across the lagoon. The dog plunges in and his head forms another v as he paddles furiously after the deer. We pull in our lines and paddle out to cut off the deer before it reaches the safety of the forest on the far side. We are fortunate. Near the bank, the deer freezes next to a fallen log. Since I have the only rifle, I shoot as we sweep alongside it. To my immense surprise the deer sinks in a rush of bubbles.

Another canoe pulls into the bank and a young boy dives and pulls up the deer. It is drawn into the canoe, and rests in front of me, dripping and still warm. Everyone comments on the wound just under its eye, and on my (lucky) marksmanship.

We return to our fishing, changing location a few times in the next few hours. The damp heat increases steadily, and the deer begins to swell and stink in front of me. We pull into the bank to roast and eat some of the fish we have caught, and then begin to descend the river, fishing all the way, until we reach the high bank once again. Some young men are there, fishing desultorily, probably waiting for us. They tie the deer to a pole, and we carry our bows, arrows, guns, line, and fish back to the village. The path is no longer a delight. It is a torture. The afternoon is terribly hot and still. The sun, when it touches the skin, burns as though it passes right through into the flesh.

When we reach the village, the young men drop the deer in the middle of the plaza, just south of the men's house, where Hwinkradi sang the night before. The fish are carried to the houses. Men who are sitting in the doorways or in the men's house give a shout of appreciation at the catch ('eeeeeyow!'). Two elderly men hobble out to examine the deer. One walks around the plaza twice, singing a deer song. I enter the cool shade of the house. Judy has been grating manioc all morning and has made a fresh manioc cake; some manioc drink remains from the morning. I drop into a hammock, only rousing myself to follow the distribution of the deer.

One of the hereditary male leaders walks to the men's house with a machete and an ax to butcher the deer. One of the responsibilities of leadership is to distribute food and other things fairly to the entire village, and not simply to kinsmen. Young boys have brought leafy boughs to put under the carcass to catch the blood and offal. Men and women are standing around, watching. So are a number of hungry hunting dogs. The deer is gutted, and cut up. It is a pregnant doe whose fetuses are given to an old woman. The head is given to an old man. There are rationales for specific aspects of the distribution. The woman, past menopause, can eat animal fetuses without having multiple births as a consequence; the old man has an itchy head and will not be affected by eating the deer head, which the Suyá say causes itchy scalp. Some fatty intestines go to another elderly woman. Suyá 'social security' consists at least in part of a relaxation of dietary restrictions that apply to younger men, women, and children. One of the hind legs is given to some boys to take to the river and cut up for a meal in the men's house. The rest of the deer is cut up and pieces of raw flesh are given to the waiting women, one piece for each nuclear family, or widow with children.

The hereditary leader carefully counts the families on his fingers, and examines the remaining pieces. He calls to some women. When he is told they are out in the gardens he summons a child or a relative to take a piece for them. This is all noted in my pocket notebook. 'Mbeni, fetus/Wikensakodo, head/. . .' Leaning against a post in the men's house, I write until the offal is dragged into some tall grass and the snarling dogs move in to feast on it.

Back in the house the few fish have also been distributed. Two were sent out of the house to relatives of the wives of the fishermen. The two largest ones are already cleaned and in a pot, to be boiled and mixed with manioc flour to make a kind of manioc-and-fish gruel. A small fish is being roasted for each of the fishermen who went on the trip.

In this way, everyone in the village receives a little of the fruits of our hunt. It may not be enough to fill them up, or even to be called a meal. Sometimes a person's share will be a small mouthful of a tiny fish and a piece of manioc cake. But since everyone's food is divided up in some way, on a good day there are many such pieces. The distribution is not equal, either. Old people without children and orphans usually receive less than the others because they lack the relatives who would give food to them. They must rely more on the general distributions in the plaza.

In a society such as that of the Suyá, a great deal can be learned by following the distribution of food, just as the distribution of money is an important datum in market economies. Most food is not stored, but rather given out. When food belongs to an individual it is given out to certain kinsmen. When it is given to the village as a whole, represented by the men's house, a leader distributes to the village and to certain age-, sex-, and name-based groups. The deer I had shot was dropped next to the men's house, indicating that it was for public distribution and a men's house meal. Suyá ceremonies are characterized by frequent public distributions and men's house feasts.

My intimate acquaintance with the way the Suyá obtain, distribute, and process their food made me appreciate the complexity of the distribution and the variety of the food itself. Brazilians often said Indian food was very monotonous: fish and manioc, fish and manioc, *ad nauseam*. They were wrong. By January 1972 it is clear Suyá eat differently at different times of year, marked by the rains and their absence which alternately fill and shrink the maze of rivers, lakes and swamps in which the Suyá live today. The gardens provide a staple diet of manioc, a starch, but lesser amounts of other crops that are seasonal. Corn ripens in February; sweet potatoes and other tubers are harvested slowly in April, May, and June, by each family. They hunt different species of fish and game in different seasons. From June through September the rivers shrink from months without rain. Fish are abundant in the drying lakes and the shallow rivers. The rains usually begin again in September, and from October through May the fishing is less certain. The rains fill the rivers and most species are increasingly hard to find. During these months the Suyá search the forests for game and honey. A family or two may make trips of two weeks or more to collect special resources such as clay, bird feathers, palm fibers, and also to hunt and fish where game is more plentiful. When they return, their canoes are laden with smoked birds and fish, which are distributed widely around the village. In March the river is at its highest flood: much of the forest is flooded with still, dark water. Hunting parties are most successful at this time. Then the flood waters begin to retreat, and the fish and game become scarcer, but are replaced by some of the new crops before fish again become plentiful.

The Suyá do not express concern about a lack of food, but it is harder to find sometimes than at others. The in-between seasons, when the river is neither at its highest nor its lowest, are the most difficult. January is a difficult time. Our fishing trip would have been three hours long in July; it lasted eight hours in January.

'It is cooked. Get your pots. The meat is ready.'

At 4:30 in the afternoon an hereditary leader summons the men to eat venison in the men's house. Men and boys converge on the men's house from all of the houses around the plaza. They carry bowls of metal or local ceramics; each brings a metal spoon. I take along a small sack of salt I brought in our baggage from Rio de Janeiro, because it is so appreciated. The leader makes sure that everyone gets served before young boys scrape the pot clean. He gives the old man who sang a deer song a heaping plate of meat. Some men send part of their share back to their wives and children. I get a much larger piece of meat than usual, and some highly valued juice is poured into my bowl. We eat in the shade of the lean-to structure. My lucky shot is described a number of times, as well as my reaction to the stinking of the deer as it lay in the canoe. The talk is desultory; soon we will sing.

An example of men talking after a men's house meal before starting to sing is given on the cassette (Example 1.2). It is typical of 'everyday speech' – conversation in which not much performed individually as in the samples of oratory given in the following chapter. They discuss the songs they had performed.

'Now let's sing,' announces Kaikwati, the ritual specialist who taught Hwinkradi his song the night before.

The men send for children who take their plates back to the houses, with some meat for their families. Childless, I take my own pot to Judy, who sits talking quietly with the women in the shade of the house, waiting for a manioc drink to finish boiling. Kaikwati brings a rattle from his house. We all sit in the men's house, older men in the back and younger men in the front, facing the center of the village. Children are sent away.

We begin a low, unison song. We sing sitting down, as it is a rainy season song (in the dry season we had sung differently), and hit our right fists on our thighs. Only Kaikwati has a rattle. I listen hard for the changes of the parts, which still mystify me. We sing first one piece, then another. We sing some 'huuuuuus' and there is a brief silence before we begin again. I try to remember what the words mean, but they are disguised by the alteration of the text typical of Suyá songs. I have them written down somewhere. I spend a lot of my time trying to remember what I have written down.

Example 1.3 on the cassette is an example of the rainy season song of the type sung that afternoon, but one I recorded instead of singing. Since this will be analyzed in some detail in Chapter 5, the complete song appears on the tape. An analytic transcription appears in Chapter 5.

Translation

Jo-jo-ha-i jo-jo-ha-i jo-jo-ha-i ne jo-ha-i ne-he tẽ
['Just song words' according to the Suyá]

First half:
Ki krüdeti na, nguwa gatüwü daw sogo daw ngre
The trairão fish (*Hoplias* sp.) sings with its face painted for log racing

Huuu, daw sogo daw ngre, huuu, huuu.
Huu, with its face painted sings, huu, huu
(Huu indicates the end of a section of the song)

Second half:
Jo-jo-ha-i jo-jo-ha-i jo-jo-ha-i ne jo-ha-i ne-he tē
['Just song words' according to the Suyá]

Samudawti na ngwa gatüwü wi sogo daw ngre
The big-mouth bass (*Cichla ocellaris*) sings with body painted for log racing

Huuu, wi sogo daw ngre, huuu, huuu, huuuuuuu
Huu, with its body painted sings, huu, huu, huuu
(The slow verse, and the three huuus indicate the end of the song)

When I make a mistake and don't sing a new line where one should be sung, the young man next to me says 'What's going on?' I pay more attention. Someone else makes the mistake the next time. The young men giggle. At the final 'huuuuuuu' one of them does it so emphatically that the others laugh. The emphasis is like that of an adult man who has killed an enemy and considers himself very belligerent; the boy is only eighteen and has never seen an enemy. The incongruity is funny. Singing is fun; it is supposed to make you happy. Eating as a group, talking together in the men's house, and singing together create the male solidarity and euphoria characteristic of ceremonial life.

When the singing is over the men return to their houses, to eat and to bathe, or perhaps to go to the gardens to hunt for birds or to meet a lover. Some men and women take heavy steel hoes and dig up the clumps of grass that have grown in the plaza and around the houses. An impromptu soccer game packs the loose earth down again as the young men race around the plaza after a ragged ball. Later the families sit in front of their houses, women looking for head lice, children playing, and everyone talking quietly. Judy and I take our medicine box and visit every house to treat the cases of malaria, colds, and other ailments that have been brought to our attention. Then we, too, sit together near the rest of the families and talk about our respective days. We do not see that much of each other; each of us is involved in the world of a different sex. Judy cools some hot starchy drink, and we finish it in the dusk.

When it is too dark to distinguish individual features, the men begin to congregate in the very center of the village plaza, not near the men's house, as earlier. Hwinkradi starts singing his song again. Another man stands next to him and begins a different song, which he has just been taught. The rest of us talk for a while. Kaikwati teaches another new song. Suddenly the plaza is invaded by clouds of mosquitoes. A deep roaring approaches from the east and a tremendous thunderstorm is upon us. Everyone runs for his house and we swing in our hammocks for a while before going to sleep. The thunder crashes and rolls, and drops fall from the thatch and spatter on the mosquito net, covering me with a fine spray.

Judy and I live in the house of Niokombedi, the strongest faction leader and the chief of the village in the eyes of the rest of the Xingu (for a discussion of leadership see Seeger 1981: 180–206). His house is the largest of the seven, and the nearest to the river. Thirty-five people sleep under its large thatch roof, in a single barn-like room without internal walls. During the night babies cry and are suckled, fires are fanned under the hammocks, and after the storm there is some quiet coming and going through the door. The woman next to us receives her future husband and the walls shake slightly as he gets into her hammock with her. Cockroaches rustle in the thatch. An orchestra of mosquitoes whines around our mosquito netting. At one end of the house a man tells his wife and children the story of how the mouse gave corn to a woman and her son, and how they eventually told the rest of the village about it. I go over some of the events of the day. Tomorrow I will not have to go hunting or fishing. I can write and ask questions. It is a pleasurable thought on which to go to sleep.

26 January

The damp reality of the next day is not so enjoyable. Although I work regularly with five different men, each somewhat better for a different kind of investigation, none is in the village. One of the men I work with is a natural linguist; another likes to talk about history; a third is a specialist in song; a fourth likes anything a little 'off-color' and although he knows less about each subject than the others, he is great for exploring new areas the questions for which I can only vaguely formulate. They are all off fishing, hunting, or traveling. I know because Judy and I make the rounds with our medicine box. We visit every house, treat the sick, see who is in the village, and catch up on the news in houses other than our own. A constant problem is finding people who are around when I am not off fishing myself. I can work with the women, but they are generally shy, and they profess no knowledge of ceremony or song. 'Ask Kaikwati' they all tell me. 'We don't know anything.' Kaikwati has two wives and heads a large household; he is often out fishing, working in the gardens, or making canoes.

Instead of interviewing, we go to pick some corn among the stumps, charred logs, and tall manioc stalks of our garden. As we walk out of the village a woman spinning cotton in a doorway asks 'Where are you going?' 'To the gardens' we reply. As we walk out the path to the gardens we meet a group of boys who are playing in the grass. 'Where are you going?' they ask. 'To the gardens' we reply again. 'What will you do there?' one of the more adventurous asks, giggling because gardens are places couples have sexual relations. 'We will gather corn.' 'All right, go,' they say. Everyone not only knows what other people are doing, but they are expected to ask about it. Gardens are the places where married couples do much of their lovemaking. Unmarried couples and lovers, who have no excuse to be going to a garden together, must manage to meet elsewhere.

In the garden we break off ears of corn and step gingerly among the fallen logs and stumps, alert for huge stinging ants. Our garden looks more like a massive confusion of bushes and weeds. It affords ample privacy. Judy carries a bundle of green corn when we return. 'Where have you been?' ask the children. 'Where have you been?' ask two women carrying manioc baskets out to the garden. 'Where have you been?' asks the woman still spinning cotton in her doorway. 'We have been to the gardens,' we answer one and all. We drop our things in the house and walk to the river. The cool, viscous and delicious waters of the Suiá-missu are ever a pleasure. As in the gardens, we can speak English to each other when we bathe. Bathing is usually a family affair, and we are left alone, although we can see other families bathing at other spots up and down the river bank, and children play in and around the canoes beached on the river's edge.

When we return to the house someone's fish is already cooking and a fresh manioc cake is on our rack. We give most of our corn away, and roast two ears for ourselves in the coals under the griddles cooking manioc cakes. We eat the sweet ears without butter or salt. This is the corn season; the Mouse Ceremony has begun because of the association of the ceremony with the origin of corn. After eating we bathe again, and I start writing fieldnotes from the day before. I note my impressions of the forest walk and the hunt, the distribution of the pieces of the deer is transferred from my pocket notebook to my journal. I enter a list of the people who sang in the evening, before it was cut short by the rain, outline the myth I heard just before I dropped off to sleep, and make notes on its performance. There is a great deal I do not write, things that will tease my memory later. But I do my best before I fall asleep in the afternoon heat.

When I awake another meal is boiling in a pot by the men's house. I walk out with my bowl, my manioc, my bag of salt and my notebook. I sit and listen to the talk, writing intermittently.

That night, when the men gather in the center of the plaza, everyone is quite excited. There is lots of laughing. One man blows his nose into his hand and rubs the mucus on his sister's son's back. Disgusted, his nephew runs away. A moment later he picks up a small bit of dog shit on a stick and hurls it toward his uncle. It lands very close to the seated men. They all jump up shouting. 'Hey! What's going on?' The would-be target runs off into the dark after his sister's son, scooping up some dust to throw at him. Everyone laughs, listens to the scuffling in the dark, then returns to his seat. A man should joke with his mother's brothers. After ceremonies have begun there is always a great deal more of it.

Tonight it is the boys' turn to learn about songs. About seven boys between the ages of seven and eleven are lined up and taught new songs by their fathers or other relatives. They go over to the men's house and begin to sing. They sing hesitantly. One refuses to sing and runs off to his mother. The adults who taught the boys stand near them, repeating the song quietly for them to hear as they sing. Everyone listens, laughs, and jokes. The village is in that desirable state of collective euphoria, or *kin* (both as adjective and noun), that should be part of any ceremony. When people feel euphoric, they are happy and want to sing. Singing makes them happy. *Kin* is a desirable state. New songs are being learned. People are acting correctly: they are being delightfully improper with their joking relatives, and behaving properly toward the others. Ceremonial food has been distributed to the entire village, and a men's house meal has been eaten. Everyone is *kin-kumeni* (the suffix *-kumeni* indicates emphasis) or 'really euphoric.'

29 January

At 5:00 in the morning some men are already off hunting and fishing. The rest of us are called to the men's house to share a large pot of manioc drink being served to all comers by Hwinkradi's relatives. After we drink they sing two rainy season songs in unison, which I record standing before the men's house, scratching mosquitoes with my foot and blowing them off my hands as I hold the microphones. Although I have never heard the songs before, their structure is very similar to the one we sang the previous evening, except they name different animals. One has a short solo section where each man is supposed to sing a line alone. Some of the young men have trouble remembering it, and women giggle in the nearby houses. At dawn we stop and most of the men go to bathe. Then we go off to fish.

In the reddish glow of the late afternoon, when I finish my journal entry, I hear boys singing from in back of one of the houses. About 200 yards down the path to some of the gardens, at the edge of a small patch of forest that has not yet been cut down, a small clearing has been made among the manioc stalks of a garden. There Hwinkradi, his brother, a sister's son, and about ten boys are stepping back and forth side by side, facing the village, and singing. After a while the older men stop and listen to the boys sing, while they roll cigarettes. The thin voices of the boys can just be heard in the village. They are singing in a 'forest camp' near the village; I know it from my reading of Gê ethnographies. It is the first time I have seen one and I take photographs. Nearly every afternoon for the next few weeks boys will be out there singing under the direction of an adult.

The Mouse Ceremony is a children's ceremony. It is all about the socialization of young boys into the ways, the groups, and the music of the plaza. A great deal of time and energy is spent teaching them to sing. After a while a few young men join us in the clearing.

When the sun is low in the west, the men and boys quietly file back along the path to the village and form a double line at the edge of the plaza. Each person pairs up with a friend of approximately the same age. Stooping over, the dancers trot into the plaza in a double line, without singing. They circle the center of the plaza. They approach the easternmost side of the men's house, back away, approach it again, back away, approach it, then stand still, stamping forward and back with their right feet, shaking their rattles in their right hands. Then all of them begin to sing the first half of their shout songs at once. The sound is a cacophony, difficult to describe but audible as Example 1.4 on the cassette. After a few minutes, each singer falls silent at the end of his verse. Following a moment's silence, starting at the back of the line with the smallest boys, each singer sings the verse of the first half of his shout song (recorded on Seeger and A Comunidade Suyá 1982 Side 1 Band 3).

After the man at the front of the line ends his verse, cacophony returns for a moment, then the singers follow the leaders and trot, stooped over, around the plaza again. They approach the westernmost side of the men's house, repeat the forward and backwards movement, slowly fall silent, then each sings the full verse of the second half of his shout song (Example 1.4), except for the young boys, whose songs have only one 'half' or part, and one adolescent who forgot the second half of his and repeated the first half. When the singers have finished their solos, they sing simultaneously again, then without singing, stooped over once more, they trot around the center of the plaza, back to the men's house, and with a final stamp, conclude the afternoon's performance. The children run to their mothers, who have been watching and listening. The men return to their houses, to eat, and then to bathe with their families.

The slow build-up of the Mouse Ceremony is reflected in the steady increase in the number of singers and the length of the afternoon singing. Example 1.4 gives an excellent sample of both individual and collective shout song singing sung by males of different ages. The differences between the performances will be discussed in Chapter 4.

The afternoon shout song performance highlights Suyá spatial domains, the identity of certain social groups, and the structure of the shout songs themselves. The first thing to be noted is the fundamental dualism in the performance: in the texts, the places they are sung, and the groups that perform them. The men sang the beginning, or first half of their shout songs (called the *kradi*), on the east side of the men's house, which is associated with the *Soikokambrigi* moiety. The word for east means 'beginning' (*kradi*) of the sky; members of the *Soikokambrigi* (red-caped) group dance at the front (called the beginning or *kradi*) of the line of dancers, and carry the lower part of a palm trunk (called the beginning or *kradi*) in log races. The association of the beginning of the songs with a particular place and a particular group is not random, but rather an essential part of the delineation of space, the identity of social groups, and the significance of singing and collective activities characteristic of Suyá musical performances.

> East (*kaikwa kradi*)
> First half of song (*kradi*)
> Moiety of the east side of men's house
>
> West (*kaikwa indaw*)
> Second half of song (*sindaw*)
> Moiety of the west side of men's house

The second part of the singing is also symmetrical. The performers circle the plaza and sing the second parts (called the *sindaw*) on the west (the 'end of the sky') side of the men's house, associated with the *Soikokeingoro* (striped-caped) moiety that dances at the end of the line of dancers and carries the upper part *sindaw* of palm trunks in log races. The dualism of Suyá shout songs is pervasive in the performance of the songs, as well as in the structure of their texts.

At dusk, when the men fetch their stools and carry them to the center of the village, they are planning a different kind of entertainment.

'Are you going to sing?' a woman asks me as I step through the doorway.

Women always seem to know everything. 'I don't know,' I reply.

'Let's sing,' a man says when I reach the group of men, carrying my stool.

'All right, let's sing,' I reply.

'No, let's sing *your* songs,' corrects another.

'All right.'

Even though we are feeling heavy from eating a lot of starch, I return to the house and tell Judy the men want us to sing. When we take our banjo and guitar into the center of the plaza, the women follow us, and form a ring of women and children around the men at the center.

Judy and I have played and sung folk music for many years, but the experience of playing for the Suyá is different from any other. We begin with a Bluegrass style banjo song, 'John Hardy,' and follow it with another in close parallel harmony and a modal tuning, 'Pretty Polly.' The women have been asking Judy to teach them some songs privately. They know the first verse of 'Pretty Polly' in English, and join in. Then we sing two audience participation songs from Africa, 'Tina Singu Lelo Votaeo' and 'Bayeza.' After all of the months we have been living with them, the Suyá sing these enthusiastically. After we finish the second one, the women tell the men they didn't sing at all. The men instruct me to announce the women have not sung. There is a lot of laughter and banter on both sides, and we sail through some sing-along songs such as 'Michael Row the Boat Ashore,' the 'Gray Goose' (a favorite, known in Suyá as the 'Tough Duck Song' because the goose is too tough to eat) and some more songs in close harmony, which they also enjoy. They like 'Michael Row the Boat Ashore' because it sounds like 'Wai kum kraw,' or 'Look out, something is rotten smelling.' They are generally uninterested in translations. They sing songs in a number of different

Indian languages which they do not understand. Ours is just another set of sounds and a different vocal style.

'Tell Abiyoyo.'

'Yes! That's right. Tell Abiyoyo.'

Abiyoyo is a story I learned from my uncle, Pete Seeger, and I have changed it to fit a pattern easily recognizable by the Suyá. I stand up and begin '*Taráma, kupen tõ da muhai ngo kam pa*' ('A long time ago, some people lived over there [pointing to the east] on the edge of a body of water'). I tell them how a giant named Abiyoyo that slept in the depths of the lake would wake up now and then and eat half of the village, especially savoring the children, then return to sleep for a long time. I tell them of a little boy whose singing is so bad it scares the animals and fish, and irritates everyone else, and about his father who is a magician and practical joker who can make things disappear.

Then I tell them how one day the sunrise is blotted out by the huge figure of Abiyoyo emerging from the lake. The earth shakes. I become Abiyoyo. Stamping around the seated audience, I describe him as 'as big as the tallest tree' with tangled hair, long claw-like fingernails, smelly feet, bushy black pubic hair and a huge floppy penis. Abiyoyo resembles monsters the Suyá have heard about from their grandparents. Children scream as I walk around shouting 'I want to eat children.' I describe how Abiyoyo can eat a tapir at a single bite, and how he squashes houses with his feet.

The audience is completely silent. I tell them that the boy suddenly wakes up, and takes his father out to see the giant. I describe how he timidly begins a song that simply repeats the name of the giant over and over again. 'Abiyoyo, Abiyoyo, Abiyoyo, Abiyoyo . . .' The giant, intrigued by the song, begins to sing. His voice (now mine) is low and silly. He begins to dance, and like a Suyá gone wild I leap around the circle, singing off rhythm and off pitch, looking out for the dogs that sometimes have to be beaten off as I work up to the climax of the story. Abiyoyo dances so long and hard that he gets out of breath and sweaty (ridiculously funny to the Suyá) and lies down. The magician father can now make him disappear and does so. The village is saved. We all sing the boy's song together: Abiyoyo, Abiyoyo, Abiyoyo, Abiyoyo. (Example 1.5 on the cassette; this version, for which only the final bit of singing is given, was performed in Portuguese at Diauarum, the Administration post, for Indians from several groups. The entire performance is recorded on Seeger 1973–86 cassette 8 side one.) 'Thus my father's brother taught me the song.'

That is the end of the evening's entertainment. The Suyá drift back to the houses, and we can hear people singing 'Abiyoyo, Abiyoyo, Abiyoyo, Abiyoyo' as we go to sleep.

Fieldwork is a delicate exchange of information and a subtle interaction of personalities, set within a larger socio-economic and political context. The Suyá thought we were quite good singers, which probably helped when it came to studying their music and myth. Singing, they were quick to notice, was one of the few things we could do quite well. As hunters, fishermen, manioc-scrapers or language-learners we were definitely inferior to their own children. But we could sing. We sang when they asked, regardless of how we felt. And we were famous throughout the Xingu National Park for our songs. Some of them, like Abiyoyo and a Seneca canoeing song, became intertribal hits.

It was satisfying to be appreciated for something besides the power of our relatives ('Would your father drop a bomb on the Txukahamae if they raided us and you were killed?' they asked), or the usefulness of our trade goods.

On 29 January we were part of the ceremonial euphoria. We provided the music that made people 'happy.' The Suyá wanted us to make our contribution. We were part of the ritual process, but only at certain moments and in certain ways. Most nights we were hardly remarked on, and the Suyá sang their own music and did other things they found satisfying and right.

30 January

'Tony, let's sing.'

At 5:00 in the morning, the men are gathering in the men's house to sing another rainy season unison song. Ceremonial periods have a greater intensity; sleeping in is considered antisocial. So I go out to sing, then off to fish. It is another day, and my understanding of the Mouse Ceremony and Suyá society slowly improves.

Judy and I lived with the Suyá for a total of fifteen months between June 1971 and May 1973. We returned for shorter periods in 1976, 1978, 1981, and 1982. In 1978 and 1981 we took our daughters Elizabeth Mapalu and Hiléia Katherine with us, which both they and the Suyá enjoyed tremendously. Between 1975 and 1982, when we lived in Rio de Janeiro, Suyá families would occasionally visit us there. We took Niokombedi and his wife and one child home to Rio de Janeiro with us once, to reciprocate the many months we had lived in his family's house. In other cases, a Suyá might get so sick that he would be sent to a hospital in São Paulo. After recovering, he could sometimes come to Rio de Janeiro. We always enjoyed these visits, although they were a burden on our budgets and a challenge to our understanding. Our own visits to the Xingu were limited during these years by the obstacles created by the National Indian Foundation (FUNAI) which made anthropological research difficult for Brazilians and foreigners alike, especially those involved in the political movement for ensuring Indian rights and concerned about the fate of native lands.

My research methods were in the anthropological tradition of participant observation, and have been described at some length elsewhere (Seeger 1981: 1–17). We participated in the daily round of activities more than we had expected. I never really enjoyed hunting or fishing. Nor was it always easy to find people who would feel like talking to me – they had their own busy and complex lives to lead, and some of my questions were unthinkable, others were unanswerable, if they could be understood at all.

As a result, I found it was best to give my full attention to whatever was going on in the village – ceremonies, sickness, death, witchcraft accusations, naming, or anything else – in order to take advantage of the general interest and conversation about whatever it was. I would ask many different people about the event, and compare what they said. Research strategies must be adapted to one's perception of field situation. As I became more fluent in Suyá, my questions became more interesting to them. Even so, what evidently was an adequate answer to a question in Suyá did not always enlighten me, and the mutual effort to understand each other was often tiring and frustrating for everyone involved.

The Suyá were not required to have us at all. We were all very much aware of this. The administrator of the northern part of the Xingu National Park had told the Suyá that if they didn't like us, he would send us away. He also told them that we were musicians who would sing for them, and that we would write a book about them, which he would read. We were not directly imposed on them by force of arms or bureaucracy. We compensated for the inevitable frustrations our presence caused for our hosts in a number of ways. One of these was our participation in subsistence activities – each of us according to our sex and our capabilities. Another was through the distribution of trade goods – fish hooks, line, .22 bullets, beads, mirrors, cloth, even tape recorders and batteries, and a variety of other things the Suyá would ask us to bring them from the cities. These were things they could not easily obtain otherwise, because they had neither money nor access to markets. For many essential items they remained dependent on uncertain gifts from the Brazilian Indian Foundation. We also administered medicines when we were asked to treat someone. If we cured an infection or a simple case of malaria early, the family would not need to seek medical aid at one of the Brazilian Indian posts, and they were grateful.

Another compensation was our exoticism and (usually) good humor. An incompetent adult does a lot to laugh at. When I capsized a canoe after casting vigorously, or when I mispronounced a word, I would laugh and listen to many descriptions of my extraordinary ineptitude. In compensation, the Suyá would recount our successes with equal enthusiasm.

In addition, the Suyá were concerned about the intrusion of Brazilians into their former lands, and curious about the ways of the Whites (or non-Indians in general, called by them *caraí*). We answered their many questions as well as we could, and showed them what we knew of Brazilian society when they visited us in Rio de Janeiro. I never knew how much they believed, but they did find us useful as representatives to the outside world. They knew of my own involvement in the Brazilian Indian rights movement, which was a constant part of my professional life between 1975 and 1982. An important part of our success in the Xingu region was our music. If we were clumsy, ignorant, part blind, and showed little obvious evidence of intelligence, we could at least make music in a way that few Whites the Suyá had ever met could make it.

The first time we played and sang in an Indian village, my whole perception of our roles as fieldworkers in the Xingu region was changed. We were invited to record some flute music in the village of the Yawalapiti, near Posto Leonardo Villas Boas. When we finished recording, the men asked us to return and play some of our own music. So the next day we went back with our instruments. The men were finishing an afternoon of singing themselves, and were covered with red body paint, brightly colored head ornaments, and feather arm bands. In the lengthening shadows we sat down by the flute house and tuned up our banjo and guitar. As we started to play, a Yawalapiti man, painted and ornamented like the others but wearing dark glasses and carrying a Sony tape recorder, walked over to us and started recording our music!

Who was studying whom? What was a tape recorder doing in the middle of the jungle? Our astonishment quickly gave way to a clearer understanding of the situation in which we were working. In the Xingu, different societies were confronting each other with curiosity and some hostility. All of my research would be two-sided. We would be watched, studied, evaluated and discussed just as I was watching, writing, and discussing. The Indians in the Xingu expected to be treated as equals or superiors. The Suyá once threatened to kill a passing anthropologist who they believed had ordered them to do something. 'Here, *we* tell people what to do,' they affirmed. One woman told us the Suyá liked us because we never told them what to do or criticized the way they did something.

What I learned that first day when we were recorded in the Yawalapiti village, and in subsequent months, applies to anthropological research throughout the world. We are not dealing with passive objects, or 'subjects.' We live in a world in which realignment of power is occurring, and in which a solitary researcher inevitably has to accede to the will of the members of the society with which he or she works or find him or herself quickly removed. If this passage from colonialism to mutual respect and curiosity can be bridged, it will be better for both anthropology and ethnomusicology (to say nothing of the peoples themselves). But it takes some patience on the part of researchers unaccustomed to having their images of themselves questioned.

Increasingly anthropologists are being asked 'what can you do for us?' by the people whose societies they are doing research on. It is sometimes a disturbing question, but generally a healthy one, indicating an end to some forms of colonial domination. The Suyá never asked us this question, partly because they knew what they wanted us for: we could become 'their Whites,' bring them things they wanted, treat the sick, answer questions they had about our world, and sing for them.

Other groups don't always perceive their need for an anthropologist, and ask outright why they should have one living with them. A positive response is simply 'what can I help you with?' It may be teaching writing or arithmetic, it may be working with members of the group to write their own history, it may be developing a self-generated development project, or it may be interceding with members of a different ethnic group to find jobs and obtain needed documents. The nature of the request may be entirely unexpected, fulfilling it can be an important part of the field experience.

Every researcher today must be prepared for questions about the utility of his or her presence and the ultimate usefulness of the project. In the case of those studying music, they can offer to document the traditions of the group, guaranteeing preservation for future generations through deposit of the materials in a secure archive, and offering copies of tapes, photographs, and any other useful materials to the group. Increasingly, part of our time and energies will have to be devoted to meeting the desires of the communities we study.

Every field experience is different. Some Indian communities are reported to dislike the music of anthropologists. It was my experience that the Suyá were very explicit about the degree to which I would participate in their lives. At their insistence we hunted together, fished together, sang together, exchanged songs and exchanged our appreciation of each other as singers, hunters, and students of each others' ways. In other spheres they set clear boundaries between themselves and us. We pretty much let the Suyá define the roles we would play, even when we found them arduous or constraining of our individuality and 'freedom.'

We were in the Suyá village at their sufferance. We were there to learn. How we would learn, and what we would learn, I pretty much left up to them at the start. Only as time went on did I begin to organize my investigations more and more in terms of the research I had originally proposed to do. At one point in our fieldwork the Suyá asked us to stop speaking English to each other, since by then we could understand them, but could not be understood. We resolved the problem by largely confining our English conversations to our trips to the gardens or baths in the river, when we were alone.

Some men and women took an active role in the research, asking us if we knew about certain things they thought we should know. Another example of collaboration was the production of a record of their music. After our return in 1975, the men asked whether I had made a record of their music. They had seen records, and had heard one of Indian music.

They wondered why I had not done so. So in subsequent visits I talked with them about what music should be on it, brought a mock-up tape, and in 1982 a record was issued that was cut and pressed in Rio de Janeiro. *A Arte Vocal dos Suyá* (Seeger and A Comunidade Suyá 1982) was the first LP record of a single Brazilian Indian society produced in Brazil, and the royalties went exclusively to the Suyá.

The intense experiences, the close personal relationships, and the total physical and intellectual involvement anthropologists tend to develop with the communities they study are essential features of anthropological research. There is, of course, a great deal more to research than that. The researcher must be able to understand what he or she is being told – not only through language, but through gesture, a glance, a brief silence, or an omission. In the case of small communities such as the Suyá a kind of dependence develops. The Suyá even reversed the common possessive form once used by anthropologists who spoke of 'my tribe' or 'my village.' They called us 'our Whitemen.' According to the Suyá, other groups in the region had their 'Whitemen' who studied them and could be counted on to bring gifts and sometimes act as intermediaries with the rest of Brazilian society. Now they had some too. In the long nights since my last visit, they have undoubtedly sat in the village plaza and remembered the things we did, the songs we sang, the presents we brought, and speculated on the size of our children. Thousands of miles away, under different stars, I often think of the rivers we traveled, the taste of wild honey, the companionship we experienced, the sights, smells, and textures of our experiences together.

The rest of this book discusses verbal art removed from the moment in which I learned of it and apart from the daily round of which it was only a part. It was, however, always embedded in days devoted to many different activities, some of which have been described here and others of which appear in Chapter 6, which were themselves further embedded in larger national, political, and professional frameworks. If these rarely appear in the descriptions it is because the Suyá were then somewhat isolated from the effects of national events. The national context will reappear in the final chapter.

2   *Suyá vocal art: from speech to song*

Any ethnomusicological study of music should begin by examining music in relationship to other art forms, because nothing simply exists in itself. Everything is always partly defined by what it is not – by the other members of a set which usually are systematically related among themselves. Definition through interrelationship is a fundamental tenet of structuralism and semiotics (see Lévi-Strauss 1963b), and yet it is often ignored in ethnomusicological studies. There are some excellent exceptions, however, in work by Charles Keil (1979), Steven Feld (1982) and Rafael de Menezes Bastos (1978).

Since virtually all the music the Suyá performed or played was song, an analysis of their singing must begin by relating song to other vocal art forms. This chapter presents and compares examples of several genres that run the entire gamut of Suyá verbal forms. Each form is presented separately, often with an example from the cassette tape. Following the individual description, the genres are compared by their texts, phrasing, pitch relations, the textual authority. Song can be clearly distinguished from the other verbal forms on all but one of these parameters.

Four nouns (and, in a slightly different form, verbs) were central to an understanding of the way Suyá distinguished different genres. These were speech (*kapérni*), instruction (*sarén*), song (*ngére*) and invocation (*sangére*). The Suyá translated *ngére* as music, but in their case music was entirely song. There are many different kinds of song, associated with specific singing styles and also with specific ceremonies. Song was contrasted with *sarén*, which I translate as 'instruction' or 'telling.' There were several kinds of instruction, including formal exhortations of children, recitative solos in public ceremonies, and the narration of myths. The third major term, *kapérni*, I translate as speech, and to speak. It was modified by a number of other words which described kinds of speech, for example 'plaza speech,' 'bad speech,' and 'angry speech.' *Sangére* were invocations or curing songs that had an effect on the body. Some of the vocal art forms are given in Table 2.1.

Instruction: the myth of the origin of the Mouse Ceremony

Suyá narratives, called 'what the old people tell/told,' were not formal affairs; they were told anywhere, by men or women, at any time of year. Some myths were specifically associated with particular ceremonies, and the example below was associated with the Mouse Ceremony.

On a sultry day before the beginning of the Mouse Ceremony Iawekidi, a woman about sixty years old, sat in back of her house, spinning cotton thread in its shadow. Nearby, one of her daughters scraped green corn to make pudding and another toasted a corn cake wrapped in banana leaves. Some of her grandchildren played around them, cobs of roasted corn in their hands. Three of her five green parrots waddled through the dust looking for fallen

Table 2.1. *Suyá vocal genres*

1. 'To instruct,' 'to tell,' 'to relate' (*sarén*). Often used in the sense of a parent instructing a child, or reporting on an entire, concluded, event. In the third person singular the form is *sarén*; in the first person it is *iarén*, as in the names of specific verbal forms, given below.

   1.1. 'Instruction' (*sarén*) of an unspecified sort usually refers to a kind of instruction. A father tells a child how to behave; a man relates the events of a fishing expedition; or a mouse (in a myth) instructs in the cooking of maize. There are no specific times or places for these events, and the phonetics and grammar are usually those of everyday speech.

   1.2. 'What the old people tell' (*mētumji iarén*) refers to narratives we could call myths. They are stories with clear narrative coherence (plot), but only a moderately predetermined performance style, which varies with the age of the performer, and the nature of the audience. Anecdotes about more recent events are not called by this term. Often performed in a question and answer form in the houses or in the village plaza, but without restrictions as to time and place. Example 2.1 on the cassette is an excerpt from the myth of the origin of maize, told by Iawekidi, considered to be a very knowledgeable older woman.

   1.3. 'Recitatives' (*huru iarén, ngatu iarén, gaiyi iarén*) refer to recitative-like addresses in ceremonies in which certain members of the village are publicly instructed through *iarén* to act in prescribed ways with respect to gardens, boys, or girls, in specific ceremonies. All of these are performed by men (usually recently initiated) in the village plaza. Example 2.2 on the cassette is a *ngātu iarén*.

2. 'Speech' (*kapérni*) refers to speech of all kinds. Public speech represents power; forms of speech both signify power and give power over people and events. Among the specifically named forms of speech are the following:

   2.1. 'Everyday speech' (*kapérni*). Speech of the most general level refers to everyday speech forms, spoken by men, women, and children. Little formality, variable length phrases. Example 1.2 on the cassette is a short excerpt from informal talk in the men's house.

   2.2. 'Bad speech' (*kapérni kasaga*) refers to the jealous speech of witches and selfish people. It is a private, rather than a public form, without a particular structure, hour, or place of performance. It is probably more talked about than spoken. I have no recordings of 'bad speech.'

   2.3. 'Angry speech' (*grútnen kapérni*) refers to public speeches made by any man (old or young) who is angry and chooses to use it to make his feelings known publicly. It is only spoken by men. When men perform in the plaza they usually walk in a circle carrying a weapon. It is a style characterized by short, rapidly spoken phrases and abrupt tone contours. Because every occasion in which 'angry speech' was used was tense, and the speaker often angrily shot off his gun as he spoke, I was unable to record any examples of this speech form.

   2.4. 'Everybody listens speech' (*mē mbai wha kapérni*) is highly structured public speech, with long phrases and cadences. It is said to be spoken only by certain political and ceremonial leaders, and exhorts the community to behave 'correctly.' It is very similar to 'slow speech,' below.

   2.5. 'Slow speech' (*kapérni kahrĩdo*) refers to the exhorting speech of any older adult man addressing the entire village from the village plaza. 'Slow speech' contrasts with 'angry speech' in the slow delivery of the phrases and the intonation. It is hard to distinguish from the 'everybody listens speech' except that more men may use it. Example 2.4 on the cassette is an excerpt of 'slow speech' spoken by Kaikwati.

3. 'Invocation' (*sangére*) is a quietly recited form that is performed over patients by adults of either sex in a number of different locations – although usually not in the plaza. It is a private verbal form, not meant to be heard by many people. Example 2.3 on the cassette is an example of an invocation.

   3.1. 'Burity palm racing log invocation' (*ngwa iangraw*) is a kind of recitative that is spoken quietly at the head of a log racing track in order to make the heavy burity logs 'light' and to keep them from injuring the runners. It is slightly different from the *sangére* as it has a song-like structure, is performed by the ritual specialist and listened to by assembled men.

4. 'Song' (*ngére*) refers to music, especially song, of any type. Songs are said to have fixed texts and generally share a similar structure of textual presentation, but there are quite a few different genres.

   4.1. 'Shout song' or 'call' (*akia*) refers to individual songs performed only by boys and adult men until they have several grandchildren. Examples 1.1 and 1.4 on the cassette present two different performances of shout songs.

   4.2. 'Unison song' (*ngére* as contrasted with *akia*) refers to songs usually performed in a lower register, and often in unison. The singers may be men, women, boys, girls, and the aged performing together or as separate groups. Some are sung exclusively by name-based groups. There are quite a number of variations in song style. The songs from different ceremonies are known by the name of that ceremony, e.g. 'deer song,' 'wild pig song,' and 'turtle song.' Example 1.3 on the cassette is a rainy season unison song, Example 6.3 on the cassette is a Mouse Ceremony unison song.

kernels and squabbling with the dogs over fish bones. It was a domestic moment with few adult men around, a good time to learn things from the women.

The myth described how the Suyá used to eat rotten wood before they learned about garden crops from the mouse. It told how a young mother took her son to bathe, where a mouse told her about corn. It recounted how the woman's house kept the corn a secret until the child could walk. Then her son carried a corn cake to the center of the village for the men. After the men tried the corn, they ran to the river and emptied it of garden crops. They threw away the rotten wood, and have eaten garden products ever since. The relationship of the story to the Mouse Ceremony was indirect, in the sense that the mouse never actually taught any songs, the way animals did in some myths. The narrative did define the principal actors and their relationships, and it revealed some important features of music itself. Recounted in the present tense by the best female performer I encountered, Iawekidi's story was also a very good example of the oral style called 'telling' or *sarén* (1 in Table 2.1 above). Example 2.1 on the cassette presents the first three paragraphs of the myth, which are transcribed below, then skips to later in the story, where the teller employs a different style, reporting several dialogues between different speakers. The two sections in the recording are indicated in the translation below.

The microphone recorded the story, the grating of the corn, the squawking of the parrots, the shrieks of the children, and the slapping of mosquitoes on the skin. 'Ne iũ' said Iawekidi, to indicate she was going to begin. The way Iawekidi told the myth was different from everyday Suyá speech. The phrases were long and she employed considerable parallel construction.

[Recording begins]

For a long time our ancestors ate soft rotten wood. They pounded rotten wood. They pounded it in pestles and ate it. They ate it baked with pieces of meat, or pieces of fish. They ate it that way for a long time. They lived for a long time that way. The evil cannibal monsters killed them, then stopped. Our ancestors killed the big mosquito monsters. Time passed. They lived for a long time like that.

The Suyá moved to the river of food and made a village there. They built a village at the river of food and lived there for a long time. There was lots of food in the water: sweet potatoes, cará, [and other plant foods]. There was lots to eat. There was corn, too, and manioc – a lot of food. When our ancestors went to the water they had to push the plants aside in order to bathe. They pushed the plants aside and bathed. That went on for a long time. They bathed surrounded by sweet potatoes. The skins of the potatoes were blackish blue in the water, but the people only looked at them. This went on for a long time.

Now, a man begins to court a young girl. He begins to court her and have sexual relations with her when she is still very small. Then she grows bigger, her breasts begin to swell [she reaches puberty]. Our ancestors are eating rotten wood, and live that way for a long time. Then the young woman becomes pregnant. Time passes.

[Recording interrupted: the following paragraphs are not on the tape]

The child is born and she lies in her hammock until the blood stops flowing. After a time she and her husband paint themselves and begin to eat fish and game again. She takes her baby to the water to bathe often. She takes it to bathe, and she bathes it. The baby grows very large and it lies with her in the hammock. Our ancestors are racing with burity logs. They bring logs into the village, and bring more logs into the village. It is nearly the middle of the log racing season [about January]. The baby cries a lot and its grandmother says to its mother 'take it to the river to bathe and distract it.' 'All right' the mother replies. She picks up the baby and takes it to the river. Together they bathe in the water. It is early morning when she takes it and bathes with it.

She enters the water to give it a bath. A mouse jumps on her shoulder. 'Hey! What kind of thing are you to sit on my shoulder?' she exclaims, throwing it off her shoulder. It comes back and jumps on again. 'Why, you bad animal, are you like a person that you fool around like this?' She throws it off again. Once more it returns and climbs on her shoulder. 'Behave, and go away,' she exclaims, throwing it away again.

Then the mouse says 'Wait, stay there, I am going to tell you something.' 'What?' asks the woman. 'I am going to tell you something,' the mouse says. 'What are you going to tell me?' she replies. 'See, I am going to tell you about something to eat. Do you see, *this* is the river of food, right here,' the mouse tells her. 'Really?' she replies. 'You are living on the river of food and you are bathing in it,' the mouse goes on. 'What is it?' she asks. 'That is corn. That is corn,' replies the mouse. 'You should take some and go back to the village with it. If someone should ask you, "what have you got in your hand? what are you bringing to the village" you should say it is your child's. Say "my child was crying so I brought this along to stop it." Then tell your mother to pound it and put it in the ashes and wait for it.' 'All right, I will,' the woman replies.

She takes one ear of corn and climbs the bank with it. Gingerly she picks one ear, holding it between two leaves, and carries it up from the river. She carries it along. People coming to the river to bathe say 'Hey, what is that bad thing you are bringing up from the river? Don't eat it!' She replies 'My child was crying for it, so I am bringing it up from the river' just as the mouse told her to do.

In her house, she puts the corn on the roasting rack and goes to her mother. 'Mother!' 'What is it?' her mother replies.

'Mother, I was down at the water and the mouse jumped on me and told me something. It came and sat on my shoulder and told me to stay still, that it would tell me something. It would tell me about something to eat. It said to take some and hide it.' 'Is that so?' said her mother. 'Yes, it said "that is corn. Take some to your mother. Is your mother alive?" it asked. "Yes, she is alive" I responded [this probably refers to part of the dialogue she left out earlier]. "Have your mother pound the corn [in a pestle], wrap it in leaves, and place it in the coals to cook." That is what he told me' the daughter says. 'All right' replies her mother.

They take the corn and shuck it. The kernels are very large, and they twist the ears to strip them off. They pound them, wrap the meal in leaves and put it in the coals of the fire. It lies there for a while and then is ready. They pull it out of the fire.

The young mother's husband arrives. 'My child's father!' the mother says. 'Yes?' replies her husband. 'Have you seen anything like this? Come here and take some; come here and take some.' He takes some corn cake and eats it. 'Huuuuuuu,' he says. The corn cake is a rich yellow. 'Only adults should eat this. Only belligerent men should eat this. Don't you eat it; we will [eat it and] be the ones to die. Don't you eat it,' he says to his wife. 'Only your old mother should eat it.' He takes some more corn cake and eats. The young mother goes to the water and picks a few more ears of corn and carries them back to the house. They make more corn cake. It is good. The house is full of rotten wood. At night they take all the rotten wood out of the house and throw it away in the forest. In its place they fill their house with corn, at night. They eat corn, sweet potatoes, *mbrai*, *ngero*, and other things they have brought from the water. They eat that way for a *long* time. They eat that way for a long time. The child becomes strong. He begins to crawl and pull himself around the floor sitting up. The corn in the water ripens and dries again [it is January again].

The men go into the forest looking for the cane they use for weaving baskets [and also for rotten wood]. Now the boy's father goes into the forest hunting for game [a man does not hunt large animals for some months after the child is born]. They eat the game baked in cornmeal. The other men go looking for cane in the forest. 'Where are you going?' they ask the father. 'I am looking for cane,' he replies. He puts rotten wood in the doorway of his house. He has some rotten wood in his hand to show the men. 'We see,' the men reply. The corn dries out and they store it in their house.

Now, after a time the child begins to crawl and walk. The mouse asks the boy's mother 'Can your child crawl now?' The mother replies, 'Yes, he can crawl and walk.' 'Your child can walk. You should pound a lot of cornmeal to make meat pies. When the men race with burity logs into the village, and throw them down in the center, you should give them some corn cakes to eat in the plaza. Then the men will see, and all of you will eat well in the village.' 'All right,' the mother responds.

In the village, the young men have all been initiated into the men's house. The Suyá have sung the *Gaiyi* song and finished it. The woman and her mother pound the corn and wrap it in leaves with pieces of meat. They cook it in the fire and remove it. When the men finish singing the *Gaiyi* song they begin to go out after burity logs. They race with them into the village. Then they finish racing. They finish racing and go to sing [rainy season unison songs] in the men's house.

[Recording resumed: the following paragraphs are on the tape]

The mother says to her son *'Wagmē* [a moiety name, and quite distinct from the address form 'baby'], come here. Take this. Take this. Go to your *ngedi* [mother's brother] and take this with you. Take this to your mother's brother.' 'All right' [the boy replies]. He takes some corn cake and walks to the plaza in the direction of the two men's houses, which are full of men.

The adult men of the *Kren* society see him coming and shout excitedly 'Hey, what is that our name receiver is bringing us? What is that reddish-yellow thing he has taken and is bringing to us? What can it be? Come here, name receiver. Come here name receiver. Come here name receiver; bring it here so we can see it. Bring it here so we can see it.' 'All right' [the boy replies].

The boy goes to the *Kren* moiety's men's house. They look at the corn cake. 'What is it?' [they cry]. 'This is a corn cake' says the boy. 'I am eating a corn cake.'

Then the men of the *Ambàn* moiety call to him 'Our name receiver, give us a taste! Give us a taste! Name receiver, give us a taste'! The boy goes to the *Ambàn* men's house and says 'Look.' [The men exclaim] 'Hey, what is that, what's that, what's that?' 'This is corn,' the boy replies. 'It is a corn cake my mother baked for me and I brought it out here to eat.' 'Where are the others? Are there more in your house?' the men ask excitedly. 'The house is full of them' the boy replies. 'Aaaaahhhh!, I want some, I want some, I want some!' shouts an old man of the *wikenyi* age grade. All the adult men run to the house, their feet thudding on the ground: rurururururururu. The boy's grandfather steps out of the house and says [in the stuttering speech of the aged], 'Hey, hey, go, go, go, go-to, go-to, go to the water. Go to the water! You have been bathing in it! You have been pushing it aside in order to bathe!'

'Let's go'! shout the men. The men run to the water, [their feet going] kru-kru-kru-kru-kru, and take all of the corn. The water is empty.

[Recorded section ends here]

They bring up squash, they clear out *mbrai*, they dig up the sweet potatoes and skin them. They bring it all up and eat it. 'Come on, companions. Let's live here and eat this food!' They take all the rotten wood and throw it out in the forest, replacing it with maize. They replace it with maize. They live like that for a long time . . .

Iawekidi continued, describing further events leading up to the planting of the first gardens (see Seeger 1984 for a complete version).

Story telling was an art, and certain individuals were generally recognized as having particularly good style, even to the extent that certain people were recommended for certain stories. The story of the origin of corn was one Iawekidi was known for. Women's versions emphasized slightly different events. Iawekidi described the young boy's mother with greater care than versions told by men. Iawekidi described the woman's betrothal, and the start of sexual relations with her husband when she was very small is described, and some aspects of the child's birth – the way the woman lay in her hammock until the bleeding stopped – that were not even mentioned in the versions I recorded from men. They were all important parts of a woman's life. The men tended to skip over the early part of the story quite rapidly. The important relationships for them were those between the mouse and the woman, and between the woman's house and the rest of the village.

There was no fixed way to tell a Suyá myth. Although in some parts of South America a narrative may be memorized – the creation myth of the Xokleng is a case in point (Urban 1986), or a performance may require a listener who will give fixed responses (as described by Basso [1985] for the Kalapalo), most Suyá myths could be told in a variety of ways. They might be narrated directly, as in the myth transcribed above and recorded on the cassette. They might be told with interruptions where people asked questions, which were answered before the teller was encouraged by a member of the audience to continue until another question was asked. Or they might simply be alluded to in a single phrase. The general plot was usually known by the teller and the audience. Most Americans and Europeans have a similar familiarity with the biblical story of Genesis, which is used in the same way – as the subject of sermons, read directly or alluded to.

Narrative performance was a 'telling' (*sarén*) that had a distinctive performance style. It had longer cadences, could use archaic forms of speech, and voice tone was an essential component. There were no 'he said' and 'she said' markers to indicate who is speaking in Suyá myths, and some stories were almost entirely in dialogue. Tone, timbre, phonetic alterations, and tempo were all devices used in telling myths – just as they are also used in musical performances.

Examining the first lines more closely, some clear rhythmic and tonal structures emerge:

1. *Hwin*	*krawi*	*krat*	*kuludaw*	*paaaaaaaaaa*	
Tree	rotten	log	ate	living in a village for a long time	
2. *Hwin*	*krawi*	*krat-chi*	*katwün*	*mà*	*kuku*
Tree	rotten	log-big	pounded	with intention	ate
3. *Hwin*	*krawi*	*krat-chi*	*katwün*	*mà*	*kuku*
Tree	rotten	log-big	pounded	with intention	ate
4. *Kàm mbru ianin kuku ne, kàm tep ku ne,*					
With game cake ate it, with fish ate it					
5. *Kàm mbru ku ne,* *sag-nin kuku ne*					
With game ate it, in cakes ate it					
6. *Niu-re daw paaaaaaaaaaaaaa.*					
Thus lived in a village together for a *long* time					

The rhythmic and tonal structures are clearest when they coincide. Thus the second half of the first line and the sixth line are nearly identical, while line three is an exact repeat of line two. Within lines four and five there are two similar patterns: *kàm mbru ku ne* has identical emphasis and a parallel semantic construction to *kàm tep ku ne*. It has a parallel semantic construction with *kàm mbru ianin kuku ne*, where two of the even beats are broken up into four. In the opening lines, the myth displays a number of tonally and temporally structured phrases quite distinct from everyday speech.

Another feature of this particular performance of the myth were the long glissandi, or sliding pitches on a single vowel. These were used here to indicate emphasis – either a long passage of time or an indicator of size. They liiiiiived; they traaaaaaveled; they liiiiiived; it was a biiiiiig baby. These glissandi all provide a kind of timeless backdrop for the subsequent events, which were largely presented through extensive dialogue and reported speech and few glissandi. The glissandi were a clear example of iconic speech: where the speech sounds themselves carry semantic meaning. The traditional separation of phonology and semantics cannot be maintained in a case like this. The actual sounds of the performance carried meaning in themselves.

Later in the story, when Iawekidi described the exciting moment when the men, sitting in the men's houses after a log race, tasted maize for the first time, the style changed. The tempo increased. There were no glissandi, but instead different uses of the voice to indicate different speakers. She indicated the different speech styles of the mother, the boy, and the two groups of men through her tone of voice and the style of the speech itself. She still made extensive use of repetition and parallel constructions. Her use of the voice to represent different speakers was another common feature of Suyá myths.

While Example 2.1 on the cassette was a striking performance, it was not unusual. The events of the story were very similar regardless of the teller's age; the use of the special constructions of myth presentation, however, varied considerably. Younger tellers tended not to use such temporally long phrases. Older adult Suyá all told myths with fairly measured phrases and repeated tonal and rhythmic features. There was considerable room for stylistic differences and plot development by different tellers faced with different audiences under different conditions.

Instruction: ceremonial recitatives

There were other forms of 'telling' or 'instruction.' Rhetorically the most formal of these were the recitatives that accompany a number of ceremonies rarely performed today (1.3 in Table 2.1). They were usually spoken by young men who were leaving their natal houses to live in the men's house, during an initiation rite. A man would be taught a certain recitative instruction before a ceremony was due to start. At a certain moment in the ceremony – usually before the final event – he would be elaborately decorated with bird down, and laden with ornaments. He would sing in his mother's house, leave it with great elaborateness, walk to the men's house, and perform his 'instruction' in which he exhorted all the members of the village to prepare the ornaments and food for the final ceremonial activity.

Example 2.2 on the cassette is an 'instruction for the young men's ceremony' *ngātu iarén* performed by Takuti. Although Takuti was not a young man, as part of a long series of log races culminating in the 'young men's burity log' (*ngàtuyi ngwa*) in 1976 he was ornamented and performed the instructions shortly before the final race. The recitative (*sarén*) took its name from the ceremony of which it was a part. I make no attempt to translate this example, as even the Suyá had difficulty making more than general observations about its content. The recitative made extensive use of a parallel melodic and semantic structure with a descending contour. At the opening and close a member of the opposite moiety from the singer (who was a member of the name-based *Ambàn* moiety) spoke a line. In between, the performer's lines consisted of a single tone held to the end of a phrase where it dropped a minor third. These are schematically represented in the diagram with a rough indication of the phrase length, shown by the length of the horizontal lines.

These recitatives were carefully prepared, and generally memorized. I collected several in private performances, but this was the only public performance I witnessed. They shared a tonal and semantic structure rather similar to the one above. Some, however, were considerably longer.

Huuuuuu, my relatives.

(member of *kren* moiety: huuuuuuuuu)

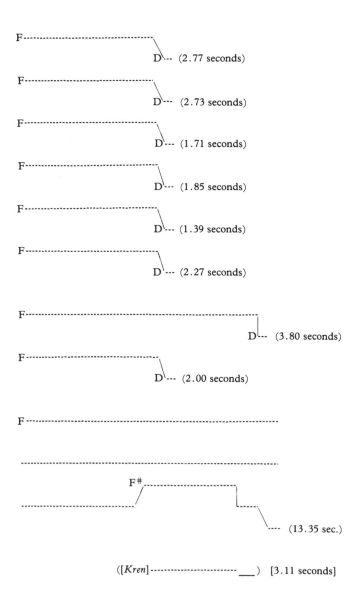

Invocations

Invocations (3 in Table 2.1) were performed in an entirely different style. They were very quiet, and might be performed without an audience at all. Their objective was to have an effect on another person's body. In Example 2.3 on the cassette, Takuti performs an invocation to enable an infant to begin eating manioc products.

1. *ã, ã, ã, ã, ã*
   Grunt, grunt, grunt, grunt, grunt
2. *ã, ã, ã, ã, ã-a*
   Grunt, grunt, grunt, grunt, grunt, grunt
3. *Ah-fffffu ah-fffffu*
   (Blow, blow)
4. *Ah-ffffu mawroma, ah-ffffu mawroma, ah-ffffu mawromaaaa*
   (Blow) goes   (3 times)
5. *Mawromaaaaaaaaa*
   Goes
6. *Wi angro mbe-ti   moro kute saw tã ku   sülü kataw daw tẽ*
   Becomes white-lipped peccary goes how come a bit eats goes to and leaves
7. *Tu kàmta, ku kàm ta, kango taikon kango tai kulu (??) ne sàrà kataw dn tẽ añitaw?*
   Root chew root eat juice drink juices takes some ready leaves and goes how come?
8. *Mbru tãw, mbru tãw, tàgà tã*
   Animal, animal, isn't that an animal
9. *Kulu taw pa kande urakta, taikon kwã kure*
   Eat master similar to, drinks and isn't affected

(Repeat lines 1, 2, 4, 5, 6, 7*, 8, 9, then repeats again 3, 4 (with one less *mawroma*), 5, 6, 7*, 8, 9.)

25. *Ah-fffu mawroma, ah-fffu-ã*
    (Blow) goes   (blow) grunt
26. *Ã,ã,ã,ã,ã,ã,ã*
    Grunt, grunt, grunt, grunt, grunt, grunt, grunt
27. *Ah-fffu, ah-fffu, ahfffu, ahfffu, ahfffu*
    (Blow, blow, blow, blow, blow)

* Line 7 is slightly different each time it is repeated. It is also very unclear exactly what is being said. The small differences are good examples of the slight variation found in many of the repeats in the invocations.

There were many reasons for performing an invocation. A sick relative, a woman in childbirth, a bleeding wound, and a toothache all called for them. So did many things that were not pathological, such as a sudden rainstorm (performed to keep it away), a disdainful lover (performed to punish), or a healthy child that they wished to grow up tall, strong, swift, and with good wind. I collected over sixty of them, and was called upon to sing 'Rain, rain, go away, come again some other day (blow, blow, blow)' on afternoons where towering dark thunderclouds threatened to dampen some enjoyable activity. (I had some surprisingly successful performances.)

The word for a large group of Suyá invocations is *sangére*. It is possible to imagine them to be a kind of song by breaking down the word into (*sa-ngére*). The Suyá, however, did not accept this etymology. They said invocations were different from songs. Because of their difference from the *ngére*, I call the *sangére* 'invocations' for convenience. (In an earlier publication I referred to *sangére* as 'curing chants' in order to stress their difference from songs (Seeger 1981: 212–19); here I call them 'invocations' as that now seems to best characterize their form and performance.)

It is quite likely that the Suyá originally learned to perform invocations from the Upper Xingu Indians. The western group of Suyá, known as the Tapayuna or Beiços de Pau, had never heard of them before they came to live with the eastern group, although they were familiar with all the other genres. The Suyá appear to have adopted the quiet performance style, dual structure, and general objectives from the Upper Xingu (mentioned in Viveiros de Castro 1977; Kuikuru invocations will be described in Franchetto, 1986). They changed the textual features considerably, making them compatible with their own cosmology, which is quite different from that of the Upper Xingu Indians. The burity palm invocation was performed in a very different style, and appears to have been an earlier, traditional Suyá form.

In the Suyá pharmacology, invocations were more important than herbal medicines. Herbal medicines were usually collected and prepared by family members, who administered them and were not given gifts in return. *Sangére* were often performed by family members, but some people had a specialized knowledge of them. If a patient recovered, the singer of an invocation was given a present by the people who asked him or her to sing it.

Invocations operated through an intricate system of metaphors. Their efficacy was the result of the insertion of an attribute of an animal, plant, or other natural object into the body of a human in order to give a particular body part or function the properties of the animal. In every case, something powerful was invoked that humans do not have, and the attribute was blown and sung into the patient's body. For instance, the invocation to allow young children to eat manioc foods without harm (above) named the wild pig, which is able to eat poisonous bitter manioc without ill effects. When the child became a little like the pig in that respect, it would also be able to eat manioc – at least the prepared kind – without difficulty. Takuti insisted that performing the invocation too often would be harmful. If it were performed more than twice for any given child, the child might develop an inordinate appetite for manioc and eat huge amounts, like a wild pig. Clearly some degree of animality is desired; too much is dangerous.

Other metaphors affected other aspects of the body. The invocation for infant convulsions named the black cayman, which lies very still and doesn't tremble; the convulsions should cease as the child becomes, at least temporarily, as still as a cayman in the water. The one for an easy birth named a small fish, which slips easily out of the hands; the infant should be delivered as easily. Another one for childbirth named a manioc 'pancake' (*beiju*). Just as women turn these pancakes quickly and take them off the fire rapidly, so the child will come out of her womb. To judge from my collection, strength was the attribute most often sought and the animals most often named were those considered to be powerful: the deer, jaguar, large otter, wild pigs, and reptiles. The attributes of fish were associated mainly with childbirth, birds were scattered among the invocations because each species had different attributes. Insects were used largely for rain; plants were for pregnancy because of the fecundity of certain palms and for growth because certain plants grow quickly to tower over the others.

Suyá interpretation and translation of invocations usually consisted of establishing what animal attributes were described and which animal was eventually named. After listening to my taped examples, and knowing that I wanted a translation into colloquial Suyá, most adults would say 'That is the invocation of the —— [an animal]; you know, it has very —— [the trait].' It was extremely difficult to get an exact translation of each line and metaphor. To the

Suyá I worked with, who were themselves performers, after the initial metaphor and the animal had been deciphered, the rest was unimportant. Indeed, the areas of variation within the performances of the same invocations by different people or by the same person at different times seemed to be in the number and type of different metaphors employed after the initial one, which is relatively fixed. What I was confronting was a different concept of translation and teaching.

The best Western parallel for the efficacy of an invocation is a hypodermic injection. The blowing injects a particular powerful essence of animality, distilled through metaphor, through the skin of the patient into his or her body. Once in the body it either rectifies weaknesses or strengthens positive tendencies that have an effect on the physical well-being of the patient. This may be one of the reasons the Suyá put so much more faith in Western medicine when it is injected instead of swallowed.

Invocations were performed by men or women, who usually blew onto the patient as they performed the invocation very quickly and very quietly. The time and place of their performance depended on the objective: *sangére* for growth were usually performed in the early morning after bathing; those for alleviating specific symptoms (pain, fever, bleeding, etc.) were performed when the symptoms were manifested. Invocation performances were extremely hard to hear for persons standing more than three feet from the patient, and they were very difficult to record except in special circumstances. My recordings were all made in the forest or gardens surrounding the village, far from the domestic noises. Even then the volume had to be turned up very high and the microphone placed near the mouth of the singer to get an adequate recording.

Invocations were usually learned by older children and adolescents who listened to adult performances. Children were able to move in close to performances in a way that adults rarely did or could. They learned most invocations by being close enough to actual performances to learn the style. The youths did not usually perform what they learned until they had children of their own. According to the adults, youth was the time when the ear was 'unclogged' and learning was easy. Most invocations were quite widely known, and had been passed down through tradition. Others were known by only a few people. These invocations were considered very valuable, and they were only taught with the understanding that a gift would be given in exchange. The invocation for scorpion bites, for example, was so jealously guarded by the only man who knew it that it died with him.

Although older men told me that people did not use invocations as much as they used to before they encountered Western medicine, it was an active form throughout my fieldwork. An invocation performance was often the equivalent of 'first aid' and prophylaxis. Certain older men were also asked to perform invocations on children from other Indian communities when they visited the local administration post, which they would do in the expectation of receiving a gift in return. In a similar fashion the Suyá would go to the administration post to consult shamans from other groups, and simultaneously to make use of the post's Western medical facilities. There is a tendency in South America for curers at a distance to be considered more powerful than local ones, and this is the case for the Xingu region as a whole.

The invocation on the cassette is fairly typical in structure and performance style. It was sung in a recording session in the gardens, but was apparently identical to a version I heard in an actual cure. The approximate transcription indicates longer pauses as line breaks. The textual structure appears more clearly in the free translation below.

1. Grunt, grunt, grunt, grunt, grunt
2. Grunt, grunt, grunt, grunt, grunt, grunt
3. Ahfffu, ahfffu
4. Ahfffu going away, ahfffu going away, ahfffu going awaaay
5. Going awaaaaay
6. The white-lipped peccary (*Tayassu tacaju*) goes, how come it can go to eat some and then leave?
7. Chews roots, chews roots, drinks juice, is finished and leaves, how is it?
8. Some animal, some animal, isn't that an animal
9. Something like the master of eating food, it drinks and is not harmed

(Repeats lines 1, 2, 4, 5, 6, 7*, 8, 9, then repeats again 3, 4 (with one less *mawroma*), 5, 6, 7*, 8, 9.)

25. Ahffu, it goes, ahffu grunt
26. Grunt, grunt, grunt, grunt, grunt, grunt, grunt
27. Ahffu, ahffu, ahffu, ahffu, ahffu

There is very clear parallelism throughout the invocation, as in the other verbal art forms analyzed so far. The first nine lines are almost exactly repeated three times, as follows:

1, 2, 3, 4, 5, 6, 7, 8, 9
1, 2, –, 4, 5, 6, 7*, 8, 9
–, –, 3, 4, 5, 6, 7*, 8, 9, 25, 26, 27.[1]

Certain lines are skipped in the repetitions – the first two lines appear in the second repeat but not in the last one. Line seven is slightly altered and virtually unintelligible in each repeat, in an apparently improvisational style also typical of the form.

Oratory

In every ceremony I witnessed there came a time when energies flagged and the initial euphoria dissipated in the daily subsistence tasks and everyday relationships. This was the moment for hortatory speeches in the plaza. On the afternoon of 2 February no boys had come out to the clearing to sing into the village. The few adult men who were there sang half-heartedly for a few minutes, then walked back to the village without the usual afternoon ceremonial entrance. That evening Kaikwati, the ritual specialist, began to orate as he walked slowly around the smoldering fire where a few men were sitting. He held a large black club in his hand, and thumped its handle on the ground. As more men arrived, they talked quietly while he spoke in a voice which could be clearly heard throughout the village. His carefully phrased speech was very different from his usual speaking style, and also from myth telling. It was a form of plaza speech called 'slow speech' (*kapérni kahrĩdo* 2.5 in Table 2.1), which has a structure of its own and involves normative exhortation. Example 2.4 on the cassette is a recording of a part of one of Kaikwati's speeches. For technical reasons I could not record the plaza speech in 1972, and I substitute for it an example recorded in 1982, orated by the same speaker. In terms of style they are quite similar, although the particular subjects discussed were probably different. I did not understand Suyá in 1972 as well as I came to later.

---

[1] I am indebted to Greg Urban for pointing out to me some of the parallel forms I had overlooked in my comparison of invocations with song.

Children, I am going to speak to you. Listen to my speech. You will perhaps listen to my speech. Our fathers, our grandfathers – not mine because I was not born a Suyá and am ashamed to speak in our language [here Kaikwati refers to his origins. He was born in a village of the Waura Indians in the Upper Xingu, but was captured as a young boy with his mother, was adopted, and has lived in the Suyá village ever since] – always spoke to their children. Your mother, our mother, your mother's brother, your father spoke to you and you listened to their speaking. You listened to their speech and behaved correctly. You followed their speech and behaved correctly. Our name givers were always like this. They spoke to their children and lived together. They spoke to their grandchildren. These weren't angry, they just listened to the speech.

Young men living in the men's house. Children, grandchildren, went to the listening place [an unusual way of referring to the men's house in the plaza where young initiates lived until they had a child, married, and went to live in their wives' houses] and hung [their hammocks]. When a man went looking for a wife, his mother's brother and his fathers and the residents of his natal house saw he wanted a wife and spoke to him. He would *follow* the speech and behave correctly. Mother's brothers, fathers, would speak to him. During the speech he would listen without anger. Men would speak to him, women would speak to him. He behaved correctly.

When he went to his wife they would speak to the husband. They never sat empty [without meaning], they spoke in the village. They spoke to him. Relatives too spoke to them thus. They did not marry with empty foreheads [without thinking?]. They spoke to their boys, they spoke to their girls, they spoke to the men. It was always thus.

(. . .)

They listened to the speaking and lived together. They followed [the speech] and behaved correctly living together.

The long phrases, the repetition of the word *kapérni*, and the lack of interruption set this form of verbal performance apart from everyday speech.

1. *Ngatureyi, aya amoi kapérni, kï aji imoi kapérni mba*
   Boys   to you I speak   do our to my speech listen
2. *ai imo   kapérni mba iantā*
   You my speech listen perhaps
3. *Wai a pam mē, ai gïtum mē*
   Your father and, your grandfather and
4. *Ai sa kre kàm i wï kupen taw   wa aya amoi kapérni*
   You house in   I am Indian another, to you I speak
5. *Ai amoi kapérni kwā whiasam   amoi kapérni*
   I to you I speak he ashamed to you I   speak
6. *A nā mē, i-wa nā mē, tukàyi mē, a pam mē*
   Your mother and, our mother and, your mother's brother and, your father and
7. *Ai amài kapérni daw pa   a kwā kapérni mba*
   To you speak and live together, you their speech listened
8. *Ai kwā kapérni mba kapérni   kot a añi mba ai a pa*
   You their speech listened speech followed behaved correctly and lived together
9. *Kapérni kot   a   añi mba*
   Speech followed you behaved correctly
10. *Wa krā tum ji da niureda, kute kra ji ma kapérni daw pa*
    Our name givers were thus, emphasis children did speak and live together
11. *Taumtwuyi, te ku ka mu pada kwā kapérni daw pa niu*
    Grandchildren (????) they spoke and lived together seated
12. *Kute, kam grüg kït ne, kwā kapérni mbai taw pa*
    How, with anger none they speech listened and lived together

Public speaking was restricted to a few adult men, not all of whom used it. Several men employed 'angry speech' in the plaza (2.3 in Table 2.1), but only Kaikwati regularly used the slower, exhortatory forms. 'Slow speech' was restricted to prestigious adult men. 'Everyone listens speech' (2.4 in Table 2.1), restricted to ritual specialists and chiefs, involved not only exhortation but suggested specific collective activities. The name 'slow speech' refers not only to the slow delivery with its long phrases and clear cadences, but also implies 'with care' or 'with attention.' Slow speech contrasted with 'angry speech' which was practically spat out, words quickly delivered, and phrases short and abruptly terminated with different tonal patterns. Although there were many different kinds of speech in the past, today very few Suyá claim to know them.

The oratory above is not only an example of the genre, it reflects on the genre itself. The word 'speech' (*kapérni*) and various uses of the verb 'to speak' (*kapérni*) appear fourteen times in the first twelve lines. This, too, was characteristic of all the examples I collected. The speaker not only appealed to the past to legitimate the present (our forefathers did this, therefore it is good and we should do it too), but he also appealed to the past to legitimate his speaking and the desired result of that speaking ('Our name givers, our fathers, they were always this way with their children. They always spoke to them and their children listened and did what they said').

There was also a larger structure to oratorical performances. Kaikwati spoke for nearly fifteen minutes on this occasion, with occasional pauses where he drew out a single syllable (as in the *paaa* at the end of the recorded sample). The structural units are too large to conveniently put on a tape. For the first seven minutes Kaikwati spoke of the speeches the Suyá used to make, and about how the young people listened to them and behaved according to what they heard: they followed the speech and behaved well. There were fairly regular short pauses of the type *paaa* approximately every minute or half-minute: 1:55, 2:24, 3:19, 3:36, 4:10, (5:00) 5:25, 6:00, 6:44, 7:01. At the 4:10 pause Kaikwati changed subjects slightly and talked about himself as a non-Suyá and his own experiences being talked to by the older people. He returned to the general statements at 5:00 minutes, where there is a very slight pause. This whole section legitimates the speaker, the speech, the subject addressed, and stresses its importance.

At the seven-minute mark there was a relatively long pause – about six seconds – where Kaikwati walked in silence, striking his club on the ground. Then he changed the topic. Although still referring to how things were done in the past, he talked about how a young man who married a man's daughter would make his father-in-law canoes and a new house; would bring him food, bird tail feathers, and other things; and would work very hard for his wife's family. He continued on this theme for over six minutes with short pauses at: 8:19, 8:55, 9:19, 10:13, 10:57, 11:28, 11:35, 11:50, 11:58 – a longer pause – 12:45, 13:18. The pauses appear to be more frequent toward the end as he seemed to be searching for ways to express himself. At 13:18 he changed the subject once again, returning to the initial theme about speaking and singing, and how he taught people songs. 'I have spoken to you, spoken well to you, listen to my words. Your fathers and your brothers spoke and you listened.' Here again Kaikwati stressed the importance of the occasion, of oratory, and of listening, establishing the legitimacy of his speech.

The long discussion of the duties of a son-in-law was not simply a general exhortation. The speaker's daughter had recently married a Juruna man, who was living in the speaker's house and he was personally concerned about the duties of a son-in-law. Even more to the point, his brother's daughter had also just married. She had married a young Kayabi man whose father was important but who, himself, did not seem to know how to fish, paddle a canoe, or show any inclination to learn. He did not want to stay in his father-in-law's village, and in a manioc beer drinking festival in August 1982 there was a long argument about his behavior, after which he left his wife, who spent hours crying during the night, audible to the entire village. As I left the field for the last time, Kaikwati's sons were trying to fix things up between them. The relations of sons-in-law to their fathers-in-law was very much on the adult men's minds at the time of this oration. At the same time as the village was exhorted to perform its ceremonies correctly, the speaker exhorted them to behave in correct ways toward their kin and affines.

Although speeches often began and ended with a conventional discussion of the importance of listening to and following the oratory of the adult men, the content of 'slow speech' and other forms of public oratory was not as fixed as in myths. Oratory could introduce topics of personal importance or public current events. While myths often recounted how society became the way it is now, oratory was used by those adult men who were permitted to perform it to legitimize particular positions through appeal to Suyá traditions and the way the 'fathers, mothers, mothers' brothers, grandfathers, name givers' and other relatives were supposed to have behaved.

Not all speeches were as serious or as emotion-laden as the speech above. Some used ridicule and broad humor to make the same points, as in the example below performed by Kaikwati on another occasion:

Our children do not paint themselves with body paint (*urucum*). They do not wear arm bands on their biceps or leg bands on their knees. Now their arms and legs are thin. All they want to do is wear White man's clothing. Shamelessly they walk around on their thin legs and show their thin arms. With their thin arms and legs the enemy Indians will no longer be afraid of us. They will say 'Let's kill the Suyá!' [and raid us] . . . We will become Whites with tiny, thin legs, like storks!

At this last image there was appreciative laughter. Kaikwati continued speaking, now about young men's sexual habits. He accused them not only of having sexual relations, but of having them with their mothers and sisters. Although it was humorous, part of this section was so obscene in its phrasing and implications that the Suyá later specifically asked me not to publish it. At that moment, probably because of the general shock at the turn of the speech, several parallel conversations broke out. Then Kaikwati continued, back to his earlier theme, extolling the grandparents of the present generation.

Your name giver [Tebnti tumu] lived correctly. He was full of respect. He always went out after racing logs [and he sang the shout song during the Mouse Ceremony]. He behaved correctly [did not have sexual relations]. When he was very small he would get up early. He would not accompany the women to the gardens. You should be like him, like your name giver. He remained for a long time in his high bed [especially constructed for an initiation ritual]. He became belligerent and tough when he was still young. He entered the men's house when the men were running log races. His grandmother and grandfather prepared white thread for his ornaments. He went to the men's house. He lived in the plaza. He sat there. He was bellicose.
Your tough grandfather, Wetkeneti, would say to young men who were having sexual relations: leave the men's house and go to your wife's father. Leave here and go to your wife's house. *We have always lived this way!* Our name givers, our fathers, they were always this way with their children. They always spoke to them and they listened.

Most of the exhorting plaza speeches I heard were very similar in style and general approach to the subjects. They referred to the deeds of deceased Suyá and exhorted people to behave like them in a style that combined preaching with humor and constituted a form of oral history. The oratory of the ritual specialist, and his castigation of the young men and extolling of the virtues of their fathers and name givers – either generally or naming specific ones – was very much a part of the ritual process. As with other aspects of ceremonies, there was room for humor in the speeches. And although no one seemed to pay any attention, the next day the young men always sang with tremendous vigor. That was true on 3 February 1972 as well.

Shout songs and unison songs

Examples 1.1, 1.3 and 1.4 on the cassette are examples of songs. There are a number of song genres, each having characteristic melodic contours, ranges and performers. They were often performed only in certain places at certain times. Two strongly contrasting genres were the shout songs (akia, 4.1 in Table 2.1, and 1.1 and 1.4 on the example tape) and the unison songs (ngére, 4.2 in Table 2.1, and 1.3, 6.3 on the example tape). The shout songs were sung by individuals or groups of individuals, in which case each sang a different song. Unison songs were sung by groups of individuals singing the same melody and words. There were a number of other contrasts as well: shout songs were sung in a high, forced voice. They usually began on the highest note, or its leading tone. The strophes (verses) of shout songs can be divided into a part with words and a part that just repeats te-te-te, although these sections differ in their length. There are between four and six discernible phrases to a strophe, which has a simple A B form and a range of about a fifth. The first two phrases usually have a more or less level contour, and the last two nearly always descend to the lowest, and final pitch, in the phrases of te-te-te-te-te-te song syllables characteristic of the genre – I once heard the shout songs referred to as te-te daw ngre or 'to sing the te-te.' Young children were taught very short phrases; teenage boys and older men learned longer ones. There are some discernible micro-intervals, especially in the tendency to slightly lower the notes of the final phrase.

Unison songs were usually performed in a low register and revealed a fairly level melody contour – although the pitch might gradually rise during a performance (described in Chapter 5). Young children could not participate with the adult men (because their voices were too high), and there was no attempt to be heard individually. Both shout songs and unison songs shared a common verse form and overall performance structure.

The melodies in the shout songs in Example 1.4 on the cassette are clearly related to one another. Since they were all taught at a single time and performed by young men and boys rather than older men, they are especially close in length and musical treatment. Recordings of simultaneous shout songs in other Mouse Ceremonies (1963 by Jesco von Putkammer, and 1972 by the author) reveal a similar unity of style. When an older adult spent an entire day singing the shout songs of his father on 2 February, there was much more melodic and textual variety, because the songs had been learned from different teachers and performed for different ceremonies (for an example of such an all-day performance of shout songs see Seeger 1973–1986: 86–316–F).

In spite of their similarity, each shout song had to be different from every other shout song.

Each singer wanted to be heard as an individual, and it was very important that each song be different enough to be distinguished from the rest. Differences were most easily heard in the rhythm, melody, text, and voice quality. When the Suyá listened to tapes of shout songs they would identify each singer and comment on the performance.

Textual features of shout songs and unison songs

Free translations of what the boys sing in Example 1.4 on the cassette are given below:

1. It is the small mouse, I leap and sing with my infant, I saw it.
   Te-te-te-te-te-te-te-te
2. It is the niati (mouse species), the mouse eats corn.
   Te-te-te-te-te-te-te-te
3. Ambe mouse, I put on my cape and leap and sing.
   Te-te-te-te-te-te-te-te
4. Big mouse, cut my cape, we leap and sing.
   Te-te-te-te-te-te-te-te
5. It is the big mouse, where are you going? We are going to put on our capes and leap and sing.
   Te-te-te-te-te-te-te-te
6. Small mouse, leaps and dances with its cape.
   Te-te-te-te-te-te-te-te
7. It is the big mouse, I put on my cape and leap and sing, we leap and sing.
   Te-te-te-te-te-te-te-te
8. The mouse is hungry, it leaps and dances with its cape.
   Te-te-te-te-te-te-te-te
9. Master of the river of food, long tailed mouse, becomes a cape and leaps and sings.
   Te-te-te-te-te-te-te-te
10. The niati mouse, I put on my cape and leap and sing.
    Te-te-te-te-te-te-te-te
11. Red mouse, paint my cape, I put on my cape and leap and sing.
    Te-te-te-te-te-te-te-te
12. The kukeni mouse leaps and sings, put black stripes on my cape, so I can leap and sing. The kukeni mouse leaps and sings, put black stripes on my cape so I can leap and sing.
    Te-te-te-te-te-te-te-te
13. Big mouse leaps and sings, I leap and sing. I put on my cape and leap and sing, leap and sing, leap and sing. I put on my cape and leap and sing, I can leap and sing.
    Te-te-te-te-te-te-te-te
14. Honey bee with stinger the headdress for the Bee ceremony, I sing with my headdress. I sing with my headdress, I sing with my headdress, I saw it.
    Te-te-te-te-te-te-te-te[2]
15. The black mouse's cape has gotten limp, I leap and sing. The cape has gotten limp, I leap and sing. I can leap and sing.
    Te-te-te-te-te-te-te-te
16. The black mouse leaps and sings; I leap and sing, I leap and sing. My cape swishes up and down as I leap and sing. I leap and sing. My cape swishes up and down as I leap and sing, I leap and sing.
    Te-te-te-te-te-te-te-te

[2] This is an 'old akia' not specifically for the Mouse Ceremony, and it therefore names a different animal. It was probably first performed as a shout song for a performance of the Bee Ceremony.

17. The big mouse can leap and sing. My cape swishes up and down, I can leap and sing. The big mouse can leap and sing. My cape swishes up and down, I can leap and sing.
    Te-te-te-te-te-te-te-te
18. Big mouse leaps and sings, take my cape and hang it up. Take my cape and hang it up, I leap and sing.
    Te-te-te-te-te-te-te-te

Every shout song text had three parts: (1) the name of an animal, insect, or plant, (2) an action associated with the animal that is particularly relevant to the ceremony, and (3) the te-te-te syllables. Song texts were supposed to be as distinctive as their melodies. When several different songs named the same animal, they did not describe the same action. In the shout songs above, six of the songs name the big mouse (*amto-ti*). All but two say different things: 'cut my cape (4),' 'we are going to put on our capes (5),' 'I put on my cape (7 and 13),' 'my cape swishes up and down (17),' and 'take my cape and hang it up (18).' Similarly, many of the shout songs describe putting on the cape and singing, but associated with different animals.

Unison texts followed much the same pattern. They contained the name of an animal, an action, and often a section of what the Suyá refer to as 'songwords' or syllables without direct referents. Songs that named the same animals usually described different actions, and those with the same actions named different animals. Example 1.3 on the cassette is typical:

1. *Kï krüdeti na ngwa gatüwü daw sogo daw ngre na*
   The trairão fish sings with its face painted for log racing

2. *Kï samudawchi-na, ngwa gatüwü wi sogo daw ngre na*
   The big-mouth bass sings with its body painted for log racing

The two halves of the song differ by the fish named and the specific action involved.

Songs were always identified by their texts instead of their melodies. I never heard a man say 'let's sing the one that goes like this' and hum a tune. Instead, the words were referred to first, and the melody later. The texts were interesting to the Suyá, who often tried to explain them by singing them more slowly and clearly to me – as though the meaning were obvious from the words themselves. It took considerable skill to decifer a song text, and in some cases not even the ritual specialist could do more than repeat the song itself. Not all songs had translatable texts. In some cases no one could explain what the Suyá text meant. In virtually all songs learned from foreigners, exact translation was impossible, although the Suyá knew they involved animals and/or spirits. They said they simply sang them, but that the people (or species) that taught them knew what they meant. Song texts were, however, central to Suyá performances.

Both unison and shout songs shared a single overall performance structure. Almost all songs began with a full verse sung only with song syllables. In a shout song this meant that one or more times the entire melody would be sung with the words te-te-te-te. Then the verse was repeated one or more times with the action words, but without naming any animal. Then the entire verse was sung: animal name, action, and song syllables. This full verse was repeated several times. The first half usually ended with a coda. The second half began in the same way, first sung with only song syllables, then action words and some song syllables, then finally an animal name, action words, and song syllables. The second part, too, ended with a coda, often more elaborate than that for the first half. This structure may be succinctly performed, or drawn out over a longer period. When Kaikwati taught shout songs, he usually repeated each verse and part twice. The structure can be summarized as follows:

Table 2.2. *Song structure*

FIRST HALF (*kradi*)
song syllables (*kwã kaikaw*)
approaching the name (*sinti sülü*)
telling the name (*sinti iarén*)
coda (*kuré*)

SECOND HALF (*sindaw*)
song syllables (*kwã kaikaw*)
approaching the name (*sinti sülü*)
telling the name (*sinti iarén*)
coda (*kuré*)

Many song texts made a parallel between the observed characteristics of the named animal species and some part of the action. In the Mouse Ceremony, the shout songs translated above repeat the verb *sarĩ* (first person *iarĩ*), which means 'to leap.' It was always described to me as the movement of a deer or mouse running along through the savannah or along a rafter. Men's movements in the Mouse Ceremony and the Savannah Deer Ceremony were also described as leaping – the right arms, holding rattles (sometimes made of deer hooves), rose and fell with the stamping of the feet. In the most dramatic moments of the ceremony everyone moved in a kind of hopping step, making the dance capes swish, rising and falling. In the songs the mice, and the singers, are all 'leaping' and all singing.

Songs often described important actions in the ceremony with which they were associated. Many of the actions described in the Mouse Ceremony shout songs above refer to the preparation of the dance capes – the responsibility of ceremonial relations called *niumbre krà chi* and *kràm ngedi*: 'hang up my cape,' 'cut my cape,' 'paint my cape (red),' and 'put black stripes on my cape, we put on our capes and dance.' These refer to a sequence of actions in the preparation of the dance capes. Once the capes were prepared and people were dancing, their movement might be described (swishing up and down) or their attributes defined (limp and rough). The songs often combined the identity of the singer and the animal: the mice leapt and sang; the human dancers leapt and sang. There was a frequent switch from third to first person in the text.

The Suyá were always telling me that they had many, many, different songs. New shout songs were introduced at every ceremony; new unison rainy season songs were introduced at every log race. Each performance began with a choice among alternative songs. When the men sat down to sing a unison song during the rainy season, the old men in the back often would discuss what song they would sing. They might say 'let's do the one with the catfish in the first half, and the big-mouth bass in the second half.' Another might ask how it went, and someone would sing it very briefly under his breath, with the words describing a certain action. The words and melody often would be inaudible in the front of the men's house. Then the song leader would begin the song. Sometimes only he would know the song, and at certain moments only he would sing, the others joining in when they had learned it.

Comparing speech, instruction and song

Examples have been given of everyday speech, myth telling, recitative, invocation, oratory and two different kinds of song (shout song and unison song). Even the untrained ear will hear some differences among them. In song, oratory, and myth telling, time and tone are clearly more structured than they are in everyday talking (Example 1.2 on the cassette). They are all named genres of Suyá verbal art, carefully performed and critically evaluated by the audiences. Yet although the Suyá were emphatic that speech is never song or instruction, they never systematically formulated the differences among them. It is, however, possible to distinguish them by the different ways they structure text, phonetics, time, pitch, and timbre. Compared to everyday speech one could say these forms are all 'musical' – they have a far greater elaboration of temporal and tonal structures than everyday speech – but not all of them are music.

Speech, instruction, song, and the fixity of texts

The forms differ in the amount of variation found in their texts. Texts in most forms of speech (*kapérni*) are relatively freer than in instruction, and songs have the most fixed texts. Everyday speech might be about any topic, and shifts of content were common. Even plaza speech, although highly formulaic in expression and repetitive in style, was not fixed. New topics were part of the creativity of the genre, which could also be used to address any kind of current crisis. New ways of addressing old subjects were also appreciated – comparing young men who don't wrap their knees and biceps to storks, for example, or developing a particularly virulent way of criticizing the young men's sexual activities.

The texts of invocations were relatively fixed. The incorrect performance of a *sangére* could be dangerous for patients, who might get worse instead of better. Although some of the metaphors in the middle of the invocation could be varied from performance to performance, the opening metaphors and the names of the animals were almost entirely fixed.

An important difference between speaking (*kapérni*) and instruction (*sarén*) was that instruction involved a prior knowledge of the entire unit by the teller and most of the audience. Although both plaza speech and the ceremonial recitative (*Gaiyi iarén*) exhorted, the text of the recitative was almost entirely fixed. The ceremonial recitatives I studied only varied in which relatives would be addressed; what would be said was fixed in an origin myth for the ceremony. Plaza speech, although highly stylized, was far more flexible.

Myths were like other instruction forms in that there was a previous knowledge of the entire structure, but the precise wording of myths was not fixed. There was no question of the order of events: they were known by most Suyá over the age of five. There was, however, considerable latitude for performers to elaborate parts of the story and briefly summarize others.

The texts of songs (*ngére*) were said to be entirely fixed, and they were legitimized by extra-human origins. They were all said to be learned from animals, plants, or enemies and should be performed as learned. When people unconsciously changed the words of any given song, they were criticized. Unlike plaza speech, nothing new should be introduced on successive performances of a song; unlike a myth the text was rigidly fixed. The sequence of parts and of actions and animal names was rigidly observed. In addition, the verses to songs were repeated over and over again, in a kind of extreme form of parallelism.

All four verbal art forms were more redundant than ordinary speech and made extensive use of parallel temporal, tonal, and semantic structures. In general, it would appear that the more formal the occasion and genre, the more highly structured the form.

If one were to place the different verbal art forms on a continuum from free text with little parallelism to fixed text with complete parallelism (repetition), they would appear as follows:

Table 2.3. *Textual fixity*

Free text
without parallelism
Everyday speech (Ex. 1.2)
Plaza speech (Ex. 2.2)
Myth performance (Ex. 2.1)
Ceremonial recitative (Ex. 2.2)
Invocation (Ex. 2.3)
Song (*ngére* and *akia*) (Ex. 1.1, 1.3)
Entirely fixed text & parallelism through repetition

Speech, instruction, song, and the alteration of speech

Speech, instruction, and song can also be contrasted in their use of language. Speech forms (*kapérni*), were all spoken in what could be called 'everyday language' in the sense that they all used contemporary pronunciation and vocabulary. The different kinds of speech were largely distinguished according to the subject talked about, the person speaking, and finally by the context and style in which the words were delivered.

Instruction (*sarén*) sometimes used words and phrases rarely employed in everyday speech, but similar to the way the Suyá said their ancestors spoke. It also employed metaphors that could be quite difficult to interpret without the performer's assistance. This was especially true of the largely memorized recitatives in ceremonies. Syllables were drawn out, pitch slides (glissandi) were frequent, and voice pitch and timbre were important stylistic features. The melodic structures of the *sarén* did not, however, alter the words themselves. The internal differences within the genre were quite large, however, as may be seen by contrasting Iawekidi's myth (Example 2.1 on the cassette) with Takuti's recitative (Example 2.2 on the cassette).

Songs present a rich complexity of linguistic alterations because the musical phrases take precedence over the text. Each note in a melodic line has a syllable, but the text does not usually have as many syllables as the melodic line has pulses. Certain new syllables were therefore inserted into the song words in specific ways to make up the difference in the length of the musical phrase and the number of syllables in the word. In addition to the inserted syllables, almost all songs had syllables with no direct semantic referent (although of course their performance itself signals something, including the type of song being performed). These were called 'song words' (*ngére kapérni*) by the Suyá, and included the Te-te-te-te-te-te found in parts of all shout songs, and the Jo-jo-ha-i of the rainy season unison song. The words that did have semantic referents were often pronounced quite differently from their present usage, but similar to the phonetics described by Karl von den Steinen for the Suyá in 1884.

Once the principle through which syllables were inserted into words is discerned, the translation of recently composed songs is fairly straightforward. This is the case of the shout song that opened the Mouse Ceremony. In the song the words sound like *a-ma-to-tu-ku-chi*. Removing the song syllables *a* and *u* it reads *amto tukchi*, which is normal Suyá for 'big black mouse.' The whole effect is not unlike singing Ha-le-lu-u-u-u-u-ia in a Christmas carol instead of Hallelujah. If recently composed songs are easy to understand, songs the Suyá said were quite old might defy interpretation altogether. When pressed, the Suyá would say that the only ones who still knew what they meant were the beings that taught the songs to the Suyá in the first place. One can go no further, for it is hard for an anthropologist to get translations directly from jaguars, birds, bees, and extinct enemies.

There is, then, a kind of continuum from verbal forms that have contemporary phonetics and free rhythm (everyday speech) to those with possibly archaic phonetics and where the rhythm dictates the form of the text itself (song). In between are a number of forms where drawn out syllables and pitch slides are frequently employed to impose a temporal pattern on the text (as in the examples of myth and curing song).

Speech, instruction, song, invocations and self-reference

Both slow speech and shout songs shared a linguistic feature of considerable interest. This was that both of them referred to themselves, action accompanied the speaking or singing about it. In the case of the shout songs, the singer who sang 'the mouse leaps and sings' was himself leaping and singing; the singer who sang about having his mask cut would have (or has had) his mask cut. In the case of oratory, Kaikwati not only made a public speech, he talked about how he was speaking to the audience, and how they should be reacting. This self-referentiality was not present in everyday speech forms, in myths, in recitatives, or in invocations. As we will see in the discussion of song texts in the following chapter, it was a feature of some unison songs.

What is the reason for this redundancy of speech and action? Why speak about it if you are doing it? Why refer to the self at the same time as the self is visibly acting? In the shout songs, it may be because the identity of the subject that is singing was itself ambiguous.[3] On the final night of the Mouse Ceremony the singers would undergo a metamorphosis in which they became a kind of being that was both human and mouse. The 'I' in the songs was thus ambiguous: it was both a human and a mouse. In several of the shout song texts given above, the song is about a mouse, but the verbs are in the first person. In number 16, for example: 'The black mouse leaps and sings; I leap and sing.' The subject is at once a mouse and a person; in the metamorphosis of the final night, the mouse and person are indeed a single being.

In the unison song texts there is a similar ambiguity. The person who taught the songs was a divided subject. His spirit lived with the animals; his body lived in the village (fully described in the following chapter). The first-person, self-referring texts there were often the words of

---

[3] I am deeply indebted to Eduardo B. Viveiros de Castro for this suggestion, as well as for some of the ideas in the following section, which he proposed after reading an earlier draft.

the spirit, speaking about the effect on it of the events described in the song. Here again, the ambiguity of the subject is an important feature of the self-reference.

In the case of the slow speech, the situation appears to be different. The speaker was not transformed. What does seem to be happening, however, is that the speaker was trying to compress the present and the past into a single moment. As he invoked the speeches of the fathers, mothers, mothers' brothers, and old Suyá who had come before, he was also seeking to put his own speech on a par with theirs. The ambiguity was not in the nature of the performing subject, clearly an adult man with status, but with time itself: this speech was at once present and past; the speeches of the past were at once of that time and now. The device of referring to the speech in the speech is a way of underscoring the ambiguity, of bridging a gap that is in other situations clearly established.

In song, the ambiguity is in the subject: is it a man or a mouse singing? Is it a man singing *about* an animal, or is it an animal singing *through the mouth of* a man? There is no simple answer. What the self-reference of the texts does, however, is bring both parties to the performance: both human and animal performers are present in the texts themselves. In the slow speech both present and past are simultaneously invoked in an effort to fuse the Suyá of today with the Suyá of the past. More attention will be paid to these juxtapositions and metamorphoses in future chapters, but clearly the texts of the different genres are rich sources for research, and vary considerably among themselves.

Speech, instruction, song, invocation, and animals

The Suyá talked about animals in everyday speech; many myths have both human and animal actors, but nowhere were animals as deeply involved in the texts themselves as in songs and invocations. All songs were learned from animals, plants, insects, or other Indians; almost all invocations invoked animals, plants, or insects, and the form itself may have been adopted from other Indians. Songs generally attributed human characteristics to the animals – they were presented as living in groups, performing ceremonies, singing songs, and so forth: fish race with burity palm logs, mice and deer leap and sing, bees have abduction ceremonies. This social side of the animals was present in the songs partly as a condition of the 'animalization' of humans that occurs in the culminating metamorphosis of the Mouse Ceremony. The men become beings that are also mice, but mice in their social roles of singers, dancers, and masters of maize.

The presentation of the social aspects of animals in songs can be contrasted with the role animals play in the invocations. There animals are presented as individual beings possessing super-human or non-human capacities. For example, they can eat poisonous manioc tubers without pain, grow extremely quickly, or swim underwater for great distances. The invocations use these non-human features of the animals to instill a socially beneficial effect on human beings: to make them grow strong or recover from an illness or injury. It is precisely the super-human or non-human traits that result in a humanization of the patient: he or she recovers from a sickness, grows, or has a child in a good and normal fashion.

Because of the importance animals play in them, songs (*ngére*) and invocations (*sangére*) may be distinguished from all forms of speech and instruction. Songs and invocations bring humans and natural beings together, songs with a predominantly metamorphic emphasis on the social and group nature of animals, invocations with predominantly metonymic emphasis on the individual. Slow speech is entirely social speech; it can be contrasted with the 'bad speech' of witches in form and content. It can also be contrasted in that oratory addresses a group; bad speech is entirely individual and anti-social. Myth narrates the passage between, or separation of, nature and society, and describes the integration of a natural product – maize, and a boy – into the heart of society itself – the men's houses.

Speech, instruction, song and phrasing

One of the most obvious differences among genres is the phrasing. As speech forms (kapérni) become more and more public, the phrases become longer and more regular – hence the name 'slow speech' (kapérni kahrīdo). In addition to their length, the oratorical phrases are more melodic than everyday speech. Subject changes are also marked by lengthening a syllable, providing a cadence.

The different types of instruction can also be distinguished among themselves by the way time is structured. Here, too, the more public the form the more structured the sounds. In addition, the more status a person has, the more structured his or her phrases are likely to be. When a myth is told by a good narrator, he or she usually uses long, carefully constructed phrases, as in Iawekidi's rendition of the origin of corn. These phrases are less clearly marked when a younger, less experienced, person tells the story. The ceremonial recitatives, performed by specially designated soloists, have clearly defined phrases and clear melodies. One might even call them more melodic than some songs, which are almost chants. The rhythm in the recitatives is also what we would call musical: the relationships among the times given to each syllable are quite regular.

The phrase structure of songs (ngére) is established by the melody and song texts. Most songs are strophic – that is a single group of phrases is repeated many times in a kind of verse form. The phrases in many songs are also structured by rattles, which further structure time, and by body movements which accompany the rattling and singing. The phrase structure of Suyá songs is usually fairly simple, and quite regular.

Regardless of the type of song, texts (both semantically relevant and 'song words') determine its division into sections. Differences may be established among the genres according to the 'song words' (certain 'song words' seem to be associated with specific ceremonies and specific seasons) and rhythmic features (for example, the shout song [akia] does seem to have a few characteristic rhythmic patterns).

As the performance becomes more and more public, and where the performer is an individual, there is an increase in the length and regularity of the phrases.

Table 2.4. *Phrasing*

Private form
with shorter phrases
Everyday speech with
same sex age-mates (Ex. 1.2)
Myth performance (Ex. 2.1)
Song (*ngére* and *akia*) and invocations (Ex. 1.1, 1.4, 2.3)
Oratory (slow speech Ex. 2.4)
Most public form with longest phrases

In addition to the general tendency to lengthen phrases with more public performances, performers of different ages tended to employ phrases of different lengths. The younger the performer, the shorter the phrases. The older, more knowledgeable, and more public the performer, the longer the phrases. Children told myths with short phrases, sang shout songs with very short musical phrases, and did not engage in any forms of public speech. It was never clear to me whether a child *could not* use the phrases, or *did not* use them. A young political leader said he didn't know how to speak 'slow speech,' but that when he got older he might be able to. I also noticed that one man changed his performances between 1971 and 1982, his phrases becoming longer and his performance apparently more confident. Adult men and women used long phrases in their narratives; adult men sang longer musical phrases, and may have engaged in various kinds of public speech forms. Only certain prestigious adult men could employ the oratorical forms with the longest phrases. Phrasing, therefore, is not only characteristic of certain genres, but also of certain kinds of performers of those genres.

Speech, instruction, song, and pitch relations

Since Western conceptions of music are predominantly harmonic and melodic, pitch relations are often considered to be music's distinguishing feature. This is not universally so. Melody is not a particularly good way to distinguish between Suyá speech, instruction, and song. The recitative (Example 2.2 on the cassette) is nearly as melodic as the rainy season unison song (Example 1.3 on the cassette), but the Suyá insisted that it was instruction (*sarén*), not song (*ngére*). Although pitch relations are important in all three genres, in myth and speech they are to some degree a question of style and emphasis. A plaza speech or myth without tonal structures would be a poor performance of those, but would be recognizable. A recitative or a song without tonal structures would be entirely incorrect. Yet the opposition of speech and myth telling to recitative and song, however, does violence to the Suyá categories. It bisects the category of *sarén*, something the Suyá do not do in the same way. Thus pitch relations may not always be a privileged means of approaching music.

Song, instruction, speech and authority

Not all verbal utterances carried the same authority. Everyday speech was the responsibility of the individual – it carried no more weight than the speaker in the immediate context. Plaza speech carried the authority of tradition and office: the old people used to speak and were listened to; today's listeners should listen to the adult men who may speak in public. Listeners may or may not accept the instructions, however, for they are recognizably from a living individual. Instruction also had the authority of the past: narratives repeat what has occurred; recitatives follow a pattern laid down in an origin myth. Song, however, has a very different kind of authority: its exact form came from outside society altogether. Songs are beyond question: they simply existed. Any doubt about a song text came up against the impossible: finding and communicating with the original animal or plant performer from which it was learned.

If the genres possessed different kinds of authority, so did the performers. Not everyone can perform every genre. All Suyá spoke everyday speech; most people would tell narratives; adult men and women would perform invocations. But other forms were quite restricted.

Only adult men and a few women orated, and some forms were supposed to be performed only by political and ceremonial leaders. Songs were originally learned by a few specially endowed men and women and might only be performed by certain sex-, age-, and name-based groups. Performers could only repeat songs they had been taught.

The authority of a genre depended to a great extent on the distance of the original text from the speaker, and on the social status of the speaker. The different genres can be placed on a continuum from identity with the speaker to identity with a non-human or metamorphosing being.

Table 2.5. *Identity of text with speaker*

Identity of text
with speaker
Everyday speech (in the present)
Invocations (from a teacher in the past)
Narratives, oratory (from the past)
Recitatives and songs (from non-human sources)
Identity of the text with a remote source

This table could be set out differently. It would be possible to invert the position of oratory and songs, since much of oratory was said to be from the past, and it was far more restricted than song in terms of who might perform it. With regard to social status, there is no question that the performance of slow speech and everybody listens speech was far more restricted than that of songs. They carried tremendous weight because of the authority of the person that performed them. Restricted forms of oratory are found in much of lowland South American Indian groups.

Conclusion

Many of the points I have described in the previous sections are summarized in Figure 2.1.

This chapter discussed some of the relationships among the different vocal art forms performed by the Suyá. Far too often music and the other verbal arts are treated in isolation from each other. The separation of the various disciplines that deal with music and speech has had a disastrous effect on the development of our thinking about them. Not only have linguistics, musicology, and studies of oral literature developed separately, they each have their own journals, their own professionals, and they rarely communicate among themselves. Since research has often begun from the perspective of a single academic discipline rather than from the speech/music event itself, it is often very difficult to reconstruct the original from the analyses of it. Linguists have often ignored the features of oral style that are not grammatical or syntactic; literary scholars have often ignored the linguistic; and ethnomusicologists have spent years analyzing sound structures, but paying insufficient attention to the meaning of the texts. All this has been done in isolation. The failure to recognize the interrelationship of verbal and musical genres and the importance of the ways they are used can result in a dry formalism which reifies the text, performance, or melody and does not begin to account for the richness and use of verbal art forms.

(All have structured tone, time, and text)

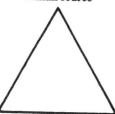

ngére (song)
Priority of melody over text;
time, text and melody fixed by non-
human source

kapérni (speech)
Priority of text over melody;
text and melody determined
by speaker. Increasing
formalization in public performances

sarén (telling) and *sangére*
Relative priority of
relatively fixed texts over
relatively established melodies

Figure 2.1   Suyá genres compared

The relationships among Suyá genres demonstrate how the separation of speech and music distorts both of them. Instruction, oratory, invocations and song all structure time, tone and timbre. The relationship of the texts to these structures (whether inserted into them or creating them) varies among the genres, and can only be understood when the entire gamut of music and speech is examined.

Rather than studying forms of speech and song singly, in the supreme isolation of different scholarly disciplines, we should be studying them as interrelated genres that employ phonetics, text, time, tone, and timbre in different but possibly systematic ways. By showing how the genres are interrelated and illustrating their use in social contexts we will be better able to analyze any given form and break out of the disciplinary isolation that has hampered the analysis of actual performances. (Ideally we would include gesture and dance in the study of these expressive forms; video recording will make such a step both practical and desirable.)

In this chapter song has been distinguished from the other vocal art forms by the priority of its melody over text, the fixed mode of its presentation, the extensive use of textual repetition, the fixed length of its phrases, the fixed relations among pitches, and the unimpeachable authority of its fixed texts. Song is clearly distinct from the other forms both stylistically and textually. The origin of songs and song texts is a topic in itself, and the following chapter investigates it in greater detail.

3 *The origin of songs*

Ideas about the origin and composition of music provide an important indication of what music is and how it relates to other aspects of the lives and the cosmos of a community. Suyá concepts of the origin and introduction of new songs can be compared instructively with those of other groups, and the answer to 'why they sing' rests in part on an understanding of what a song is and how it is learned.

According to the Suyá, songs had been introduced in three different ways. Some songs they considered very old, and their origin was described in myths referring to very early times. Some songs were new at any given ceremony, and were taught by men called 'men without spirits' who in some ways resembled what we would call 'composers.' Other songs were introduced by learning them from foreigners. As a group, all songs were said to come from outside Suyá society. Each form of introduction, however, had its own characteristics.

Songs in myths

Certain unison songs and recitatives were said to have been learned a very long time ago, in the period in which Suyá society was taking its present form. The formation of society as it is today was described in a number of myths, including some where songs were learned from partly human partly animal beings in the process of metamorphosis. A man who was slowly turning into a large deer sang a song that has since always been sung in the Savannah Deer Ceremony; a man who became a wild pig/person sang a song that became the Wild Pig Ceremony for the initiation of young boys; an enemy child captured by the Suyá taught the children a naming ceremony that the whole village began to perform after he became an adult. (For versions of these myths, see Seeger 1984: 191–194 [Savannah Deer]; 252–254 [Wild Pig]; 203–209 [Enemy Child].) The origin of Suyá songs and ceremonies described in myths is quite different from those of many other South American Indian groups, where they were taught by culture heroes or spirits.

The lack of transformation in the myth about the origin of maize may be why the myth included no songs. The story involved no metamorphosis. The mouse remained a mouse; the infant grew into a boy (but remained a human); the maize was just maize. I recorded one version of the origin of maize where the teller went on to describe the origin of planted gardens. The origin of the gardens (distinct from taking the crops from the river) involved the metamorphosis of different parts of a woman's body into garden products after she was burned alive when the clearing for the first garden was set ablaze. Before she burned, she sang a song that was sung by the men almost every year just before they ran to their gardens to set them afire at the very end of the dry season. Among the Suyá, where there was metamorphosis, there was song.

Songs from men without spirits (mẽ katodn kïdi)

Although certain songs and ceremonies were part of the construction of Suyá history, new songs were also constantly introduced. As one Suyá said 'if we sing the same thing over and over again, it is boring. So we sing a new song, then another, then another, and we are happy/euphoric (kin).' New songs were taught by specialists who had undergone a partial metamorphosis, and had acquired a kind of permanent marginality. Two different kinds of persons were involved in the introduction of new music: a witch and a 'person without a spirit.'

How, I asked a number of Suyá, can certain people teach songs to other people? Takuti, an older man whose answers were often organized into long narratives – almost lectures – of a normative sort, gave me the most easily understood description. He told me that witches are very jealous. They get very angry if they are not given what they want, and in revenge remove a person's spirit from his or her body. When a witch sees someone come into the village with a lot of fish, game, honey, birds, arrow cane, or other desired item, it becomes very angry if it does not receive some. That night the witch will transform itself into a bat or some other nocturnal animal, enter the culprit's house, and take the spirit of the person who failed to share the desired item, while he or she sleeps. The witch takes the spirit and throws it where the thing it is angry about lives: it will throw the spirit to the village of the bees if it is angry at not receiving any honey; it will throw it in the river if it received no fish; it will throw it into the place of some animal or to the birds, or to the trees and arrow canes. Spirit loss causes illness. The now spiritless person will get very sick, lose weight, and suffer fever and convulsions. If the spirit does not return, the person becomes a 'person without a spirit' and a teacher of new songs. Here are his words:

When there were still many Suyá alive, it was very frightening because there were many witches. If a young boy came back with some fish and a person said to him 'Give me one' he might answer 'No, I am taking these to my mother.' The witch would get angry and throw the boy's spirit in the water. So we tell our young children, 'when someone asks for something, give it right away. Do you want a witch to throw your spirit to the fish?' We tell them: 'When someone over there [in another house] asks you for bird feathers, honey or whatever, you say "A-ha! A witch!" and give it.'

Witches, who might be male or female, were said to cause all deaths – whether from disease, attack, old age, or even automobile accidents – by removing a person's spirit and taking it to the village of the dead. Although death was said to be the normal result of the removal of the spirit to the village of the dead, when the spirit was removed to an animal or plant community, the patient might continue to live. Takuti described how:

[A witch takes a man's] spirit to the birds. He has convulsions and lies in his hammock for a long time. He lies in his hammock while his spirit is with the birds. A vulture takes the man's spirit flying with him in the sky, and the man has convulsions. Then he sees himself [discovers that his spirit is with the birds in a dream or delirium vision]. 'Oh ho! So some witch took my spirit to the birds!' he says.
Another person, whose spirit was taken to the birds long before, will tell the man 'Some time ago I saw the spirits of many of your belongings in the bird village [the spirits of belongings also may be taken by the witch to encourage the owner's spirit to stay wherever he or she has taken it]. That is why you have been having convulsions for so long.'
Then the man begins to hear the birds' shout songs (*akia*), and the birds' unison songs (*ngére*). He hears the birds singing about themselves. His health improves and he lives as before.

Then [one day] someone comes into his house. 'What are you coming for?' the man asks. 'I come to see you.' 'What are you seeking?' the man inquires. 'Will you tell (*sarén*) me a shout song?' the visitor asks. 'All right.' The man sits and listens [to the birds]. When he has finished listening, he teaches the shout song he has heard to the man [in the manner described for the opening of the Mouse Ceremony]. When he has finished teaching it he says 'Go and sing, that I may hear it.' The man does.

Everyone in the village hears the new song. They say, 'Who told (*sarén*) that shout song?' 'Our companion has taught it to him. Our companion has become a bird' [meaning his spirit resides with the birds] someone replies. They say, 'Our companion has lost his spirit! He has become a person without a spirit! He has lost his spirit among the birds!' [they can tell all of this by the song]. Now other people come to ask him for shout songs. 'Will you teach me a new shout song?' each asks. 'All right.' He listens and learns the song, then he teaches it. 'Sing, that I may hear it,' he says.

Then the men say 'Let's learn one of his unison songs' (*ngére*). They go to him and he teaches them a unison song. If the song is beautiful the men say 'Hey! That is beautiful!' When they want to learn another song, they go to him and learn one. When they want another, they go to him. His companions seek him out. He teaches beautiful unison songs of the fish and beautiful shout songs of the fish. [Takuti started talking about a man who lost his spirit to the birds, then concluded talking about fish. He is describing a general process, and I think he simply forgot which he was using as an example.] He has become a man without a spirit. They keep coming to him for songs.'

Sickness, and especially serious illness or injury involving possible spirit loss, was of great concern to members of the community. Whenever a Suyá would become quite ill or was injured, members of the family would spend many hours speculating on who might be the witch responsible, and what might have caused him or her to become angry. The sick person's female relatives would evaluate each suspect by name and make a kind of ranking by likelihood. Heavily armed male relatives would stalk around the plaza, speaking angry speech (*grútnen kapérni*), sometimes firing their rifles in the air, asking all witches (without mentioning any names) to stop making their relative sick. If the ill person died, one of the suspects was sometimes held responsible and killed in retaliation. If the sick person improved, the concern temporarily subsided, but fear of witches always lay just beneath the surface. Five accused witches were killed between 1972 and 1984. The fear of witches encouraged Suyá to distribute things, and accusations of being a witch probably inhibited people from asking for things. One old woman refused the present of a dress from my wife saying 'I don't want the cloth, because if I accept it people will say I asked for it and they will say I am a witch.' Suyá society was based on networks of sharing and reciprocity, and giving to people who asked was a fundamental social skill that had its own sanctions. If one did not give, a witch could make one ill; if one asked for too much too often, one could be considered a witch and killed.

In spite of the fear of witches, they were necessary for creating the men without spirits who introduced new songs. Without witches there could have been no introduction of songs from animals after the episodes described in the myths, whereas new songs were a constant feature of Suyá ceremonies. Witches, capable of transforming themselves into animals at will, created composers, whose transformations were partial but often final, through their jealous retaliation for imagined slights. This process illustrates a complementarity between the 'bad speech' of witches and the socially valued songs men without spirits learned from the animals and taught or sang themselves. A village without one would be without the other – a kind of complementarity typical of Suyá dualism in general.

Teachers of songs, the people without spirits, were men and women in a state of what might be called 'halted metamorphosis.' The person's body was alive in the village; the person's spirit lived with some natural species, accompanied their activities, and learned their songs. People without spirits are examples of liminal figures, characterized by Victor Turner as 'neither here nor there; they are betwixt and between the positions assigned and arrayed by law, custom, convention . . . Liminality is frequently likened to death, to being in the womb, to invisibility, to darkness, to bisexuality, to the wilderness, and to an eclipse of the sun and the moon' (Turner 1968: 95). The men without spirits were truly neither here nor there; they were alive but not whole; and their spirits were intimately associated with a natural species. I was repeatedly told by Kaikwati that to be without a spirit like himself was bad. There was a term for men with spirits that could be translated as 'whole' or 'healthy' (mẽ tĩrĩ). Composition, or the introduction of new animal songs, could only begin after liminality was permanently established. When the sick person discovered where his soul was, after he 'saw himself' in Takuti's words, his metamorphosis into a dual being – living in the Suyá village and living in an animal village – would be completed.

Certain individuals who had lost their spirits and who were also respected for their knowledge of songs were given a high status as 'masters of Suyá ceremonies' (mẽ ro kïn kandé). Such a person usually decided when a ceremony would be performed; he exhorted everyone to perform it correctly; he often organized collective hunts and fishing parties. Every historical Suyá village had both one or more political leaders and a single 'master of ceremonies' (see Seeger 1981: 180–205 for detail on historical villages). Political leaders and masters of Suyá ceremonies were quite different. A political leader was rarely a person who had lost his spirit. He was supposed to be an ideal man, whose legitimacy resulted from his actions and behavior in everyday life and his inheritance of the leadership role, rather than from the kind of knowledge characteristic of teachers of songs and ritual specialists.

There is a single principle at work in both the introduction of new songs and the myths of how songs were learned from animals in the past. Suyá composition reproduced in a living person the way songs were introduced in the myths. In the myths a group of men would learn a song from a metamorphosing person. The body of a man without spirit would learn the song from his own metamorphosed spirit.

People who had lost their spirits could only teach or perform songs they could hear. A person whose spirit was with the bees could only teach bee songs, one whose spirit was with the birds only bird songs, and the same for fish, plants and the other possibilities. Each kind of animal or plant had its own language, and usually sang about itself. The bees usually sang songs about bees, birds about birds, fish about fish, and so forth. It was easy to tell which animal taught a song from the species named in it. When people learned songs from several different composers, they sang about different animals. An exception to this general rule was the Mouse Ceremony, which was also performed by a number of different animals, plants, and insects. Thus Kaikwati learned the Mouse Ceremony shout songs he taught from the trees and arrow canes that also perform the ceremony at the ripening of the maize. The songs did not come from the mice named in them, but from plants singing about them.

Sometimes a person's spirit moved from one place to another within the natural realm. In the previous generation, approximately thirty percent of Suyá men and women had spirits living with bees, birds, fish, and trees. In several cases their spirits moved during their lifetime. One man's spirit fled from the trees to the arrow cane after he was shot in the leg; another moved from the birds to the arrow cane after an arrow pierced his eye. One old man's spirit went from the armadillo village to women's vaginas: in his old age he only composed songs naming parts and actions of women's genitalia, which were considered obscene, funny, and highly appropriate for an old person to sing. These changes of location usually accompanied accidents, sickness or changes in social status.

Not all Suyá visits to the animal realm were permanent. A number of people described how their spirits had been with birds, bees, or fish for a short time when they were very sick. They would recount the experience in very convincing detail to fascinated audiences. One man described how he found himself to be a bird. He described what it was like to ruffle his feathers prior to flying – making movements with his arms and hands and a sound with his voice that was unmistakable. He said the birds were having a ceremony, and singing. They invited him to sing with them, and he did. He sang the song for the audience, under his breath. They then flew off to hunt for the food that is an important part of most ceremonies. He described circling high over the ground. People asked him questions: 'Were you afraid?' 'Could you see very far?' 'What did you eat?' He answered each question, expanding on things he had mentioned. He reached the high point when he and the other vultures had plunged their heads into the entrails of a rotten carcass. 'Yummmmm, good ceremonial food' said the vultures (to the disgust of the audience). They flew to a stream, and he described how they drank and threw water on their feathers. 'I was very hot and thirsty.' Then he said 'I wasn't any longer.' Suddenly the bird he had been was no longer, and he was lying in his hammock croaking 'water, water, water.' His mother brought him water, and when he got well he sang the song he had learned, dancing with the birds. Since his spirit had returned to his body, he did not learn any further songs or teach them to other villagers.

The unison songs (*ngére*) were the most important song forms to be learned from animals. Their texts provide another path toward understanding the interaction of men without spirits and animals. They describe parallels between the human and the animal. Many unison songs indicate parallels between the animal world and the human world and create new metaphors of relationship between them. The areas of white fur on the coati are called its 'bird down' for a ceremony; a fish's fins are likened to burity palm frond dance capes, which wave with the movements of the dancer as the fins wave in the water; a swarm of a certain bee species arrives and they dance with their arms over their heads, while another species watches; a catfish wraps its head with cotton and sings. A fish species 'wriggles through shallow water, making ripples.' A wasp 'carries mud to its hanging nest and builds it.' 'A honey bee dances back and forth' ('the way they do on their trees' according to a singer). These derived from direct observation. The coati has patches of white, as do humans with bird down on them; fish fins wave like capes; bees swarm and dance; the 'whiskers' of a certain catfish look as though it has wrapped its head with cotton string.

Other songs are almost short stories. 'A tall tree looks for its formal friend and says "Cut my cape so I can dance."' 'The water turtle says to its formal friend "let's go to the Suyá village and sing the Kahran *ngére* with them."' 'The vulture comes [to the Suyá village] and sings, circling the plaza with its arms in the air [as vultures usually fly] and the men are very happy/euphoric.' 'A certain bee species swarms to the [Suyá village] log racing path, sees the Suyá women on the path and sings about them.'

Finally some texts describe the emotions of the composer's spirit in the natural world. One of the most striking of these was the first song taught by Kaikwati after he had been accidentally shot in the thigh in the confusion surrounding the assassination of a witch. After he recovered he taught a new unison song, and there was considerable excitement among the listening women. They commented among themselves, and explained to my wife, that he was singing a new song. They said, on the basis of it, that his spirit had fled the trees and was living with arrow cane now. The song could be freely translated as 'The bullets arrive in the arrow cane village to sing, the arrow canes are afraid and leave' for the first half and 'The wide tipped arrows arrive in the arrow cane village to sing, and their [arrow cane] mother is afraid and leaves.' These refer to the way his own spirit became afraid and fled to its new home. Other songs describe the spirit's fearful reaction to situations it encounters: 'a [huge] catfish species muddies the water with its tail and it is frightening'; another species of catfish 'has little fish living in its gills, and they are frightened.' The fright refers to the spirit of the person who taught the song, which was very frightened by the power of the catfish.

The essential reality of the spirit realm was constantly reinforced because Suyá kept going there or had their spirits there, and they discussed what it was like among themselves (this has been described for other Gê-speaking societies as well by C. Nimuendaju [1942] and J. C. Melatti [1974]). The supernatural features of the spirit and animal realms were as real, for example, as Europe or China to Americans who have never been there. We play music written in Vienna, we hear descriptions of life in China, we are quite certain that people have gone there and that those places exist. We have seen travelers leave and have spoken to them when they came back. Different travel accounts emphasize different things, but we do not question the existence of the countries because of that. We know that travel there is filled with unusual experiences and sometimes perils, and that life there is quite different. Those places become part of our lives and experience even though we may never have been there. The same thing was true of Suyá experiences with spirits.

I have no explanation for why some people lost their spirits permanently, and others only temporarily. It was clearly not inherited, as political leadership was. From my discussions with Suyá, it appeared that people without spirits often lost their spirits temporarily as youths, only to lose them permanently later. Political status may have had something to do with it. The children of political leaders were expected to be political leaders also, and would not be as likely to say they lost their spirits, while captives and half-siblings of leaders tended to lose their spirits more frequently. This suggests that although it was not considered 'good' to be without one's spirit, it was a way to become a prestigious adult for those who did not inherit the right to be a political leader.

In 1982 only Kaikwati, the ritual specialist, was a man without his spirit. All the others had died, and no new ones had appeared. When I asked why there were so few today, Takuti attributed it to demographics:

When there were many Suyá alive, it was very frightening because there were many witches . . . In the old days when there were many Suyá it was very frightening. Now there only a few Suyá, [and it is not very frightening].

Without witches there could be no new men without spirits. However, Takuti's sister had been killed because she was believed to be a witch, and three other women in his house were considered to be witches, and feared by women who lived in other houses. Life in the 1970s and 1980s was not free of the fear of witches and retaliation against them.

Several factors probably contributed to the decline in the number of men without spirits, among them the death of many of the older men, the abeyance of the full initiation ceremony, the popularity of Upper Xingu ceremonies during the 1960s, and the increased possibility of learning other kinds of songs from human beings, rather than from animals. The intertribal (and interethnic) community that had developed since the Suyá were peacefully settled into the Xingu National Park in 1959 diminished the importance of the animal realm as a source of novelty, learning, and musical innovations. The best younger singers traveled extensively to other Indian groups as well as to Brasilia and São Paulo. They returned with new songs – often recorded on cassette tapes – which were often learned by the entire community. The same men were often the first to pick up new songs from visitors to the village. The disappearance of men without spirits may have been as much the result of an alternative source for powerful things. Until recently, the animal realm was virtually the only source of power from outside the village.

Foreign songs

The third way new songs were introduced represents a kind of inversion of the first two, yet it is intimately related to them. Instead of a song being learned by an individual and brought to the village, foreigners (enemy Indians, peaceful Indians, or non-Indians such as ourselves) were brought to the village where they would teach a song or ceremony to the entire community. The Suyá have incorporated foreign songs on a grand scale: they sang the songs of over ten different groups with whom they have had contact over the past two hundred years. They sang songs they learned from the 'White Indians' (identified by them today as the Munduruku), from the Manitsauá and the Iarumá (now both extinct), from the Kamayurá, Waurá, Trumai, Juruna, Kayabi, Txukahamae, and then from Brazilians and Americans since their 'pacification' in 1959. At that pacification, when the leaders of the expedition reached the Suyá village, the Suyá and the Indian members of the pacification team sang songs for each other. During my stay, when non-Suyá men visited the village they were usually invited to recount news and stories, and to sing. In the 1980s they usually brought cassette tapes recorded in their villages, which they would trade for those recorded by the Suyá of their own ceremonies.

Why would the Suyá want to perform the songs of so many different groups? Part of the answer lies in the significance of foreigners' songs to the Suyá, and the continuities between this mode of learning music and the other ones already described. According to Suyá oral traditions, before they met the Munduruku in the nineteenth century, they had learned songs from a man becoming a deer, from another man in the final stages of transformation into a wild pig, and from a woman who had a penis growing on her right thigh. Clearly, we are not dealing with 'objective' history, but with a pattern of learning songs from outsiders that includes the present and recent historical past but has equal continuity with the 'mythical' past described in 'what the old people tell.' Historical experience cannot be arbitrarily separated from myths, since each influences the interpretation of the other.

The balance of power has shifted during the past hundred years from the power of animals to the power of enemy Indians (who almost wiped out the Suyá in the early part of this century, and from whom they stole captives to survive), to the power of non-Indians today, about whom they were very concerned. Knowledge is an important form of power in most South American Indian groups, and the Suyá were no exception. By taking and performing other groups' songs, the Suyá incorporated some of those groups' power and knowledge into their own community. They did this first with animal songs, and more recently with foreigners' songs.

Suyá understanding and representation of their own past provide a clue to their incorporation of so many foreign songs. They described their past as the gradual incorporation of items taken from monstrous outsiders that are used for the benefit of the Suyá in their enduring circular villages (that themselves have no myth of origin). Myths recount how the Suyá obtained fire from the jaguar, corn and garden crops from the mouse, names from enemies underground, body ornaments from cannibals, manioc varieties and pots from the Upper Xingu Indians, and so forth. Rarely did they obtain songs alone. Contact with the Indian groups in the more recent past added new material culture (new crops, different ways of processing manioc, new technologies of fishing and hunting) and also songs. The material culture was part of production; songs were part of social reproduction. Suyá history reports the steady and simultaneous acquisition of the means of production and reproduction from first animals, then historical Indian groups, and now from non-Indians.

Although new songs were introduced from outsiders, the social groups that performed them were the same as those that performed the traditional Gê-style Suyá songs and ceremonies. They were based on the fundamental Suyá distinctions of sex, and age (which have no myths of origin), and name-based ceremonial groups. Regardless of their origins, all songs were sung in basically the same social space. Thus while the text and tune changed over the years, the location of the performances and the identity of the actors continued to be the groups of collective social life. The new songs or ceremonies were often performed in the long preparatory periods between the opening of a rite of passage such as the Mouse Ceremony, and the grand finale of the ceremony – at precisely the time they asked us to sing for them on 29 January 1972. When Suyá introduced the new songs, a great deal remained the same.

One result of learning many songs from other groups was that some decision had to be made about which of the many songs to sing. While many Suyá songs were regulated by season and social group membership, this was not the case with performances of many foreigners' songs. It also appeared to me that the Suyá more frequently and more seriously sang songs from groups with whom they had recently intermarried or from whom they had stolen many captives, or had obtained a fairly large amount of material culture. Thus they sang more from the Upper Xingu Indians and Juruna than they sang from the Panará, Kayabi, or Txukahamae, and the Manitsauá and Iarumá songs were sung quite infrequently, now that the captives from these groups have been dead for several decades.

There has not always been agreement about which ceremony should be performed. I was told that the explanation given for a 1984 dispute in the Suyá village that led to the establishment of a second village by a sizeable faction was that the members of the community disagreed over the kinds of ceremonies they were going to perform. One faction was interested in performing mostly Upper Xingu women's songs, while the other wanted more traditional Gê-style Suyá ceremonies. Although there were multiple motives behind this factional dispute, the selection of ceremonies was clearly also a political event.

The contemporary Suyá adoption of foreigners' songs was a way of incorporating the power and material resources of strangers into the social reproduction of their own society, while they simultaneously established the otherness of the others (who were on a par with animals) and the changing, growing, creative, self-ness of themselves.

Men, animals, and music

Suyá ideas about composition are fundamental for understanding their cosmology as well as their music. Suyá musicology involved central cosmological concepts and processes, and the origin of songs reveals how the very epitome of the social world (a ceremonial group of men singing in the center of the plaza) is linked to the domain of animals and non-Suyá through contrast and reciprocity.

In *Nature and Society in Central Brazil* (Seeger 1981), I argued that many aspects of Suyá cosmology rested upon the fundamental distinction they made between animals and human beings. Although I glossed these as 'nature' and 'society,' the real basis of the opposition was the relationship between fully social adult men and animals. While the argument is presented at length there (Seeger 1981: 21–35), I will summarize it here.

Humans and animals were carefully separated and contrasted in many aspects of Suyá life, including the delineation of space and time, the characterization of persons, the conceptions they had of the life cycle, and the definition of sickness. Nature and society were principles expressed through specific attributes such as spatial relationship to the plaza or classification by odor. In space, animal classification, and other domains there was a clear gradation between the extremes of the social and natural. But nature and society were not fixed realms containing categories such as women, parrots, anthropologists, and jaguars. Instead they were principles that organized thought and action, which the Suyá used in dynamic and creative ways.

Nature and society operated on each other constantly, transforming each other. The transforming process might make something natural into something social, or something social into something natural. Nowhere were the dynamic and creative aspects of the interaction of the natural and the social clearer than in food and song. Carefully isolated from the social world in some domains of Suyá life, the animal domain was essential to both subsistence and ceremony. The earlier book dealt extensively with food and the classification of humans and animals, but not with song. Singing transcended the purely human, it participated simultaneously in the social and the animal realms. In ceremonies such as the Mouse Ceremony, the performers themselves transcended the purely human, becoming simultaneously men and animals. Both food and song were parts of the natural world that were introduced into Suyá society at its very center: rites of passage such as the Mouse Ceremony. They shared other aspects as well: both were oral. Eating and speaking (including singing) are central features of the cosmologies of many South American Indians.

A corollary of the power of nature is that it could be dangerous (this applied to foreigners as well). The Suyá observed extensive restrictions on the animals they could eat, including those that could not be eaten at certain moments of their lives or by certain sexes and ages (see Seeger 1981: 92–120). Singing, too, was restricted to certain times, places, ages and sexes. Suyá musical genres did not include domestic songs, lullabies, protest songs, or work songs. Domestic performances were restricted to myths or descriptions, and the songs reported then were sung very quietly. Musical performance had a ceremonial purpose – controlled and associated with certain social groups. When a ceremony was being planned, and later during its realization, there were constant injunctions against 'fooling around' or not taking the ceremony seriously.

Claude Lévi-Strauss, in his famous volume *The Raw and the Cooked* (1969) described at great length the importance of transforming raw flesh into cooked meat in the cosmologies of many native South American groups. Fire, which effects that transformation, is central to many of those cosmologies. The Suyá were no exception. For them, both fire and songs were obtained from the animal realm. Fire transformed raw food to cooked and edible food (they abhorred raw or rare meat), and song transformed humans.

Nature thus had two aspects. On the one hand nature was represented as individual game animals (food). On the other it was represented as collective and social – by groups of animals singing. Certain animals were rarely eaten, but were often sung about or invoked. The Suyá avoided the flesh of the jaguar, the giant otter, the sloth, and the vulture; they highly restricted the consumption of the flesh of the deer; they placed restrictions on the flesh of the wild pig and many other mammals. These same animals appeared in the invocations, where their power was used to cure a patient or improve a human body, and in songs. The very power that made those species dangerous to eat made them powerful tools for curing: they transformed humans, making them more like animals. The incorrect performance of an invocation, the indiscriminate eating of animal flesh, or the improper performance of a ritual could transform a patient, an individual or an entire society in undesirable ways.

The appearance of powerful, sometimes dangerous, and ultimately transforming persons or objects is common to ceremonies around the world. In the Catholic mass and the witches' coven, powers are brought together and used for different ends. The common association of the sacred with the taboo or dangerous led to the consideration of the sacred and the tabooed as a single unit (Hubert and Mauss 1964 [1898]). The Suyá were little different from other groups in this. What did distinguish them was that the principal items reintroduced from the powerful and transforming domain of nature were food and music.

It should be clear that Suyá song meant much more than what we call music today. It was far from being simply entertainment. Songs were obtained from dangerous beings through an intermediary who had lost his or her spirit through the actions of a witch, or who had con-fronted foreigners and learned from them. They had to be performed carefully and seriously. Ceremonies and their associated songs transformed members of the society and also each individual's experience of self and social relationships. Song was associated with euphoria and with personal and society-wide transformations. Songs, and the Mouse Ceremony among them, were not something at the periphery of essential experience, but at its very center.

Kaluli, Suyá, Ancient Greeks, and Americans

Ideas about the origin and nature of music can be fruitfully compared among different societies. They can provide some instructive contrasts. An interesting comparison would be between the Suyá and other Gê-speaking groups. Unfortunately, too little has been written on Gê song composition and ideas about music except for the Xavante – whose songs apparently consist entirely of song syllables without direct semantic meaning and are heard in dreams by adults and taught to younger men (Aytai 1985). Not much else is known. Looking further afield, an excellent description has been provided for the Kaluli of New Guinea, and an instructively different one is attributed to the Pythagoreans in ancient Greece.

Among the Kaluli, as they are described by Feld (1982, 1984), music is modeled on a metaphor of bird song. As with the Suyá, most Kaluli music is song. One Kaluli myth recounts the transformations of humans into birds, where the metamorphosed human sings

Kaluli words to the melody of a certain bird call. Feld's analysis details how certain songs (and other forms of verbal expression such as weeping) have the same melodic structure and range as the cries of specific birds. The Kaluli apparently talked a lot more explicitly about verbal art than the Suyá did, and Feld brilliantly explicates a number of Kaluli metaphors in several chapters on song and weeping.

Kaluli and Suyá ideas may be compared in a general way to those of Pythagoras. Relationships among tones were declared to be a 'natural series,' and harmony was thought to derive from formal mathematical relationships among tones. Lewis Rowell describes it as follows:

Harmony was also a symbol of universal order, uniting all levels of the cosmos – the four basic elements (earth, water, fire, air), higher forms of life (man), and the structure of the universe (the planets, sun, and moon). As Aristotle testified with respect to Pythagorean doctrines, 'they supposed the elements of number to be the elements of all things, and the whole heaven to be a musical scale [harmonium] and a number.'   (Rowell 1983: 41)

Music was also said to unify opposites:

The Pythagoreans, whom Plato follows in many respects, call music the harmonization of opposites, the unification of disparate things, and the conciliation of warring elements . . . Music, as they say, is the basis of agreement among things in nature and of the best government in the universe. As a rule it assumes the guise of harmony in the universe, of lawful government in a state, and of a sensible way of life in the home. It brings together and unites.   (Theon of Smyrna, cited in Rowell 1983: 41)

Although comparisons across time and space inevitably run the risk of caricature, comparisons are as essential to anthropology and ethnomusicology as in-depth understanding of single cases. The Suyá, Kaluli, and Pythagorean ideas about music emphasize some important similarities and contrasts.

First, in all three cases song is the result of a particular relationship between humans and the rest of the universe, involving an unusually close relationship and merging of states of being into a single combined state of being expressed through music. When humans, birds, animals, or other aspects of the universe are conjoined, the result is song.

Second, the non-human order provides a model for music. For the Kaluli the model is bird song, for the Pythagoreans it is the harmonic scale that provides natural relationships, and for the Suyá it is not the apparent sounds of individual birds but the songs natural species are said to sing when they are in groups that are taught to the village by specialists who are the only ones who can hear them.

In all three musical traditions, music provides an emotional experience of considerable force. Kaluli songs arouse sadness and anger, Suyá singing arouses sadness in some and creates euphoria in the rest, for some Ancient Greeks music produced a gradual approach to absolute beauty.

There are some essential differences, however. A Kaluli becomes a bird by decorating himself with feathers and singing 'like' birds in melodies 'like' waterfalls, identifying places in the surrounding forest which play on people's emotions. The surrounding forest, and the real birds and sounds in it, provide the textual and melodic model for human song. Although the Suyá learn music from the natural kingdom, what they sing (and therefore what the natural kingdom sings) bears no sonic relationship to the sounds of animals, plants, birds, fish, or insects that a tape recorder could capture. Animal songs – what the people without spirits hear in the villages of the animals – are entirely different from their calls in the forest, which are called *kà*, and might be translated as 'cry' or 'bark.' To 'become a bird' in the sense that a person loses his spirit which then lives with the birds, is to be able to see and hear the essential social reality of bird life – which is in many ways the same as human life today and radically different from the animals' apparent natural habitat and sounds. There is a myth in which a woman literally becomes a bird (Seeger 1984: 499–502). When she does so, however, instead of singing as the bird sings (as the Kaluli might have told it) she simply gives a 'cry' (*kà*) and flies away. The differences between the way humans and animals are juxtaposed are probably the essence of larger differences between the Suyá and Kaluli cosmologies.

Suyá and Kaluli rituals both reduce the distinctions between men and animals. Kaluli songs are based in part on observations of what we call 'nature' – their songs are similar to the cries of certain forest birds. Suyá songs are not. In Pythagorean theory harmony was a symbol of a universal order to which men should become attuned. It existed in nature, and could be expressed through music. The later idea of the 'harmony of the spheres' described in medieval texts proposed that the operation of the universe itself produced music. Kaluli and Pythagorean ideas of music were partly based on observations of nature and mathematics, and human song is said to reproduce something natural. Suyá ideas of nature are fundamentally based on observations of (or interpretations of) society, just as their animal songs do not mimic observable nature but rather the true sounds of the communities of animals that live much like human beings.

These ideas about music as fundamentally 'natural' can be compared with contemporary American ideas about musical talent. In everyday discussions with Americans about music, it is clear that to a certain extent music is related to a 'natural' force rather than a purely human one. While among the Suyá every member of the society was at some time a performer but only a few lost their spirits, many Americans appear to believe that although most people can be taught music, only a few of them are musically 'gifted.'

In a very interesting dissertation on musical values at a music conservatory in the United States, Henry Kingsbury (1984) discusses the concept of talent as an essential component of modern ideas of music. Music at the conservatory is said to be something created by certain individuals who have been 'naturally endowed' at birth with something that other people may or may not have. Technique is of course essential, but there is more than 'mere' technique in the evaluations at the conservatory. In fact, 'pure technique' is a strong criticism of any performance. Music is conceptualized as a kind of natural gift, and a considerable amount of anxiety at the conservatory revolves around whether one 'has' or 'doesn't have' talent which is expressed in 'feeling.' Kingsbury writes of a certain master class:

A fundamental principle of Goldman's teaching was that students *must* play what is printed in the score, and yet that they *must not* play something simply *because* it is written in the score, but rather because they *feel* it that way.   (Kingsbury 1984)

The 'feeling' required of musicians is quite distinct from their intellectual grasp of the musical system, and relates to an American contrast between what has also been called nature and culture. In the United States, many features of life are considered to be part of the natural order – and therefore legitimized and ordained. David Schneider, writing on the symbolism of American kinship, observes 'kinship is the blood relationship, the fact of shared biogenetic substance . . . This is nature; these are natural things, these are the ways of nature. To be otherwise is unnatural, artificial, contrary to nature' (1968: 107). His discussions of the difference between 'natural kinsmen' and 'in-laws' and between 'American born' and 'naturalized' citizens, parallels the distinction between talent and 'mere technique.' Musical genius, feeling, and talent are somehow innate, in the blood (and therefore justified), the others are learned through self-discipline, training, and (in the case of citizenship) legislation.

Composers are often said to possess a special kind of genius. The introduction of new music is the result of individual experience among the Suyá and the result of a genetic lottery among Americans. Yet in both groups musical innovation is broadly 'natural' or beyond the control of the individual involved. For the Americans music is the result of the genes; for the Suyá it is the result of a witch. One society's individual gift is another society's individual evil transformed into a benefit.

All of these ideas may be contrasted with the North American Plains Indian vision quest. There, an individual purposefully sought a vision through isolation and fasting. The visions experienced were somewhat similar to those described by the Suyá (Native American cosmologies have many broad themes in common), but meant something quite different. A Plains Indian who saw a vision was a complete adult with powerful spirit. In a similar pattern, shamans in many of the Tupi-speaking groups in Brazil sought spiritual journeys and were often political leaders as well. A Suyá who lost his spirit, on the other hand, was less complete than adults who had them. He would almost never become a political leader, and the fate of his spirit after his physical death was quite uncertain – many people said that his spirit would never join its relatives in the village of the dead when the body died.

Music, in a great many places, is said to come from beyond the mind and beyond the body – from the natural order as it is differently conceived by different peoples. This gives music a pre-ordained, transcendent, and often unquestionable reality. The following chapter will describe how singing is part of the construction of the Suyá world, and thus part of the creation of certain social, spatial, and personal processes, forms, and ideals.

4 *Singing as a creative activity*

In two preceding chapters we have investigated the distinctive features of musical form and the transcendent origins of Suyá songs. But music is more than sound and cosmology. It is performed by members of a community in certain places and at certain times, often with an audience composed of other members of the community. Music is the entire process of conceptualization, realization, and evaluation of music. Each performance re-creates, re-establishes, or alters the significance of singing and also of the persons, times, places, and audiences involved. It expresses the status, sex, and feelings of the performers, and it brings these to the attention of the entire community, which interprets them in a variety of ways.

The Suyá village can be likened to a concert hall, its annual round equated with a concert series, and its population equated with an orchestra. I will investigate these analogies by discussing musical space, musical time, and the social relations involved in musical production. Then I will describe the musical expression of individual identity, and the kinds of choices a singer might make during his performance. Finally, I will summarize some of the recent work on the ethnography of musical performance which provides a methodology for the study of music and performance genres more generally. Above all, this chapter focuses on what singing does for the individual, the social relationships he or she establishes, and the community as a whole. Far too few descriptions of musical traditions consider the broad social and symbolic contexts of which music is a part. By situating singing in socially defined space and time, this chapter presents the sounds discussed in the previous chapters in their social framework.

The village as a concert hall: the sonic re-creation of spatial relationships

The Suyá village resembled many others in lowland South America: it was small and sounds traveled easily within it. Native communities in the tropical regions of South America typically consist of small populations living fairly densely packed in a single house or in villages separated from one another by large stretches of gardens and uninhabited forest used for hunting and gathering. Populations of less than one hundred are common today, and even in the past settlements of over one thousand were quite rare. Although there are exceptions, the village is usually the most important social and political unit. Communities were (and in some cases still are) composed of a single large house (the Northwest Amazon region, Yanomami, some Tupi groups), or a circle of houses (the Gê-speaking groups, the Upper Xingu, some Tupi-speaking groups). Probably the best description of the space and time of everyday life is to be found in Gregor's description of the Mehinaku (1977). In these small communities, sounds made in one part of the settlement can often be heard by all of its members. With its circle of thatched houses around the cleared plaza, the Suyá village resembled a theatre in the round (see Figure 4.1 and Illustration 1). Orators circling the plaza,

65

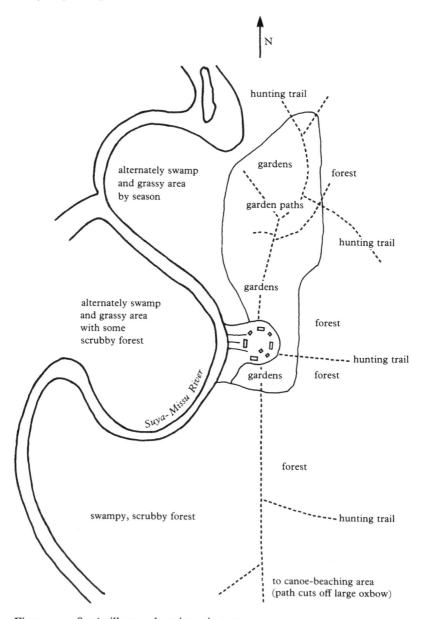

N

hunting trail

gardens

forest

garden paths

hunting trail

alternately swamp
and grassy area
by season

gardens

alternately swamp
and grassy area
with some
scrubby forest

forest

hunting trail

Suya-Missu River

gardens

forest

swampy, scrubby forest

forest

hunting trail

to canoe-beaching area
(path cuts off large oxbow)

Figure 4.1   Suyá village and environs in 1972

women mourning the dead inside their houses, and old men shouting from their hammocks could be heard throughout the village by the entire membership of the society.

Living as so many of us do in houses with solid walls, windows, and the soft noise of fans and running motors, it may be hard to imagine a society as acoustically transparent as the Suyá village. One could hear what was made public (loud) in every house, but one could not necessarily see it. Thatch and upright log walls hid quiet activities, but the cry of a newborn child announced a birth to the entire community, a shout indicated a successful hunt, the wailing of a mourner might indicate a death. Lying in their hammocks the Suyá had a pretty good idea what was happening in their village. As a consequence, things that were not supposed to be public were virtually always silently undertaken. Silence was characteristic of anger, of lovers, and of witches. While noise was characteristic of the public, the collective, and the euphoric, silence was the mark of strong but socially disruptive emotions. When sounds were to be heard, what they were and where they originated were essential features for their interpretation.

The villages of the Gê-speaking communities in Brazil are famous in the ethnographic literature for the clarity of their spatial domains and the importance of their village plans for a sociological and cosmological understanding of their societies (see Lévi-Strauss 1963b; Seeger 1981: 66–80; Maybury-Lewis n.d.; Sá 1982). Many of the essential features of Gê cosmology are laid out horizontally on the ground, in concentric circles from the hard-packed earth of the central plaza to the nameless stretches of distant forest. Their village plan is also the basic outline of social relationships. This is not true of all native Brazilian groups, some of which have far more elaborate cosmologies with hundreds of spirits but far less significant village designs. Inversely, compared to other language families in the region, Gê concepts of spirits and levels of the sky are very little developed (for a comparison with the Tupi-speaking Arawete, see Viveiros de Castro 1986). Gê cosmology is geographic.

The different village spaces and their relationships must be constantly re-established and re-created. This would occur each time the Suyá constructed a new village or planned and executed a ceremony. A ritually active village was one with clearly defined spatial zones; it was almost possible to measure the collective activity in Suyá villages by noting the condition of the plaza and the main paths leading into it.

At certain times of year there was often little ceremonial activity in the Suyá village. The period from August through November was one of those times. Families were often out of the village on long trips to gather wild products, taking advantage of the low waters to kill many fish, gather a lot of honey, and eat the eggs river turtles laid in the sandbanks. Communal activities were rare, and the village plaza literally lost its clarity. Clumps of grass grew up within the circle of houses. The log racing track narrowed as bushes grew into it. The paths to the canoe-beaching area also became overgrown. One of the first activities after a ritual began was to begin a general clearing of the village. Men and women in each house would clear and sweep the earth on all sides. Virtually no grass would remain in the plaza, the racing path would be widened and smoothed, the paths to the canoe-beaching area would be cleared. While this clearing had a practical aspect – the Suyá mentioned snakes and spiders as being good reasons to keep large clear spaces around the houses and on the paths to the water – it was regularly part of ritual activity. The physical state of the men's house also showed the effect of a long period without ceremonies. The men often burned the men's house thatch during the cold dry months of July and August, leaving only the bare poles standing. When the men's house was in poor repair, or even non-existent, one of the early activities after the start of a ceremony would be to rebuild it. During the years I visited the Suyá they constructed three of them, two to the southeast of the center of the plaza, one to the northwest.

The plaza was above all the domain of men and public performance. It was the location of their evening meeting place and the men's houses. Angry speech, everybody listens speech, slow speech, ceremonial recitative, and most songs were performed in the plaza. The plaza had several components, a night-time meeting place in the center and one or two men's houses off to one side. In a large village there were two men's houses, one in the east and one in the west side of the plaza, each associated with a moiety. In a village with a small population the two moieties shared a single structure on one side or the other. When the plaza was overgrown, there would be paths leading from the doors of most houses to the center of the plaza. Around its edge another path would link the front doors of each house to the other.

The plaza stood in vivid contrast to the largely female dominated kinship-based residence houses that surrounded it, and in a sense defined it. The houses were the homes of the primary audience – the women. In them people employed everyday speech, muttered 'bad speech' (selfish gossip), mourned, and quietly performed invocations. When men were performing in the plaza, women often sat in front of their houses, watching, or remained inside and listened to them. Men did sing inside the houses, but only rarely, and either as a prelude to leaving or as a collective group. Children spent much of their time in and around their natal houses. Traditionally (before the 1960s), every adolescent boy was removed from the house he was born in and slept in the men's house until he married and moved into the house of his wife's parents. Barring separation or death, he lived there for the rest of his life. When a couple's children were grown, their married sons would reside in other houses, and their daughters' husbands and children would live with them. The result of this arrangement was that the core of continuity in the houses was provided largely by a group of women. Recent studies of the Northern Gê groups – especially those by women – indicate that there may have been a male-oriented and plaza-oriented bias in some earlier studies. They show that the houses are tremendously important social units with symbolic continuity through individual names (for the Eastern Timbira see Ladeira 1982; for the Kayapo Verswijver 1985; Lea 1986) or house names (for the Suyá see Seeger 1981: 73–75). This group was not exactly a matrilineage, since the whole concept of lineage is problematic in the region (Seeger 1980b: 127–135, Rivière 1985). Lea, however, has amassed considerable evidence for matrilines among the Northern Kayapo (1986).

The circle of houses was enveloped by a zone of silence. The area directly behind the houses was called 'the dead side' or 'the black side.' This did not mean that people spoke in hushed voices there, but rather that things done there were private, not ceremonial, and were often undertaken in silence. Men and women in seclusion bathed there, food not shared with the community was often eaten there, and some domestic work was done there. Invocations were performed there sometimes, to cure ill patients. Non-relatives seldom entered the areas behind each other's houses. Just beyond the cleared area behind the house were the trash dumps, and a transitional zone of bush and a few plantings of pineapple or sweet potatoes that thrived on the refuse thrown there. They were well picked over by the parrots, chickens and dogs that wandered freely, as well as by the groups of children who played there. Beyond the dumps people defecated and urinated, and perhaps met lovers on the maze of over-grown paths. Music was never sung in the dead side. Ceremonial groups passed through them in silence, as when the boys who had been singing in the forest camp on 29 January came to the edge of the village circle. In two years in the village I never saw a group sing there.

The gardens lay beyond the private area, trash dumps, and defecation trails, except on the river side where there was no room for them (see Illustration 1). Entering the dense bushy gardens, the acoustic clarity of the village disappeared. Only gunshots, cockcrows, and the barking of dogs could be heard once a short way into them. Far more striking were the sounds of birds and insects. Since the Suyá cleared new gardens every year, and did so progressively further from the village, the point where the gardens began changed. Old gardens might be partly replanted to manioc, but they were usually overgrown with scrubby second growth and fruit trees, cut by trails leading to more distant gardens, hunting spots, or water sources. Ghosts were said to wander in the gardens, and women usually went there only in groups.

The concentric ring of gardens was not important in ceremonial activities except as a source of food. The gardens were never sung in as such; they were simply a place to cross on the way to a very important space – the forest. I suspect that the unimportance of the garden space was the result of an historic tradition: most Northern Gê villages were located on savannah, quite far from their gardens, whose products were important but whose space was not part of the village design. This was almost certainly true for the Suyá before they moved into the forested Xingu region where they could clear gardens at the back of their houses.

The forest was the domain of animals and spirits; the more distant forest was the home of enemies and powerful monsters as well. The forest stood in strong contrast to the plaza. The plaza was cleared of all growth and was the place where adult men sang collectively. The forest was entirely overgrown, where animals roamed, enemies lived, and where adult men usually traveled individually and silently. It was also in the forest that humans became transformed into animals and their songs were learned.

This is not to say the Suyá were not quite at home hunting in the low, bushy forest of their present homeland. Nor should they be imagined as terrified wanderers in it. Instead, the forest was represented by them as a place of unexpected encounters, unusual events, and radical transformations, among them the death of both humans and animals. Ceremonies used the forest as a place to transform human beings as well, and a number of them involved movement to and from a forested area. This was the importance of the forest camp in the Mouse Ceremony, where on the final night the dancers were transformed.

The Suyá sang in forest camps, in the houses, and in the plaza, and danced (or sneaked) from one domain to the other in very systematic ways. Their use of space was strikingly different from what has been reported for some Tupi-speaking groups that lived nearby. Among the Arawete and the Kayabi, there is no alternation between houses and plaza, or between village and forest. Most of the performance occurs inside the house, and the major events usually involve possession and transition to a spirit realm above the village or house (Lins 1984; Viveiros de Castro 1986).

The way Suyá sang in space was significant. The different parts of their cosmos were marked by the sounds performed there (or the silence observed). The empty space in the middle of the circle of houses became a plaza when it was the stage for public performance. The houses took on their significance by supplying ornamented singers and the audience. The envelope of silence sealed off the village activities from those outside, except for those in the forest and the forest camp. The forest was the place for shouts and shout songs, but not for low unison songs. These spatial domains were endowed with meanings and associations by singing, dancing, and ceremonial activities. In this way, singing and silence were part of the constant re-creation of significant space. Everyday life tended to blur some of the distinctions between plaza and periphery; ceremonial activity and song re-established them.

The year as a concert: creating time through sound

The anthropological investigation of time has revealed it to be socially constructed rather than a universally shared concept. Evans-Pritchard's study of Nuer time as it relates to their ecosystem and the needs of their cattle (1940) is a classic in the field. Yet time not only reflects seasons, lives, and other processes, it imposes order on them. Time as a socially relevant experience is created by societies and individuals acting within them. Although the Suyá could use the sun, stars, moon, and constellations to calculate time, its important social markers were imposed with song. Just as singing, dancing and other ceremonial activities clarified or re-defined certain spaces, so they re-established periods of time and some of the relationships among them.

The Suyá regulated themselves with a social calendar, rather than an astronomical one. The year was characterized by a wet and a dry season, and their musical year was also divided into two parts: rainy and dry season songs. Yet the seasonal songs did not simply follow the vagaries of rainfall and drought, but rather established a change of season. When the new season's song had begun, it was really that season – whether or not the rains suddenly stopped or began to fall once again. The day, too, presented a continuum of dark to light in the morning, the gradual movement of the sun during the day, and a change from light to dark in the evening. The Suyá marked these gradual changes of day and year with musical events of distinct types, presented by distinct performers with distinctive styles. As in the case of space, the time when music was performed was part of the creation of the regularities they apparently marked.

The Suyá talked easily about how ceremonial periods structure the year. I was often presented with descriptions of the annual cycle, the rain, and the ceremonies that were associated with them. A recording of Takuti was the most coherent presentation.

The men sing the dry season songs for a long time. The rain comes. Thunderstorms explode in the sky. Then we begin to sing the rainy season songs. We sing the rainy season songs. One of the men walks around the village all day singing his shout songs. A tough man sings all day, and in the afternoon the men all sing a rainy season song. They sing the rainy season songs. They sing the rainy season songs, they sing the rainy season songs.*
'Well, what shall we do?' the men ask each other. 'I don't know.' 'Let's race with logs.'† We finish planting the gardens, and then travel out of the village.‡
When the berry *wai iō sü* is red on the banks of the river the men say 'Let's go back. Our corn is already ripe.'

[I omit a description of the return]

The men race with logs for a long time. They only sing the rainy season songs. They race with logs until they begin the Gaiyi Ceremony. They do the Gaiyi Ceremony for a long time. They sing the rainy season songs and run many log races. Then they say 'Let's run the Gaiyi log.' They go on a long hunt, and bring fish and game back to the village. They arrive in the evening and the *ngātu iarén* soloist performs his ritual instruction. The rest of the men look for a big log. [I omit a description of this particular race]

---

* The use of repetition indicates repeated action over a period of time, and is a stylistic alternative to Iawekidi's use of stretched syllables in the myth.
† This summarizes the moment when the men decide what ceremonies they will perform during a given season.
‡ Before steel tools, and since their introduction only when the gardens have not done well, the Suyá left the village after planting the new gardens and returned only when the corn was ripe.

Then the formal friends paint each other's feet. The Gaiyi Ceremony is over. They only sing rainy season songs now. In the rainy season we only sing rainy season songs. That goes on and on. At the start of the dry season we still sing rainy season songs. We sing them even though the Gaiyi Ceremony is over. Then it is the dry season. It is the dry season; and we sing the dry season songs. It is always thus.

It may have once been thus; by 1970 it was no longer. The Suyá ritual calendar never really recovered after the Juruna and their rubber tapper allies raided and burned their village to the ground around 1915. A number of ceremonies requiring especially large numbers of people were never performed after that, and the overall number of ceremonies diminished. In addition, more and more Upper Xingu ceremonies were introduced that did not require as many people, and they came to dominate at certain times of year. Nor did one ceremonial period always follow immediately upon another. When there was no ceremony in progress, Suyá men liked to turn on their radios at high volume from about 4:30 a.m. to about 6:00, perhaps substituting one form of music for another, observing the correct hour, and playing for the entire community to hear. Yet between the time an extended ceremony was initiated – for example after the first shout song of the Mouse Ceremony – and the time it was concluded, in the 1970s and 1980s the days still passed as Takuti described.

Ceremonial periods varied in intensity and length, leaving considerable room for innovation through the introduction of new segments. The Mouse Ceremony was fairly short in 1972. In 1976 the Suyá performed a Mouse Ceremony, followed it immediately with a Savannah Deer Ceremony, and then a Small Bow Ceremony. In the middle of all these they performed a whole series of smaller ceremonies, each with its own name and specific obligations between brothers, sisters, name givers and name receivers, the different moieties, and men and women. The Suyá would often perform a ceremony that belonged to one moiety and then one that belonged to its opposite. They would also sometimes insert several evenings of Upper Xingu ceremonies into the weeks of preparation for the end of a longer ceremony.

The Suyá did not usually repeat ceremonies in consecutive years. They said they did not like to sing the same thing all the time. Thus not every year was the same, and the decisions of what would be performed would depend on the membership of the ceremonial groups most involved.

Each season had particular ceremonies that were appropriate to it. The Bee Ceremony would be performed when the gardens were cut; the Garden Song when the men set fire to the clearings; the Mouse Ceremony when the corn was ripe and drying on the stalk. Log races were only run during the rainy season. The Gaiyi ceremony was performed only at the very end of the rainy season. Table 4.1 summarizes the seasonality of Suyá ceremonies.

The songs of the two seasons – the rainy season songs and the dry season songs – formed the backdrop for all other ceremonies. No matter what other small ceremony was being planned or performed, the mornings and late afternoons were punctuated by the seasonal unison songs. This seems to be a characteristic of a number of the Gê (see Aytai 1985 on the Xavante). The seasonal genre *agachi ngére* and *kahran kasag ngére* were interchangeable during their respective seasons, and new ones were introduced fairly often to the repertory. The morning song would begin after cockcrow, when the men either spontaneously went or were called quietly to the men's house where they sang facing the center of the plaza. The ritual specialist usually would lead the singing. Those who were not singing usually lay in their hammocks listening to the song.

Table 4.1. *The annual round and the accompanying ceremonies*

Month	Season	Agricultural cycle	Seasonal songs	Agricultural cycle songs	Upper Xingu songs	Season-specific ceremonies
April	Dry season begins	Cut gardens	Dry season songs	*huru iarén* (garden recitative)	*judnti*	Begin *pebjitugu* and *angrochingere*
May				*mben ngére* (bee song)		
June						
July						
August					*iamuricuma jawari*	
September	First rains	Burn cleared gardens & plant		*huru ngére* (garden song)		End *pebjutugu* and *angrochingere*
October						
November	Heavy rains begin		Rainy season songs			Certain rainy season ceremonies may be begun. Log races begin
December						
January		Corn ripe		*amto ngére* and other songs		Many rainy season ceremonies terminated at corn harvest. Others continue
February						
March		New sweet potatoes		Rainy season ceremonies concluded, if not before this		

The terms may be translated as follows: *amto ngére* = Mouse Ceremony; *judnti* = an Upper Xingu ceremony called by the name of the hummingbird; *iamuricuma* = an Upper Xingu women's ceremony; *jawari* = an Upper Xingu ceremony learned from the Trumai; *pebjitugu* = a traditional Suyá initiation ritual (literally the black initiates); *angrochingere* = a traditional Suyá male initiation ceremony (literally the wild pig song).

When it was light enough to see easily, the men would stop singing and disperse, some to bathe, some to hunt, some to the gardens, others to domestic activities. This was also the time when the men would stop singing if they had been singing all night. Actual sunrise came later; often the morning mist made the sunrise difficult to discern.

From sunrise until about 9:30 the village would usually be quiet. I was told that no unison songs were ever performed until noon. All that could be heard was the sound of manioc being grated, corn pounded, children playing, sometimes the distant barking of a dog or boom of a shotgun, the playing of a radio or cassette recorder, or the solo performance of shout songs.

While there were never any unison songs at this time of day, solo singers used these hours to prepare themselves for all-day performances, sitting on their mother's or sister's bed and singing shout songs while being painted by their female relatives. Then, at about 10:00, the solo singer would emerge from his maternal house (not where his wife lived), and begin to walk clockwise (if in the *Kren* moiety) or counterclockwise (if in the *Ambàn* moiety) around the plaza. As he left, his mother or sister would weep. Solo singers would continue to sing the entire day, stopping every once in a while to rest in the men's house – where they were also singing. They might sing a certain deceased relative's shout songs all day, or their own.

I was told there was sometimes unison singing at noon. I never saw any. Instead, the solo singer would continue circling the plaza under the scorching sun. In the late afternoon, often after a men's house collective meal, the men would comment 'It is already late afternoon' or 'the sun is very low' and they would meet in the men's house and sing another unison season song. The soloist would keep walking around and singing until the men finished. Then with a final coda, he would walk to his sister's or mother's house and sit down.

The men would disperse once again, going to bathe, to eat, to talk with relatives. They would return to the center of the plaza at dusk, carrying small wooden stools and often some tobacco. This was a gathering rarely missed – no one remained in the forest or on the river at this time if he could avoid it, and a man's absence would be remarked upon and was usually the result of illness or an overnight excursion. This was a time of public oratory, the 'slow speech' of elders and the 'everybody listens speech' of political leaders. Sometimes the men would sing then, and go on into the night. Or they might sit around and smoke and talk, until some of the elders would say 'I'm cold' or 'It's already late at night' and leave for their houses, abandoning the plaza to the young men who would continue talking, joking, shouting, and disappearing on silent amorous pursuits. Silence, and silent activities, usually reigned until the pre-dawn singing (or radios) began the following morning.

The days were not separate, but linked through a series of interrelated performances. If a solo singer had performed on a given day, a solo singer from the opposite moiety would sing the next day. After that, one from the first moiety would circle the village, singing to the rest. These voluntary performances could go on for some days until it seemed as though there was constantly singing in the air. Shorter ceremonies were often inserted in longer ones. When the men were in the state of euphoria that defines ceremonies, they would perform one short ceremony after another, embedded in the larger ritual period. They were regularly up early to sing, and stayed up late carousing. The men's energy amazed me, and I would usually run out of tape, batteries, or physical energy, and be left swinging in the hammock as day after day they kept singing, hunting, finding racing logs and carrying them in, and assembling the materials for the ceremonial costumes of the final night. Night after night they would sing or play rough games long after dark. The more excited they got, the more energy they had. Suyá ceremonies tended to snowball in complexity and enthusiasm, with occasional lulls, at some point during which they would be harangued by the ritual specialist and they would start up again.

The way the Suyá related one performance to the next turned both days and years into musical performances. If the day began with morning singing, it would end with an afternoon unison song; if a solo singer began to sing at 9:00 in the morning, he would finish at the end of the afternoon group performance and be followed by another the next day. During the day there were times of unison sound, of domestic work, of silence, and of individual song. During the year dry season songs followed rainy season songs and were themselves followed by rainy season songs, each punctuated by appropriate seasonal rituals and some 'free floating' ones that might be performed at any time of year.

The relationship of performances to one another should lead us to re-think the concept of a 'piece' of music. To say that the Suyá year was a concert series is only partially correct; it was also a single concert. In one sense, the year was a 'piece' with two movements (rainy and dry season unison songs). Each seasonal song was defined not only in itself, but also in relation to the other part – already sung or as yet to be sung. In another sense, each season was a complete musical 'piece' in itself, with a clear musical beginning, duration, development (through a series of cumulative ceremonies) and conclusion. In a narrower sense, each component of the series of smaller ceremonies performed during a given season was a 'piece' and the season a string of such pieces. In the narrowest sense, each individual unison or shout song performance was a unit – structurally complete and performed in the space of approximately half an hour. Each of these delimitations is correct, but each is incomplete by itself. Suyá music consisted of small units that were conceptually (and in sound, gesture, and dance) integrated into larger units that were often described to me as a succession of seasons. Both longer and shorter periods of time were marked through song. The musical units must be considered in all of their various lengths and the musical performances studied as parts of a long series of such events.

Society as an orchestra: the vocal re-creation of social relationships

What and how a Suyá sang was largely defined by membership in groups determined by age, sex, and name set. Who would sing what kind of song today, and who would sing tomorrow, who would mourn for the dead and who would shout falsetto shouts was determined by group membership, rather than by 'talent,' 'personal inclination,' or 'experience.' Suyá society was an orchestra of voices whose characteristics were more limited according to sex and age than their biologically determined characteristics demanded.

Different individuals or groups contributed different sounds to create a vocal orchestra. Listen to the fairly complex sound of Example 4.1 on the cassette, a selection from the conclusion of the Bee Ceremony. After singing Bee Ceremony songs in the evening for weeks, all the men painted elaborate designs on themselves and ran (like swarms of bees, they said) from house to house, singing in each and in the plaza as well. This recording, just outside a house, captures not only the unison singing of the adult men, but also the sound of a young solo shout-song singer and the falsetto cries of an old man. In another house a woman was crying over the memory of a dead relative who liked that ceremony especially, and in yet another a different group of men was singing. Since thatch walls are not barriers to sound, sounds can be produced simultaneously in a number of different places and still contribute to the whole. It is difficult to capture simultaneous sounds produced in widely separated places on a tape recorder. The human ear is far better equipped to hear and interpret simultaneous sounds with very different degrees of loudness than a microphone is able to record them.

The excerpt from the Bee Ceremony may sound uncoordinated and anarchic, but the performance was creating and expressing a specific social order and community experience. Our orchestras are comprised of a group of musicians who sit close together and play under the direction of a conductor who coordinates their entire performance. No one in Suyá society, not even a political leader, had the control over other people's actions that a conductor has over his orchestra. When the Suyá performed, each person would participate according to his own role, sometimes only loosely articulated with the particular melodic movement and meter of the other singers, but intricately coordinated in terms of sex, age, performance style, and the space and time of the performance. Their sounds were complementary, and together created the euphoria of community participation. The contributions of different age-, sex-, and name-based groups to the orchestra were distinctive, and are described in Table 4.2. The contributions listed in boldface indicate how those groups participate in the Mouse Ceremony. The others refer to their activities in other ceremonies but not in the performances of the Mouse Ceremony witnessed.

Although there are differences in performance style according to age, the biggest contrast in Table 4.2 is between men and women. In many Suyá ceremonies, men were the performers and women were the audience. Shout songs were sung 'for sisters and mothers' who in fact listened and commented on their relatives' songs. Sisters and mothers had specific important roles in almost all ceremonies, but they did not sing. In the Mouse Ceremony, for example, young women whose names were part of a male name set accompanied the men on the final afternoon, but did not perform any shout songs. Painted with red body paint, but without dance capes, they accompanied the name set to which their name belonged with their eyes downcast, stepping back and forth instead of stamping. Sisters and mothers might provide food for their brothers or sons, receive food from them, hold their bows while they raced, paint them in their houses, and so forth. Women were central actors in all Suyá ceremonies, which often emphasized the relationships between a man and his real and classificatory sisters and his mother over other kinds of kinship ties, such as those with his wife and in-laws. Women in their roles of wives and lovers, although essential to physical reproduction, were de-emphasized in ceremonies that stressed name-based relationships. In certain ceremonies, the men took a few unmarried women for cooking and sexual services on a hunting trip, leaving their wives at home. The women were called 'wives of the group' and all the adult women in the village were considered sisters, rather than wives. Many ceremonies involved a general realignment of relationships to de-emphasize the everyday sexual division of labor and marriage relationships, and to replace them with natal family ties.

Women's participation in ceremonial life was not all silent. They had a ceremony of their own, learned from Upper Xingu captives, called Iamuricumã. In it, they aggressively preempted the public performance space, and chased the men out of the center of the village, where they sang in unison. Another female contribution to the total aural effect of ceremonies was crying. Adult women often cried at the start of a ceremony, when they remembered and commemorated their dead relatives who used to enjoy it particularly, or when a brother left their houses after being adorned for his solo singing. The traditional crying (as distinct from non-melodic sobbing), performed regularly by only a few older women during my stay, was somewhat similar in form to a shout song. It had a descending melodic line. It was sung by individual women, but several of them might cry at once, creating a cacophony which recalls the men's collective singing of their individual shout songs. The words were composed by the woman who performed it, and usually referred to features of the dead. 'Oh, my grandson, my grandson. You were sick and now you are dead. My grandson, my grandson' is an example. Since these were most often performed in the tremendously emotional and often volatile situations immediately after a person's death, I never recorded the group crying sessions.

Every song had a 'master' or 'owner,' which could be an individual or a group. Shout songs belonged to individuals and unison songs belonged to groups, although they both had origins from the animal domain. Certain groups either had the exclusive right to sing a certain song, or the right to refuse to authorize its public performance, in which case members of other groups would always ask them for permission to sing the song before doing so. Unison songs were sung by specific ceremonial groups, never by kinship-based groups. The groups could consist of all the adult men in the village (or women, or both), or a single moiety, or the

Table 4.2. *Musical performances and Suyá groups defined by sex and age*

Age grade*	Types of musical activity

MALE

Ngàtureyi (from 3–10 years of age.†)

>**short shout songs, no participation in seasonal unison songs**, played at performing adult ceremonies, on the periphery of the performance.

Ngàtuyi (from 10–15 years)

>**longer shout songs, participation in seasonal unison songs after voice change. Prepared food for men's house meals**, shouted bird calls in Jawari.

Sikwenduyi (from 16–22 years)

>**long shout songs, solo shout song performance, unison singing**, solo 'recitatives' (*iarén*), this age group was most associated with all forms of singing. **Active and intense participation** in all ceremonies, with considerable laughing and enthusiasm.

Hen Suyapé (1 child to 3 children)

>**long shout songs, unison songs, day-long performances of solo shout songs**, occasionally performed invocations.

Hen Tumu (3 or more children to 2 grandchildren)

>**sang shout songs lower in the throat than sikwenduyi; sang unison songs**; few solo performances of shout songs, but could **orate**; are considered to be knowledgeable **myth tellers**; **perform invocations**. May choose not to participate in Mouse Ceremony after their name receiver is an adult, in which case they sit in the center of the village and watch.

Wikenyi (more than 2 grandchildren)

>**Gave characteristic wikenyi shout. Sang funny, obscene shout songs. Danced and sang in a clowning style.** Keened for dead; clowning pantomime.

FEMALE

Pureyi (from 3–10 years of age)

>**No specific musical activity.** Might sing songs from other tribes, accompanied young boys in the play performance of adult ceremonies.

Puyi (from 10 years to first child)

>**Accompanied male dancers but did not sing.** Silent participants in several ceremonies as sexual partners, and took important roles in ceremonies of Upper Xingu origin.

Hen Suyapé (1 child–3 children)

>Fully active in Upper Xingu singing. Performed female Suyá songs, but did not lead them. Were important as an audience for men's singing. **Prepared food for Mouse Ceremony and other ceremonies.**

Hen Tumu (3 or more children to 2 grandchildren)

>Led singing of both Upper Xingu and Suyá female songs. Told myths; keened for dead; performed invocations.

Wikenyi (more than 2 grandchildren)

>Old people's shout, clowning shouting and **keened for dead. Helped in performances but without singing.** Were considered to be especially knowledgeable tellers of myths; performed invocations.

MOIETIES‡

Ambànyi	Sang more slowly, in east side of plaza, their songs name 'good' animals, from edible species. Walked counterclockwise around the plaza when they sang all-day shout songs.
Krenyi	Sang more rapidly, in west side of plaza, their songs often named 'bad' or inedible animal species. Walked clockwise around the plaza when they sang all-day shout songs.
Soikokambrigi	**Sang in east side of men's house or plaza and danced at the front of the line of dancers.**
Soikodnto	**Sang in west side of men's house or plaza and danced in the second part of the line.**

* This table summarizes Suyá sex- and age-based groups (for a full discussion see Seeger 1981:106–147), and indicates their musical contribution to ceremonies. These age grades appeared not only in musical events, but in economic and political life, in conversation, oratory, and myths. They were one of the fundamental organizing principles of Suyá social life.

members of a single name set within a moiety. The songs of a given group often had something in common – or were said to share a trait by Suyá. One moiety (*Kren*) sang rainy season songs more rapidly than the other (*Ambàn*). Their songs also named different animals.

Each name-based moiety or plaza group had its own songs. The people who sang together might be brothers-in-law who never spoke to each other, political opponents, or the best of friends. The way they felt about each other had nothing to do with the way they sang except in extreme cases when a man might refuse to sing entirely. Factional disputes did sometimes come to a head in ceremonies because suddenly what had been covered up came out in the open (literally into the open because it was displayed in the plaza).

When the entire social orchestra was mobilized, a number of distinctly different simultaneous sounds built through juxtaposition to create an entirely different effect than any one of its parts – as in Example 4.1 on the cassette.

The importance of simultaneous sounds that are not necessarily rhythmically coordinated or even performed in the same place has been largely unrecognized in lowland South American music. Sometimes these 'extraneous sounds' have been carefully avoided in making the recordings, or edited out when the recordings were turned into a record. To unaccustomed ears, the simultaneous sounds are distracting. Anyone who has listened to records from this region has probably wished the shouts and cries didn't 'obscure' the 'music.' These cries have, in the past, been called 'incidental,' 'extraneous,' or 'non-musical' sounds. Their non-musicality, however, was sometimes over-emphasized in recordings where the technician had set the recording level to the level of the singing rather than the shouts, which were therefore distorted in the subsequent recording. Yet shouts, cries, weeping, and animal sounds are an essential part of the musical performance.

I discovered this when I was trying to make the best possible recording of an Upper Xingu song (known regionally as the *jawari*) the Suyá were performing in August 1982. After witnessing several performances of a given song series, I knew the adult men in the center of a long line of singers were the only ones really singing the unison melody. The young men, bachelors, and boys on the ends of the line were imitating bird calls, shouting comments to each other, and giggling. By using a directional microphone, I was able to make a recording that consisted largely of the unison singing. This was, to me, the 'music.' But when I played the recording back to the Suyá that night, they were terribly disappointed with the result. It wasn't beautiful, they said. It wasn't euphoric. It excluded an essential part of the performance. They insisted that I record the song series again, to get it right and make a 'beautiful' recording.

The Suyá reaction to my recording was one of the clearest statements I obtained about the importance of the different parts to the total sound. The melody line – the clearly organized tone and rhythm being performed by the older men – was only part of the desired total effect, which also included the apparently irreverent calls, shouts, and giggles. Every age group

† The ages in this table are approximate. Young people were classified according to their size, while older people were classified according to the number of children or grandchildren they had.

‡ The reason there are two pairs of moieties is that they appeared at different times, and have different membership. The *Ambàn/Kren* pair appeared in some ceremonies, the *Soikokambrigi/Soikodnto* pair appeared in others. The *Kren* and *Ambàn* name sets were mixed together in each of the *Soikokambrigi/Soikodnto* pair. This is one of the complex aspects of Gê social organization, where cross-cutting ceremonial ties bound all members of village together in several different ways.

contributed to the total effect, if not to the melody, and they were all important. I suppose my recording sounded a bit to the Suyá as if I had recorded only the strings in the performance of Beethoven's Ninth symphony, and ignored all of the woodwinds, brasses, percussion and voices.

The lesson to be learned from this is that our recording techniques can often be inappropriately selective. When, for example, we use particular microphones and set them up in a particular place, we are in fact making assumptions about the music itself. Selective recordings have their place. If one intends to analyze drumming, it is important to have the drummers clear and underplay the vocalists. If one wants to study the bird call imitations, it is distracting to have the men singing. It is essential, however, to evaluate the recordings with the people recorded. When the Suyá obtained cassette tape recorders, which were ubiquitous in the 1980s, the tape recordings they made were different from mine and very instructive as to the parts of the singing that were of interest to them.

A Suyá participated in a ceremony according to who he or she was: what sex, what age, and what name group. Of the three, only an individual's age could change. Thus each time a person sang he or she reaffirmed (or established for the first time) a certain age status. A young boy might learn a long shout song for the first time. An adult man might begin not to force his voice as high as before. An older man might begin to clown before he had more than a single grandchild, or an old woman might retain the sober demeanor characteristic of a younger woman. Every ceremony was thus an opportunity to reaffirm not only what one was (a male and a member of certain groups) but what one believed one was or wanted to be.

Every performance of a ceremony re-established social relationships in other ways as well. A dramatic example of this occurred in certain log races, where each man received a little food from all of his biological and more distant 'sisters' in the way Suyá figure relationship (classifying parallel cousins as sisters). Sexual relations with distant sisters were not publicly accepted, but they appeared to gain piquancy and allure from the public approbation, and people who had addressed each other as brother and sister sometimes took each other as lovers. At the next log race, however, the sister-turned-lover was not supposed to give food to the man, nor should he ask for it. The possibility that certain men might not receive food from women from whom they had taken it in the past made that episode in the log races a dramatic one for revealing often hidden sexual relationships. The Suyá watched everyone very carefully. This occasion was just one more example of how ceremonies made public what had been private, and clarified some (often intentionally) ambiguous relationships. Performances established and re-established important relationships between groups and among individuals in very concrete ways.

The body as a musical instrument

The body is involved in music in several ways. The performer learns the song, performs it with accompanying body movements, and an audience hears it. The significance of the faculties of hearing, speech, and movement, as well as the body parts associated with them, are emphasized through ornaments. The decoration of the body is never arbitrary; certain body parts are singled out for attention because they are important.

The most important Suyá body ornaments were those associated with hearing, speaking and singing, and dancing. Earlier in this century, both men and women used to wear large discs inserted in the lobes of their ears. In the 1970s the older men wore the ear discs as well as a wooden disc inserted in their lower lips (these are clearly depicted in Illustration 4). A person's ears were pierced around puberty; a man's lip was pierced several years later. These were the major body ornaments of the Suyá. Contact with Brazilian national society, depopulation, and the death of most of the older men, resulted in the abandonment of full initiation, and the end of ear and lip piercing. What follows is a description of body ornaments as they were used by adult men, and had been used by the entire population before 1960.

Ear discs were associated with hearing and the moral qualities of proper social behavior. The Suyá maintained that people who heard well also knew, understood, and acted properly. The verbs 'to hear' (*mba*) and 'to behave morally' (*añi mba*) are very close, the latter resembling a reflexive form. They said that a person who listened (*mba*) to the speeches of the elders would behave correctly (*añi mbai mbechi*). The moral component of hearing was one of the reasons oratory was so important: if hearing and behavior were associated, then both speaking and listening would be tremendously significant. Kaikwati, in the example of 'slow speech' in Chapter 2, repeated over and over again that the elders 'listened to the speaking, followed the speech, and behaved correctly.'

All adults must listen, hear, understand and behave. Adolescence was an important phase for both sexes. Young men were initiated and entered the men's house, and young women eventually had a child and married. It was a time of life in which moral teaching was especially intense. Before that age, Suyá were quite lenient with their children and did not emphasize the importance of obedience as much as they emphasized the importance of sharing and the obligations of kinship relations. In addition to being a time for moral instruction, adolescence was the age when both sexes traditionally had their ears pierced.

The ear was also important in the physiology of knowledge. The Suyá said knowledge entered the ear and rested in the 'ear hole' (*mbai kre kàm naw*). A song was said to 'lie in the ear' when it was learned, as did a weaving pattern. Knowledge, some of which in other societies is associated with the eye, was for the Suyá consistently an aural phenomenon. People who found learning difficult were said to have 'swollen ears' or, more lightly, to have 'frogs in their ears.' The ear was the conduit of knowledge and moral understanding, essential for correct behavior.

The lip disc was associated with public speaking, song, bellicosity, and adult manhood. Men had their lips pierced shortly before they left their mothers' houses and took up residence in the men's house. The association of the lip disc, the removal from home, and song were all clear in the activities of young men after they entered the men's house. They were supposed to sing constantly, to make larger and larger lip discs to insert in the hole in their lower lip, and to engage in few subsistence activities. The lip disc was a central symbol of masculine identity. They were worn day and night by the men who had them; ear discs were worn on public occasions but were often not worn in the domestic sphere. In all ceremonies the men inserted new ear discs and lip discs whose bright coloring contrasted with the everyday ornament.

The mouth was the principal means of instruction. As we have seen, the Suyá had many different kinds of instruction. In native South American groups there is often a variety of speech styles restricted to certain social roles. Leaders have few institutional resources other than speech: there are no police forces, immediately applicable punishments, or other clear forms of coercion. They rely on exhortations. When many members of a village no longer follow their suggestions, they are no longer chiefs. Kinship ties and exchange relationships provide the underpinnings of political leadership among the Suyá (discussed in Seeger 1981:180–206). In terms of publicly accepted leadership behavior, however, speech is the primary activity. Among the Western Suyá, the brothers of a political leader are called 'political leaders who do not speak.'

Given the importance of the ears, hearing, and morality and of the mouth, speaking and masculinity, it is easier to appreciate the importance of instruction, oratory, invocation, and song. To a certain extent, the interrelationship of this group of concepts relating to speech and hearing also explains why the Suyá had not developed much of an interest in instrumental music. The voice was their most important musical instrument, and the main object of critical evaluation, and the word (embodied in song) was an essential part of knowledge. Even though the Suyá had known of the Upper Xingu Indian flutes for over a century, they did not adopt flutes or flute music as part of their permanent repertory the way they adopted Upper Xingu singing. Nor have they adopted any non-Indian instruments.

The only kinds of musical instruments regularly played by the Suyá were rattles. With a rattle the body itself becomes an instrument. Rattles were held in the hand, tied behind the knees, hung on belts, and worn down the back. They were made of animal hooves, fruit pits, gourds, brass shotgun shells, and small metal bells. Attached to different parts of the body they all sounded quite differently. A rattle shaken by a hand was very regular and controlled; a leg rattle sounded when the leg moved, even when that was not in the rhythm of a song. A woman's hair could be adorned with empty brass shotgun shells that rang occasionally when they hit each other; a man could wear gourds hanging on strings from his neck that clashed against rattles tied to his knees in a totally different pattern from the rhythm of his steps. Rattles made a variety of sounds according to the material they were constructed from, the way they were attached to the body, and the movement that propelled them. The Suyá managed to create considerable variety in each of these.

Percussion instruments can only be played through movement, and dance is therefore an essential part of musical performance. The Suyá described their ceremonies in a number of ways, but one way differentiated between the kinds of movements involved in them. 'Up and down' (*Iarĩ*) indicated that the dance was an up and down leaping movement, characteristic of certain animals – mice and deer among others – and the ceremonies associated with them. Thus the Mouse Ceremony was leaped. Other ceremonies were simply 'everyone together' (*wudn twú*). Descriptive phrases were used for movements of groups of dancers – a line across, a long double line, and a movement in a circle – as well as for many kinds of arm movements. It appeared that a number of the more complex dance movements were no longer practiced. In a number of cases only the old men could perform them, and the young men were ashamed of their own attempts. The two sexes never danced and sang in a single line. If they performed together, it was as two parallel lines of dancers. When women joined men in a line of dancers – as at the Mouse Ceremony – they did so in silence, accompanying the movements of the dancers but without song and without rattles.

Suyá body ornaments and rattles created a socialized body that expressed fundamental aspects of correct behavior for adult men and women – speaking and singing for the men, listening and correct behavior for both sexes. The initiation rites that accompanied biological growth shaped the moral person just as they shaped the body by piercing the ears and lower lip. Although body paint, leg and arm wrappings, and other ornaments donned in ceremonies were significant in the parts of the body they covered, the permanent ornaments indicated moral features that were physically expressed.

The concept of person

The concept of what a person is, the makeup of the biological and social individual, can be very important for understanding social processes. A number of studies of the concept of person in different societies have appeared recently, and it is quite clear that in lowland South America the concept was especially important due to the lack of other social institutions commonly associated with tribal societies such as descent groups.

The Suyá concept of person had three components. One of these was the body, associated with the individual's parents. Another was the social identity which was received with names from a more distant relative, and the third was the 'spirit' or 'shadow' (*mēgaron*) that was entirely individual.

The Suyá said their bodies were formed from their fathers' semen, which accumulated in their mother's womb and formed the fetus. Parents, children, and full siblings were said to maintain a kind of physiological identity throughout their lives, signaled by dietary and activity restrictions on the others when any one of them was sick. For example, when a man had a fever, none of his children, his siblings, or his parents were supposed to eat certain red-fleshed animals because ingesting them would have a direct heating effect on their relative and raise his fever even higher. Many aspects of interpersonal relationships were based on kinship and physical identity. Yet only certain kinsmen were important in song. Specifically, a man would sing for his sisters, and ceremonial activity intensified relations between a man and the women of his natal household. Most relationships stressed in ceremonies were those based on names.

An infant received its social identity through the names it received shortly after birth – from a member of the group of mother's brothers if it was male, or father's sisters if it was female. Name sets were not kinship-based groups; parents took care to alternate the *Kren* and *Ambàn* moiety names for their successive sons when they selected the mother's brother who would give his names. That put their sons in opposite ceremonial groups for the rest of their lives. Names conferred (especially on males) an entire social identity – ways to paint and dance, songs to sing, ornaments to wear, and so forth. This social identity was painted on the skin and both covered and altered the unique identification of the physical body with the immediate family. The social identity was most often represented by various body paint designs (for an excellent article on Northern Kayapo body ornamentation, see Turner 1969). The name-based identity was passed intact, it did not change as the child grew older except that some individual nicknames might be added to the name set. Singing, dancing, and body ornamentation were the most important ways the name-based groups were activated.

The third component of the person was entirely individual. Every person had a different spirit or shadow, already possessed by the unborn fetus. This spirit was not itself formed by the parents, nor affected by the names, and was located inside the body, apparently in the chest. The spirit usually stayed in the body. When it left (or was taken from) a person's body, he or she sickened (and might become a 'person without a spirit') or died. After death, the spirit traveled to the east, climbed to the sky, and traveled to the village of the dead and apparently lived forever in that huge village. The spirit was unique, and its misadventures caused some of the individualizing tendencies of Suyá life. When a child's spirit left its body, it could be found and brought back into the body by a 'good' witch. Or a bad witch could steal someone's spirit in anger, causing sickness and eventually creating a new teacher of songs.

When an infant was born it already had a body and a spirit. Within days it was given a social identity. From that time on, it grew and devoted more and more time to activities associated with its social identity – with painting, dancing, and singing. Suyá song emphasized the social identity of the participants. When Kaikwati made fun of the young men in one of his public speeches by saying that they no longer painted themselves or wore arm and leg bands and thus had arms and legs like storks, he was pointing up the essentially creative and socializing aspects of body paint. Wearing the ornaments was said to thicken the limbs. To 'become a Whiteman' for the Suyá in the 1970s meant to stop painting the body, to wear clothes instead of body paint in rituals, and to refuse to participate in ritual life. Being a Whiteman, like being a Suyá, was a question of ornamentation and what was on the skin. A person's biological identity was given, as was his or her spirit. What had to be constantly affirmed and reaffirmed throughout life was a person's social identity.

Every ceremony was a re-affirmation of the social identity of the name-based groups, as well as of certain age- and sex-based groups that otherwise rarely acted together. Every ceremony involved different details that identified the groups and provided some of the differences and interest (for the Suyá) of their social identity.

Studying music as process

If music is to be studied not as sounds but as the production of sounds, approaches to musical performance must provide a great deal of ethnographic data in order to present the social processes of which music is a part. The last decade has seen the publication of a number of articles and books on the ethnography of musical performance (for examples see Herndon and Brunyate 1976; Seeger 1979 and 1980a; Herndon and McLeod 1980; Stone 1982; and Béhague 1984). To a large extent these studies were inspired by linguistic and folklore research into performance (described and illustrated in Bauman and Sherzer 1974) and the writings of Erving Goffman (1973). While most authors agree that until recently the context in which music is actually performed has been ignored in favor of structural analysis of what is performed, they recommend different ways to reconcile the form of analysis with the nature of the object.

Norma McLeod and Marcia Herndon have repeatedly emphasized the importance of the notion of performance for ethnomusicology. Norma McLeod conceives of performance as the 'real behavior' of the specific musical event, not only its ideal behavior. Real behavior is the result of the interaction of players among themselves and with the audience and includes mistakes, dissatisfaction or satisfaction, and so forth. Too often the reality of performances is ignored in preference to describing the ideal: what a performance aspires to, or how it relates to some ideal (Herndon and Brunyate 1976: 2–3). This may recall Platonic philosophy, but it is closer to the distinction between *langue* and *parole* in language and *culture* and *action* in social life. McLeod proposes that ethnomusicologists study actual performances rather than the ideal to which they may aspire. The suggestion is developed further by Richard Bauman who describes the act of performance as 'situated behavior, situated within and rendered meaningful with reference to relevant contexts. Context is another way that performance is patterned in communities' (in Herndon and Brunyate 1976: 35).

The concept of performance can itself create difficulties, however. Frisbie (1980) points out that there are ambiguities in the concepts of 'performance' when applied in music to all genres. Members of a given community may consider some musical events public performances (in which case they and the ethnographer agree) while other events are considered 'playing around' and not performance (contrast an aria in a concert hall with one in the shower; only an ethnomusicologist might insist that both were performed). Contexts, whether formal or informal, are defined by each society and isolated in time, space, and degree of public evaluation. We have not only to define the concept of performance, we have to discuss what kinds of performances occur in any society.

Gerard Béhague summarizes the study of musical performance as follows:

Ideally, then, the study of music performance as an event and a process and of the resulting performance practices or products should concentrate on the actual musical and extra-musical behavior of the participants, and the rules or codes of performance defined by the community for a specific context or occasion.   (Béhague 1984: 6)

Béhague is right. That is where the investigation should start. The issue of what is 'musical' and what is 'extra-musical' remains problematic, as we shall see below, and the issue of the extent to which performances are the result of fixed rules or make the rules must be established. Most of the contextual studies of music have focused on the influence the context has on the performance, and on searching for the extra-musical influences on the performance practice. This entire book is an argument that the musical performance is as much a part of the creation of social life as any other part of life, and that the creation and re-creation of relationships through the ceremonial singing creates a social context which influences other such contexts. Other authors, among them Herzfeld (1979), have made a similar argument for the impossibility of separating context from text in general. The context is part of the text. The points made here for music are applicable far more broadly to social life.

The analysis of musical performances as events is easier to suggest than to accomplish. In an earlier paper (Seeger 1980a) I suggested that one way to approach the context of musical events was to dissect it somewhat arbitrarily into the answers to the basic journalistic questions: 'what, where, how, when, by whom, for whom, and why.' The advantage of this approach is that anyone can begin an ethnography of performance without great difficulty, and the data so produced are far richer than we have been provided for most musical traditions.

When asked of Suyá song, these questions reveal important contrasts among the different genres. Table 4.3 summarizes data on performance practice for a shout song (Examples 1.1 and 1.4 on the cassette), a unison song (Example 1.3), and an invocation (Example 2.3) performance, which includes the answers to the questions 'what, who, how, where, when, to whom, and why?'

The Suyá men said they sang shout songs for their sisters (described at length in Seeger 1980b). When I asked them for whom they sang unison songs, they responded that they simply sang them. They weren't for anyone. A man did not sing a unison song as a brother, lover, or individual. He sang it as a member of a group, whose identity was partly established

Table 4.3. *'What, who, how, where, when, to whom, and why?' Shout song, unison song, and invocation compared*

What?	*Shout song:* individually sung with loud, high, tense voice, at a variable tempo according to the body movement, accompanied by a rattle. Strophic form, characterized by descending melody contour. Structure of two halves, each naming a different animal and presented with a clear progression.
	Unison song: sung with a group in a low, usually quiet, unison following the cues of a song leader who established the tempo, often with a rattle. Strophic form characterized by a terraced melody contour. Structure of two halves, each naming a different animal and presented with a clear progression.
	Invocation: performed by an individual without accompaniment in a very quiet voice. Non-strophic form characterized by a flat contour with use of glissandi. Parallel formal structures that progressed from blowing through referring to an animal trait, to naming the animal, to ending with further blowing.
Who?	*Shout song:* performed by boys, adolescents, and men (not women or old men). Taught by adult men and women, usually people without spirits.
	Unison song: performed by men whose voices have changed (not boys except for Mouse Ceremony unison song), men and women together, women together. Taught by people without spirits. Led by a ritual specialist.
	Invocation: adult men or women (not boys or girls). Taught by a person who knows it to an adolescent boy or girl interested in learning it, often in return for a gift.
How?	*Shout song:* performed with rattles and accompanying body movements, sung loudly and according to performer's age by individual singers.
	Unison song: performed by a group usually sitting, standing, or dancing fairly close together, in unison and in a low register. There were clear attempts not to be heard as individuals except in a few songs where there were solo parts.
	Invocation: performed in a very quiet voice, accompanied by blowing and sometimes a light massage, in a middle register with glissandi, with no attempt to be heard by audience.
Where?	*Shout song:* in the village plaza, in the forest camp, and in the residential houses only as a prelude to leaving them.
	Unison song: in the village plaza and the men's house, occasionally in the residential houses. (Never in the gardens or forest or 'for fun'.)
	Invocation: inside the houses, in back of the houses, in the bathing areas on the river bank. (Rarely or never in the plaza.)
When?	*Shout song:* during the day in solo performances, all night long during group performances, whenever an individual feels euphoric in 'for fun' performances. Less fixed than the unison genres.
	Unison song: before dawn, in the late afternoon, and sometimes during the night on the final night of certain ceremonies. Times were fairly regular.
	Invocation: at dawn, in the evening, and at the appearance of the symptoms.
To whom?	*Shout song:* sung 'for sisters' by men and boys.
	Unison song: sung for the collective audience by the group.
	Invocation: sung for the patient, and also for the efficacy of the song itself – it is not necessarily intended for ears at all. Patients are most often sons and daughters, grandsons and granddaughters, or other persons related through kinship ties. When only one person knows a particular invocation, then all members of the village may use that person.
Why?	*Shout song:* to reaffirm social ties to sisters and mothers, and to express emotions.
	Unison song: to reaffirm the identity of the collectivity.
	Invocation: to instill a particular animal trait into the body of the patient so that a desirable physical change could take place.

through the song. Thus they sang for a general audience: the act of singing was the statement. In some sense, invocations had no audience at all. What set them apart from the other vocal genres (with the exception of a witch's 'bad speech,' which I never witnessed during my fieldwork) was that they were specifically not intended as public forms of address. The intended target of an invocation was not so much anyone's ear – as with all the other vocal genres – but the patient's body. Unlike other genres of Suyá vocal art, invocations could be effective even when they were not heard.

Invocations suggest we must be sensitive to certain forms of discourse whose object is less to be heard and understood than to be performed and seen. Their efficacy is in the fact of the performance, and to some degree in their success at relieving symptoms, rather than in the aural reception of the sounds and their direct evaluation. The invocations themselves were not faked: they were really performed and they had a very elaborate system of metaphors which were employed in a highly structured way. But they were not performed to be heard by more than a very few people, one of whom could be quite sick.

Shout songs were public and directed at certain relatives and shared a loud performance style and a number of specific musical features that helped ensure that the singer would be heard. Unison songs were public and directed toward the community as a whole, their musical features encouraged a more perfect unison. Invocations were private and directed at a physical body more than anyone's ears, performed so quietly practically no one could hear them. Although the ethnography of performance breaks down a performance by asking a number of different questions, the answers will often all be interrelated. The performance style is related to the intention, and to the spatial, temporal, and sonic context of which the performance is a part.

The creativity of singing and ceremony

Ceremonies are not simply strict obedience to a set of rules. Ceremonies and music are performed by conscious subjects who are creating something that is at once a re-creation and a new creation under unique circumstances. A number of ways in which Suyá ceremonies achieved this have been described. The comparison of the genres reveals their similarities and differences. But the performers were not singing simply to establish contrasts. Their singing was part of the creation of their society and their cosmos. To a certain extent singing positioned each person in relationship to those. Suyá musical performance was a 'structuration' (a creation of the structures) of sound, place, time, person, and meaning in particular circumstances. A new song was new but shared an old structure. An old ceremony, performed by men acting according to set patterns, was also somewhat new because it was never performed exactly the same way twice.

Social scientists have become increasingly critical of approaches that overemphasize the fixity of social life and underemphasize the interpretive role of the members as thinking actors (Bourdieu 1977; Giddens 1979). Although small-scale societies are often believed to be bound by tradition, without a written tradition codes can only exist to the extent that they are somehow created through performance. There was no library or ultimate text in the Suyá village. Instead, continual performance was essential to the reaffirmation or transformation of values, relationships, practices, and ideas that were essential to both the most mundane and the most exalted aspects of life.

The creation and re-creation of social life are accomplished in the details of everyday life as well as in ritual. Sharing a piece of fishline with a brother maintains that relationship as clearly as singing over a name receiver. Not everything, however, can be created in everyday life. If it were, ritual would have little innovative force or interest.

The Suyá continually re-created their society in a number of ways. These forms of social reproduction included the re-creation or redefinition of spatial and temporal relationships, the establishment and re-establishment of social relationships, the formation of the body and the expression of the continually developing social persona. Just as the introduction of new songs reproduced the long-standing relationship between men and animals and men and other Indians, so their performance at the appropriate times and in the appropriate places by the appropriate people re-established the fundamental individual, sociological, and cosmological parameters of Suyá society.

The ethnography of performance has justifiably renewed ethnomusicologists' determination to study music in its social context. I have suggested that asking the journalistic questions of what, who, how, where, when, to whom, and why, provides a useful, practical approach to the difficult task of defining the context of a performance. The answers to those questions are not the end of an analysis but rather the means to one. An ethnography is not an end in itself. Ethnographies tend to fix the forms of social action rather than see in them the elements of choice and creativity because the anthropologist is often unaware of the changeability of what he or she observes. A creative act, a strategy, a choice among alternatives appears to the anthropologist as a rule because there is little temporal analysis. The Suyá, for example, liked to experiment. At each performance a person was older and had opportunities for doing something new. He or she could try new ways of dancing or singing. Or a person might do the old things in an unusual space 'just for laughs.' If something were particularly successful, it could become part of a group's (name set, sex, or age group) activities in future ceremonies. Or it might simply be remembered with fondness, admiration, or scandal for decades to come. Creativity was part of the fun of social life, and ceremonies provided ample range for the creativity of humor, the creativity of speech and song, the creativity of self-decoration, and the creativity of degree of participation or lack of it.

All social actions are creative and re-creative. Suyá singing was a particular kind of re-creation. It morally weighted the times and spaces of social life. Singing created musical relationships between silence and sound, low and deep and high and tense, between fast and slow, between unison and solo, between shout songs and weeping, between the short silly songs of youth and the long serious songs of adults, the public songs of the plaza and the invocations of the periphery. Singing also established relationships among movements: between sitting and standing, walking counterclockwise and walking clockwise, approximation and removal from the residential houses, leaping and standing. It established relationships among groups: between men and women, between the *Ambàn* and *Kren* moieties or the *Soikokambrigi* and the *Soikodnto*, and between affines and consanguines. Thus space, time, the body, and social identity all defined, and were defined by, vocal art. The relationship was intimate and formative, not simply reiterative and expressive of other realities.

To consider song and ceremonial life to be mechanical products of other aspects of social life is to miss the essential nature of musical and ceremonial performances. Suyá ceremonies created euphoria out of silence, a village community out of a collection of residences, a socialized adult out of physical matter. If a myth were not told it could be forgotten; if a relationship were not activated it could fall into abeyance and domestic relationships replace it. If the plaza were not cleared, the village could simply disintegrate into its constituent families or into very small settlements. In a village without ceremony, more food was brought in through the back door, grass grew up in the plaza, men delayed coming out to the center of the village at night because life centered on the domestic group, and families drifted off leaving their houses standing dark, silent, and empty in an unmarked succession of days, seasons, and years.

5   *From lab to field: the mystery of rising pitch in a rainy season song*

So far we have been addressing some of the larger features of Suyá music, including general aspects of song structure and performance, and its role in re-creating time, space, and person. But what is the relationship between these general features and the sounds of the music itself? To demonstrate how specific sounds can be related to some of the more general values that have already been presented, I will analyze some fairly minute musical features of a single song.

The ensuing discussion of a slow rise in the absolute pitch during a performance of a rainy season unison song is presented as a mystery. It seemed like one from the start. There was a physical fact – a microtonal rising – but with no indication as to why it occurred. Not unlike a latter-day Sherlock Holmes I searched for clues to understand what had happened. The search took several years, and may not be entirely satisfying, but it did lead to a better understanding not only of the musical feature itself, but of some of the values expressed through the sounds of Suyá music.

Three important issues in ethnomusicology are also addressed through the analysis of microtonal rising. These are the use of our own analytic categories versus the use of native categories for musical analysis, the role of musical transcription in ethnomusicology, and the usefulness of using several approaches to musical phenomena rather than one or two.

The problem

The acoustic problem is quite simple: what was the reason for the gradual rise in the absolute pitch of the Suyá *agachi ngére* (Example 1.3 on the cassette). Listen again to the entire piece. It is a unison rainy season song performed in the men's house by members of both moieties. A partial transcription appears in Figure 5.1.

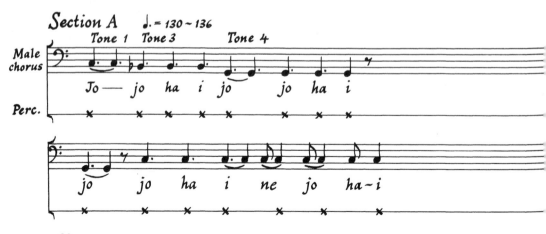

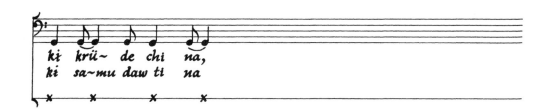

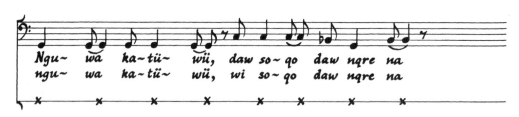

Figure 5.1   Transcription of rainy season song (adapted from Roseman 1977)

This particular rainy season song was composed not more than forty years ago when Takuti was a bachelor living in the men's house. Its text is typical of the rainy season genre, *agachi ngére*. *Jo-jo-ha-i*, and its permutations, are what the Suyá call 'song words' because they have no direct referents. These particular syllables are specific to the *agachi ngére* and less frequently found in other kinds of unison song. The 'telling the name' of the first verse is simple, 'the catfish is singing with its face painted for log racing.' The song is a fish song; it was taught by someone whose spirit lived with the fish. The second half, nearly identical in many ways, changes both the name of the fish and the kind of painting sung about. Freely translated it would be 'the big-mouth bass is singing with its body painted for log racing.'

Body painting and face painting were important parts of the preparation for ceremonies, and they were markers of the social identity passed through names and worn on the skin. Log racing was a combination of ceremony and sport, where the ceremonial moieties ran relay races carrying heavy logs into the village. Membership in the moieties was visually represented through body paint and some ornaments, and orally expressed through songs. The texts were highly condensed symbols of the log racing season, of rainy season activities in general, and of social identity. When I asked about these fish, I was told fish also have log races, and that they sing these songs before and during them, 'just like men.'

There is something unusual about the singing in Example 1.3 on the cassette. Advance the tape to Example 5.1, and listen to a recording of the first lines of each verse. The men go steadily sharp of the initial pitch, then drop down for each of the codas. This gradual rise in the 'absolute pitch' occurs while the relationship of the notes to each other remains nearly constant. In other words, the melody remains the same, but the whole thing rises.

Marina Roseman, a graduate student at Columbia University, prepared a detailed analysis of this rainy season song for a graduate course in musical transcription and analysis. In 'To try and catch the wind: notation of shifting pitch in a Suyá example' (Roseman 1977), Roseman transcribed the entire song, and carefully noted the level of the pitches for each section. I was in Brazil at the time. She sent me a copy of the paper.[1]

Roseman divides the song into sections based on musical and linguistic features. These parallel, but are not identical with, the Suyá divisions of the song. She divides the opening section into two parts (A i and A ii) for the *Jo-jo-ha-i* part the Suyá give a single name; B is equivalent to the 'approaching the naming,' C' is the 'naming of the animal' and full verse, and A' is the coda. In the second half, Dr. Roseman did not notice the semantic change in the B section (which should be B'), but she did hear the change in the C section, which becomes C'. Her transcriptions of the major sections of the first half of the song are given in Figure 5.1. I also analyzed parts of the song at the acoustic laboratory of the Université du Montréal with the aid of Charles Boilès in 1984. The machine analyses confirmed the general tendencies indicated in Roseman's analysis, which was performed using less sophisticated equipment but whose results are easier to understand.

In the transcription the tones have been assigned a constant pitch, and the transcription was prepared as though there were no microtonal rising. Accidentals hold through the stave unless otherwise indicated. The capital letters [A, B, C] indicate sections of the piece, which has an ABABACACACACA; ABABACACA form (but with slightly different text in the second half). The initial pitches of the five tones, 1, 2, 3, 4, and 5 are:

Tone 1 = A sharp plus six cents
Tone 2 = C plus seven cents
Tone 3 = B flat minus thirty-nine cents
Tone 4 = F sharp plus thirty-five cents
Tone 5 = F plus seven cents

Following her initial transcription, Roseman measured the pitch of certain notes at the

---

[1] Dr. Roseman recently received her Ph.D. from Cornell University. She knew something about Suyá music from work she had done with me when she was an undergraduate at Pomona College. She has reviewed this chapter, and has kindly given her permission to quote extensively from her paper and to use her diagrams.

same points in each repetition of the verse form. The results of this are summarized in Table 5.1. This table clearly demonstrates that although the notes of the melody remain relatively stable in relationship to each other (tone no. 1 is an exception, in that it rises more than the others), the pitches gradually rise in the course of the song. Tone 1, which starts 6 one-hundredths of a semi-tone above B-flat, rises to nearly an F, before dropping down at the very end. Tones 2, 3, 4, and 5 rise approximately 4 semi-tones, which we may say is the general rise of the whole melody. Roseman notes that while the rise in pitch is gradual, there are three points in the song where the absolute pitch descends fairly abruptly. There is a slight lowering of the pitch at the start of the coda (the last C) in the first half, and at the start of the second half in relation to end of the first. There is a much greater lowering of the pitch at the beginning of the coda in the second half. She suggests that the places where the pitch is lowered indicate that the rising pitch may be an important feature of Suyá music.

Anyone who has sung in a choir, or who has listened to amateur choral groups will be

Table 5.1. *Additive and cumulative readings of pitch rise in hundredths of a semi-tone (cents)*

SECTION	Tone no. 1 B-flat + 6 cents		Tone no. 2 C + 7 cents		Tone no. 3 A-sharp − 39 cents		Tone no. 4 F-sharp + 35 cents		Tone no. 5 F + 7 cents	
	Additive	Total	Additive	Total	Additive	Total	Additive	Total	Additive	Total
A	+169	+169	initial pitch		+0	0	+100	+100	initial pitch	
B	+66	+235	X	X	+104	+104	+34	+134		
A	+113	+348			+97	+194	+83	+217	+146	+146
B	+0	+348			−25	+171	+0	+217		
A	+42	+384	+137	+137	+11	+187	X	X	X	X
C	+12	+396			+100	+287	+48	+265		
A	−69	+465	+110	+247	+19	+306	+31	+296	+31	+177
C	+0	+465			+13	+319	+30	+326		
A	+45	+510	+71	+318	+49	+368	−15	+311	+102	+279
C	−12	+498			−37	+331	−46	+265		
A	+33	+531	−23	+295	+62	+393	+46	+311	−34	+245
C	−33	+498			+0	+393	+15	+326		
A	+76	+574	+11	+306	+12	+405	+0	+326		

(End first half)
Values of initial pitches of second half:

	Additive	Total	Additive	Total	Additive	Total	Additive	Total	Additive	Total
	−43	+531		+531	−12	+393	−30	+296		
A	+0	+531	+35	+341	+24	+417	+75	+371	+51	+296
B	+0	+531			−24	+393	+0	+371		
A	X	X	X	X	X	X	X	X	X	X
B	+22	+553			−12	+381	+30	+401		
A	+53	+606	+89	+430	+71	+452	+14	+415	+33	+329
C	+0	+606			+47	+499	+43	+458		
A	X	X	X	X	X	X	X	X	+98	+377
C	+0	+606			−23	+476	+0	+458		
A	+51	+657	+22	+452	+34	+510	+28	+486		
C	−448	+209			−556	−46	−439	+47		
A	+114	+323	−395	+147	+201	+155	+121	+168		

X = a reading was not taken in this section
Blank box = tone did not appear in the section

familiar with the problem of gradually rising or falling pitch. In Euro-American choral music, the problem is usually revealed by the fixed-pitch instruments such as piano, organ, or woodwinds. Rising or falling pitch appears to be a widespread phenomenon in choral groups. It has been reported for a number of North American Indian groups. What makes the rising pitch important is that it does not always occur in every society, that some societies have both rising and falling floating pitches while others reveal a greater degree of one or the other, and that some societies appear to make it a conscious feature of their musical structure. Frances Densmore described a Seminole informant who said that his grandfather had taught him to raise the pitch of certain songs, saying that it should be done in old war songs (Densmore 1956: 212).

Roseman suggests that further ethnographic research is necessary to explore why the shifting pitch occurred in the song she had analyzed. 'Exploration of other *ngére* [unison songs], as well as other Suyá categories of orality, might reveal the generality or uniqueness of this phenomenon' (Roseman 1977: 17). She raises a number of specific issues for investigation, among them (1) Do the Suyá recognize the pitch is rising then falling? (2) Do they have a terminology for the rising and falling? (3) Are there specific associations with rising and falling pitch? (4) Are changes in pitch used as cues among performers? (5) Who controls the shifts in pitch? and (6) What is the role of the performance context in the shifting pitch?

I took Roseman's questions to the field with me, along with many others, when I visited the Suyá in 1978, 1981, and 1982. One might expect the investigation to have been relatively simple. I had already spent over fifteen months with the Suyá, spoke their language well enough to carry out all my research in it, was considered by them to be one of the best non-Suyá singers of Suyá music they could remember (compared, for example, to captives they had taken in the past), and had good rapport with the community. To my surprise, the task was not easy at all.

One of the most difficult problems was to discover how to ask questions about a musical feature for which there was apparently no term in the Suyá language. They did not talk much about any melodic features of the music. Most of their talk about music referred to the song texts, their origins, and who was singing. I never heard them, or could get them to, speak about the rise. Nor would they necessarily wish to speak about varying pitch. They played no fixed-pitch musical instruments (such as flutes), which would call the changing pitch to their attention. It was possible that the Suyá had a concept without a term for it, but the absence of fixed-pitch instruments made it quite possible that the phenomenon was not an object of attention to them.

I was faced with a phenomenon I could not find a way to discuss with the Suyá. Failing in the direct approach, I cast about for other means to discover information that might address the issue, even if indirectly. Four fundamental clues led to a greater understanding of the musical phenomenon. These were (1) an analysis of other musical examples; (2) my own participation in musical events of a similar sort; (3) a defective recording, and (4) the masculine aesthetic of unison song.

Rising pitch in other Suyá songs

Since Roseman had transcribed only a single example, it was possible that the rise was unique to the recording she analyzed. Slowly weakening batteries would have resulted in a gradual rise in absolute pitch. There might have been a defect in the tape recorder itself. The recording might have been an unusual performance of the song. Sometimes expert singers do not perform well; less trained singers may make mistakes in their performance; pitch rising or falling might have been entirely random.

There were, in fact, some unique features about the particular recording that Roseman analyzed. She could not tell it from the notes that accompanied the tapes, which were deposited in the Indiana University Archives of Traditional Music in 1973, but the recording was the first rainy season song performance of the year. It was unusual in that only four men sang, instead of the entire adult male population. At first I thought the song had been sung out of season, for recording purposes alone, but I discovered that was not so. It was possible that the reduced number of singers and the primacy of the performance had resulted in an unusual performance.

As a test I selected several other songs of the same genre that were performed by a large group of men during full-scale ceremonial events, and analyzed them only for rising pitch. They had been recorded in different years, on different tape recorders, at different points in the tape and with different batteries. The results, summarized in Table 5.2, indicate that the rise in absolute pitch is common to all of them. The pitch is approximate; the important datum is the degree of rise.

Table 5.2. *Rising pitches in three rainy season songs* (agachi ngére)

	Agachi 2 Tape 17 Side 1	Agachi 3 Tape 38 Side 1	Agachi 4 Tape 67 Side 1
First half opening	A B flat	B	A B flat
First half	B flat	B	B flat B
End first half	B flat	B	C
Second half opening	G sharp	B	C
Telling name	A B flat	C sharp	C sharp
Final coda (low)	G	A	A

Note: Song parts were described in Chapter 2. Where two values are indicated for a given part, they were measured at different times.

These three examples show a slow rise of slightly more than a single semi-tone (*Agachi* 2), two semi-tones (*Agachi* 3), and four semi-tones (*Agachi* 4). On the basis of these measurements, I decided that the gradual rise was probably to be found in all performances. Of all the examples I analyzed, none of them descended. Questions about batteries, other mechanical causes, and the unusual influence of the particular performance could all be dismissed. Nor was there an apparent correlation between the time of day the songs were sung and the degree of rise, which had been suggested.

As important as establishing that all the rainy season songs showed a gradual rise in absolute pitch (as well as descents in the codas) was the irregularity of the rise. *Agachi 2* rose nearly the same amounts in each half, and the initial pitch of the second half was unusual in that it is nearly as low as the initial pitch of the entire song. *Agachi 3* hardly rose at all in the first half, but did rise considerably in the second half. *Agachi 4* inverted the rise: the first half rises considerably, the second hardly at all. I did have an explanation for the unusually low pitch of the second half of *Agachi 2*, which was the only such case in my sample. At the end of the first half there was an unusually long pause, and a bit of discussion among the singers, before they started the second half. That might have caused (or allowed) the lead singer to start up again at the initial pitch. In other examples the pause was quite brief and the drop less. What appeared from the analysis of the other rainy season songs was that the pitch rise was regular; the degree and location of the rise was not.

The pitch rise might have been a feature of the unison rainy season songs alone. Since Suyá music was so dualist, it seemed that if the rise were purposeful there should be a group of songs without one. The logical candidates were the unison dry season songs. Sung in the other half of the year, paired with the rainy season songs in usage, they might have been quite different. They were not. Table 5.3 presents the results of the analysis of four dry season songs:

Table 5.3. *Rising pitch in dry season songs* (kahran kasàg ngére)

	Kahran 1 Tape 38 Side 2	Kahran 2 Tape 38 Side 1	Kahran 3 Tape 38 Side 1	Kahran 4 Tape 39 Single side
First half begins	A	A	F	A
Telling the name	B flat B C	B flat B C C sharp	G G sharp A flat A	B flat C C sharp
End first half	C sharp	D	B flat	D
Second half begins	C sharp	D	B flat	D
End second half	D	E flat	B flat	D

Note: Dry season songs had no long coda with a return to a low pitch, characteristic of the rainy season songs.

All four unison dry season song examples rose considerably during the first half, but very little during the second half. It is striking that so many of these songs start near the same pitch, although they were sung months or years apart. The Suyá never spoke of any attempt to begin on a certain pitch (as I indicated, I found no way of discussing the concept with them), and I can only attribute the constancy of initial pitch to the habitual voice placement of Kaikwati, the ritual specialist.

Random testing of other genres also revealed gradually rising pitch. From these analyses a fairly clear pattern emerged of a slow rise, more often greater in the first half. Yet the pitch did not rise equally in all songs, or at the same speed. There was at once a clear pattern and a undefined degree of rise. A number of suggestions were made over the years, including the length of the song, the time of day, and the temperature. Of those features about which I had information, these did not appear to vary with any regularity. The phenomenon clearly merited further investigation.

Participant observation

Although direct interviewing failed, I became more sensitive to the vocal technique used to perform the rainy season songs. I reflected on my own learning process, and sang rainy season songs with the Suyá a different year. The physical context of the singing seemed to be important.

When the rainy season songs were performed in the morning, the men gathered in the men's house before the rise of the morning star (see the description in Chapter 1). Sometimes a few glowing coals warmed the older men, but no flames illuminated the dark interior of the men's house. If there had been a conductor, he or she would not have been visible in the dark. The Suyá had no conductor, however. They did not even sit facing each other. Figure 5.2

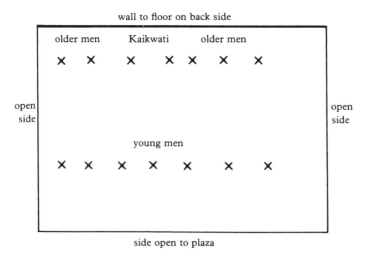

Figure 5.2   Position of singers in the men's house

sketches the layout of the men's house and the orientation of the singers. They would sit in two parallel lines, facing the center of the village. They did not look at each other, even when there was enough light to see, as in the afternoon performances. There was some segregation by age: the older, more knowledgeable, and prestigious men sat in the back, and the younger men sat in the front. The ritual specialist, who held the rattle and led the singing, would sit in the middle of the back row, with good singers on either side of him. The center of the front row was usually occupied by the better singers among the young men, and I usually sat off on one side, with the less expert singers.

When the Suyá first invited me to join them in the unison songs, I could not figure out what to sing. It seemed that everyone kept changing what they were singing, and I made obvious mistakes every time they changed. I found that in order to follow the changes in the song I had to listen to the ritual specialist behind me. What I learned to listen for were slight emphases in his tone, and a slight rising of the pitch in the middle of a syllable, something like a grace note. This feature was mainly a question of the 'attack' of the note. Instead of being sung as a straight pitch, it was sung with a short pitch rise, with a forceful attack.

I made fewer mistakes after learning the aural cues. When I discovered the names and nature of the sections of every song, singing in the men's house became even easier. But even Suyá made mistakes. My companions in the front line sometimes did not change sections when the ritual specialist did. They would mumble through the phrase, or even fall silent until they caught on to the new part. There were even times when the old men in the back made a mistake, and the ritual specialist would start the new section alone. When this happened there would be comments of consternation and the performance was not considered a good one.

Another thing I found from my own experience was that it was hard for me to keep my throat 'open' enough (or keep my larynx down) for the duration of the song. Suyá songs were supposed to be sung in a deep, resonant, unison. The singer should force his voice a little, and sing with a low larynx (approximately equivalent to singing with the Adam's apple kept as low as possible in the throat). Singing without these physiological and acoustic features was considered a feminine and a boys' style, restricted to women's song or young boys' imitations of adult song. It required some physical effort to keep singing in a man's style. The forced, slight rise at every attack was also tiring. These aspects of male song were said to represent strength, masculinity, and assertiveness. My own experience singing them indicated that they did require considerable strength, if only in the vocal chords. The Suyá themselves said that singing was 'hard' and that you had to be tough to do it well.

Participant observation in actual performances of the rainy season songs provided some important information on singing. First, the cues given to the singers that indicated when they should change from one part of a song to another were aural. It was impossible for the singers to see each other, whether they were singing in the dark or during the day. The cues seemed to be given through a slightly greater forcing of the singing and rise in pitch. Second, a considerable effort was required in order to sing as the Suyá thought men should. This vocal tension, even though not related to high pitch, seemed to be a possible factor in raising the pitch. Third, in spite of the cues, Suyá did make what they considered mistakes, most of them being made by the young men, and some of them being made by virtually all the singers.

The defective record

While I was working on my analyses of Suyá music another issue came up that ultimately contributed to my understanding of rising pitch. After my initial work, when I had recorded a lot of Suyá music, I came across a record that included two songs by the Suyá. These had been recorded by Harald Schultz in 1960, very soon after the first peaceful contacts with the Suyá, and some 10 years before my own visit. There was something very strange about the sound of the men's unison song, 'Suyá, men's choir, rhythm with hoof-rattle' (Folkways Record FE4311 Side 2 Band 3). The pitch was lower than any song I had recorded, and the rattles had an unusual timbre: they sounded strangely slowed-down. I could almost hear each pit in the rattle hit the others (Example 5.2 on the cassette).

I was certain a recording error had been made somewhere between the performance and the pressing of the record. My suspicion was that a tape recorded at 60 cycles had been copied at 50 cycles, and thus slowed down. So I made a cassette copy of the recording and took it to the Suyá village. One night, when all the men were gathered in the center of the plaza and wanted to listen to some of their music, I played them the recording from the record. Attentively they listened to the entire song.

When it ended, Kaikwati – the ritual specialist and the only one of the four singers on the original recording still alive – leaned back a little and said:

'It is beautiful, Tony. That is the way the Suyá really sang in the old days.'

One of the most stimulating things about doing fieldwork in another society is that just when you think you understand something, the answer to a simple question opens entirely new vistas and raises many new questions. The Suyá reaction to the recording was exactly just such a moment. I had expected them to recognize the recording error and criticize it, but instead they praised the piece as though it were a good performance accurately recorded. What was I to make of their answer? Did the old people really sing so much lower 'in the old days'? How was I to integrate the 'native point of view' with my analytic approach? The Suyá audience remembered the person who made the recording, had known the singers, who were famous for their songs, and they thought the recording lovely.

I had no way to follow up on the issue for several years. Then, in 1979, I was able to obtain other recordings of the same singers, made by Jesco von Putkammer within two or three years of the Schultz recordings (the originals of Putkammer's recordings are deposited in the museum of the Catholic University of Goiânia, Brazil). I did not have time to analyze the recordings extensively, but it was clear that the singing was not noticeably lower than on my own recordings made a decade later, nor did the rattles sound the way they did in the Schultz recordings.

In 1983, I used a voltage regulator at the Indiana University Archives of Traditional Music to speed up the Schultz recording to the point where the timbre of the rattles sounded the way I thought it should. That was just eleven cycles above the speed of the recording on the record – just about what one would expect from making a copy of a sixty-cycle recording on a fifty-cycle machine. My reconstructed recording is Example 5.3 on the cassette.

In 1985 I reviewed Jesco von Putkammer's recordings and recognized one of the songs he recorded as the one that appears on the faulty record. The pitch of Putkammer's recording, made in 1961 or 1963 (he was there both years and the recordings are difficult to date), is very close to my estimate of what it should have sounded like.

The results of an examination of Jesco von Putkammer's recordings are summarized in Table 5.4.

Putkammer did not usually record both halves of a song, and there is only one full rainy season song in his collection. It rises more in the second half than the first, but within the same general range as the ones I collected. So are two separate halves of other ones. The turtle songs name only a single animal, they do not have the dual structure of nearly all other song

Table 5.4. *Comparison of rising pitch in examples recorded by Jesco von Putkammer with the defective recording on Folkways FE4311.*

	Agachi 5 Tape 1 Side 1 No. 12	Agachi 6 Tape 1 Side 2 No. 6	Agachi 7 Tape 2 Side 1 No. 8	Turtle 1 Tape 2 Side 1 No. 9	Faulty recording (Turtle 2) Folkways FE4311
First				B-flat	G
half	**	B-flat	B C	B (+)	A-flat
		C	C-sharp	C	A
Second				C-sharp	
half	A		B		
	B-flat	**	C	XX	XX
	B		C-sharp D		
Coda	**	**	B-flat	XX	XX

Notes:
The tape numbers refer to Putkammer's original tapes.
** indicates this part of the song was not recorded.
XX indicates there is no second half; Turtle songs are unique in having only a single part.

genres. The defective recording and version recorded by Putkammer rise about the same amount during the course of the song, the only difference being that the defective record begins a minor third below the von Putkammer recording.

The recording the Suyá liked so much was not an accurate example of the way they had sung in 1960. Something else was getting involved in their statement 'that is the way they sang in the old days.' Why did the Suyá like the faulty recording so much? Several factors were involved. One was their idealization of the past. The Suyá maintained that in the past the village was larger, the men were taller, the women more womanly, and the entire population sang more and behaved correctly. These statements were common in oratory, such as in the example in Chapter 2, and in their oral history. The idealization of the past was partly the result of the depopulation and other changes in Suyá society that occurred following their pacification and settlement in the Xingu National Park. The present, in a number of ways tragically clear to the Suyá, was indeed a pale reflection of their past. The idea that the present is only a shadow of the past is, however, a common sentiment in many societies and cannot be unquestioningly related to historical events or to musical styles.

When the recording of the deceased singers was played for them, what the Suyá heard fitted their expectations of a past that was 'better' and closer to their ideals. They heard the men singing at a lower pitch than they themselves sang, the rattle sounding lower and bigger than rattles today, and since it was a tape recording (tape recorders 'hear and remember' accurately in their experience), they probably concluded they were hearing the way men really used to sing in the old days. The recording reinforced their expectations about the past in general, as well as their ideas about the present.

Another factor that might have affected their evaluation of the faulty recording was the relative difference in the way men of different ages sang. When they sang shout songs the young men would sing in a very high, forced tone. Older men sang at a lower pitch. It is possible that since the men on the record were (at the time of the recording) older than any of the men in the audience, and since no young men at all were singing, the Suyá expected them to be singing at a lower pitch than men today. All four singers on the recording were said to have had 'big throats' (or low resonant voices).

There were thus two possible explanations for the Suyá appreciation of the faulty recording: an idealization of the past and expectations due to the age and voice quality of the performers. The observation of the relative pitch of a song and the age of the performers led me to one of the final clues – to an area that I had been investigating for some time: the aesthetics of Suyá singing.

Deep throat: the aesthetics of Suyá song

When the Suyá discussed the way individuals sang, they did so by talking about their throats. Since all their music was song, the throat (what we would call the voice) was the most important instrument. In discussing the throat with them, it became apparent that this organ was somewhat different than it is conceptualized by Americans. Called *sõ kre* (*iõ kre*, my throat; *ngõ kre*, your throat; *sõ kre*, his throat), the throat begins just behind the teeth and lips and extends down to the collar bone.

An admired singer would be described as having a 'beautiful throat'; a poor singer as possessing a 'weak throat'; when a person was hoarse or had too bad a cold to sing he or she would be said to have a 'bad throat.' A very loud singer would have a 'strong throat' while one who could not be heard clearly would have a 'weak throat.' Children would have 'small throats' and old men 'big throats.' People often talked about singers' throats when they listened to tapes, or when the women were talking while the men sang. Yet when asked directly 'what kind of a throat do you have?' singers always responded doubtfully: 'I don't know, ask someone who hears me.' The aural correlates of some of these were quite clear – as in the difference between children's voices and those of adult men. Other evaluations seemed to rest more on the identity of the singer than on the voice quality. People tended to admire singers in their faction and the singing of important political figures. Whatever the reasons for evaluation, however, the attribution was to the throat of the singer.

Suyá musical genres could be classified by where in the throat they were sung. Shout songs were said to be sung 'at the upper end (*sindaw*) of the throat,' or 'with a small throat.' The unison songs were sung 'at the base (*kradi*) of the throat' or with a 'big throat.' These two ways of phrasing the differences were basically equivalent. One was locational – at the top as opposed to the bottom. The second described the feeling of the positioning of the vocal chords – the open throat was precisely the position I found it difficult to maintain; the small throat was the tight, forced position for shout songs. As with virtually everything in Suyá society, positioning in the throat was fundamentally dual: the position of the throat was either very low or very high, in the lower half or upper half of the throat (*kradi* and *sindaw* were the same words employed for halves of the songs).

Suyá evaluations of what made a beautiful song and a good performance included more than the throat. It also involved the identity of the singers. The answer to the mysteries of rising pitch in the rainy season song and the Suyá enthusiasm for a poorly recorded song lies partly in the relationship of age to the positioning of the throat when a person sings.

Young men were said to have smaller throats, while old men who were good singers were described as having 'big throats.' Since the men who were singing the song on the record were older at that time than most men today and renowned for their singing, their throats could be considered *very* big. The faulty recording confirmed the Suyá attitudes. Old men should always sing lower than younger men, and those in the past could sing lower than those today. On Folkways FE4311 that is exactly what they heard.

In the case of the floating pitch, age was important since the initial pitch in most unison songs would be set by the ritual specialist, an older man with a 'big throat.' The pitch might rise quite quickly in the first strophe (in the transcribed example nearly one quarter of the rise occurs between the first two A sections) when the young men joined in. The ritual specialist also set the pitch for the beginning of the second half (where the pitches drop slightly) and in the final coda (where they drop to within a semitone of the initial pitch).

While the Suyá apparently were unconcerned with absolute pitch, they were very conscious of relative pitch, which they used to establish differences among individuals and between age groups. Since the unison songs were supposed to be low, they would be started quite low by the ritual specialist, an older man with a big throat. Children (with small throats) were not permitted to sing them. When the younger men joined in, the pitch rose, and continued to rise until the ritual specialist set it again. At the final coda the pitch was set again by the ritual specialist.

Did the young men's singing then raise the pitch? While it seemed likely, they did apparently not raise it by themselves. In 1978 I recorded Kaikwati teaching a new rainy season song. That was the only complete recording anyone apparently ever made of teaching a rainy season song. It began on G and rose to B flat before the second half, which in turn ended on B. No coda was taught, as it could be deduced from the rest of the song. In this unique example Kaikwati sang by himself. In spite of this, the song rose in an entirely characteristic fashion. This left me quite dissatisfied, for the mystery did not have as neat a solution as I had hoped for. It is quite likely, however, that age and aesthetics did have a great deal to do with the pitch rise, which was built into the structure of the song itself. In the final analysis, it appears that the rise was a regular part of most unison songs, regardless of how and by whom they were performed, in spite of my inability to get the Suyá to talk about it.

The investigation of the throat, and its relative size according to age, was the final step in marshalling the evidence to respond to Roseman's questions. (1) The Suyá apparently did not verbally articulate the slowly rising pitch during the song, or express any concern with absolute pitch. The rise was, however, a regular feature of their songs, even when sung by a single older man for the first time. (2) They had no name for the rising pitch. (3) It was unclear whether the rising pitch was 'meaningful' or not, in the sense of being consciously performed. The rise may simply exist as the result of other, verbalized, and conscious values. (4) Participant observation established that the pitch changes were, as Roseman suspected, partly cues used to coordinate the performance. (5) It was not obvious who controlled the shifting pitch. The ritual specialist controlled the initial pitches. (6) The role of the immediate performance context in affecting pitch rise appeared to be small.

Lessons to be drawn

This discussion has illustrated some general features of Suyá music. First, the Suyá did not talk about absolute or rising pitch. A rise in absolute pitch, so important to *our* musical values, was itself neither commented upon nor criticized. This was partly because they played no instruments on which to measure pitch. They were very interested in *relative pitch* (higher or lower than the mid-range), which was associated with age, genre, and the authenticity of the singers.

Second, the rise in pitch which Roseman's transcription documents was the physical result of other conscious values and processes, rather than an objective in itself. The rise may not have been meaningful in itself, but the things that caused it were. These included the aesthetics of masculine song (which should be in unison with a tense low sound) and the relative age and performance style of the singing group. Many aspects of musical performance may be the result of similar general values, which is why musical values must be considered in all musical analyses, rather than just the physical sounds that result from them.

Third, if I had investigated only the native categories of music, I would never have found a discussion of the rising pitch, even though it turned out to be a regular feature of Suyá song. Careful musical transcription can reveal aspects of the performance that native categories do not highlight. A good musical transcription can raise many questions. These questions may or may not lead to a greater understanding of the music, but they are usually worth asking. It is precisely the confrontation of our musical parameters (with their emphasis on absolute pitch) with the different ones of the Suyá that can produce a productive group of questions and a comparative approach to music.

Ethnomusicologists have argued for decades about transcription (for a review of some of the literature, see Herndon 1974). I believe transcription should never be an end in itself, but rather a tool for raising questions. When copies of recordings are easy to obtain, the documentary quality of transcriptions is greatly reduced. But their analytic quality remains as an important – although limited – tool in ethnomusicology.

There are always aspects of music that are not revealed by musical transcriptions. Our transcriptions are notably poor in describing tone quality. They do not show that old people sing lower than young people, with difficulty would they catch the difference between male and female approaches to notes. The issues raised through the examination of Suyá song can be asked in both directions. Why do we pay so little attention to tone quality? Why does our presentation of rhythm make it so hard to see cross rhythms (Koetting 1984)? Are there any consistent relationships between sex, age, values, and pitch in our own society? (There are, at least in popular music.) Just as our ideas of pitch raise questions for Suyá song, their ideas of aesthetics raise questions about music for our own musicologists.

Fourth, this investigation of rising pitch is an example of fruitful collaboration between a person in a laboratory and another person in the field. When comparative musicology began, it was similar to much of anthropology: one group of people usually collected the data, and another group of people analyzed it. Like Frazer or Tylor or Morgan, Erich von Hornbostel spent most of his career in his laboratory. This pattern changed dramatically with the students of W. H. R. Rivers in Anthropology, and with those of Jaap Kunst and George Herzog in Ethnomusicology. But it is important not to extend too radically the maxim that the analyst should always be the collector. A good analysis may be very stimulating to a field researcher, for it may reveal things initially uninteresting to him, her, or the society with whom he or she may be working that may be worth following up.

There is a corollary to the point that laboratory analysis can be valuable in itself. If valuable laboratory work can be done by people who have no personal experience with a musical tradition, it is important that recordings be preserved in publicly accessible locations – such

as sound archives. Modern recording techniques have resulted in an abundance of recordings, and not all of them are accessible. In addition to the arguments that the recordings
should be preserved in the interests of the people recorded (whose children or grandchildren
often would like to hear their elders' voices), they can also be a valuable resource for
laboratory–field interaction.

Fifth, and finally, my investigation of rising pitch among the Suyá employed various
approaches, which is essential for all ethnomusicology. I used musical transcription to
document rising pitch in other songs. I used my experience as a participant in Suyá singing to
elucidate the role the aural cuing might play in the unison performances and to reflect on the
physical strain of singing with a 'big throat.' I used earlier recordings – and discovered that
some care was needed with drawing conclusions from them. And I used native concepts of
appropriateness and beauty. Each of these methods has had its exponents in the history of
ethnomusicology. Using them all, rather than a single one, brings considerably more data to
the analyst and more power to the analysis. The sum of these will undoubtedly lead
anthropologists and ethnomusicologists closer to an understanding of the musical traditions
in other societies. Methodological rigidity – when this implies the use of a single mechanism
for obtaining data – is always inferior to the use of a number of different ways of obtaining
perspectives on a given problem.

From a series of questions we have moved to a series of tentative answers. There is little
certainty in ethnomusicology or anthropology, or even physics or biochemistry. The answers
will be satisfying only until previously unconsidered aspects of the phenomenon challenge
them. The question of rising pitch is to some degree a false one: for to answer it we had to go to
details of Suyá performance and ideas about sound that are a concrete development of ideas
presented in a more general way in earlier chapters. Here, challenged by the transcription of a
single song, some of those values have been clarified and their implications for sound made
concrete.

6 *Leaping, dancing and singing the Mouse's song*

'Red Mouse, hang up my fronds to make a mask'

Two weeks have passed since the opening of the Mouse Ceremony, and four chapters have intervened. Both the Suyá and the reader should be ready for the finale. Almost every afternoon the boys have sung shout songs in the gardens and the men have sung unison songs in the men's house. Before dawn on 25 January, male relatives of Hwinkradi's name receiver left for a long hunting and fishing trip to obtain food for the singers. On the 26th a man went to the men's house at about 7.00 a.m. and began to sing solo shout songs, which he kept up all day. Many of the men were out of the village getting burity palm frond buds (the growing spike at the top of the burity palm) for making the dance capes, but they were back in time to sing in the afternoon and bring the all-day shout song singing to a close. On 27 January a man from the opposite moiety was painted and ornamented sitting on his sister's bed. When he walked out to the village plaza to sing, his sister wept as she recalled dead relatives and ceremonies of the past. Rattles tied to his knees, gourds hanging on strings down his back clashing at every step, feathers tied to his arms and the back of his head, carrying a bow and a sheaf of arrows, he walked slowly around the plaza in a counter-clockwise direction until the men sang a rainy season unison song in the late afternoon, after which he returned to his sister's house, took off the ornaments, went to his own house, and slept. In the evening the men sang shout songs and entertained themselves with lively talk, shouts, and euphoric happiness.

In the houses women opened the burity palm buds and then stripped the very fine fronds of their hard edges and dried them in the sun. At every sign of rain women hurried out to bring them in, for dampness would destroy their softness. On 1 February most of the older men had been working at weaving the dance capes. The afternoon singing in gardens and entry into the village had taken on a more formal air: more adult men came, and everyone was painted with more care and wore some kind of burity ornament. Preparations for the ceremony continued each day, as had the singing. Food was distributed in the men's house most mornings and afternoons.

Visitors began to arrive. The Suyá women who married men in other Xingu groups returned with their families for the final night of the ceremony. These included the two Juruna men who married Suyá women, who hung their hammocks in our house. Manioc pancakes were toasted for them, and they were given generous portions of food. The women talked excitedly for hours while their children played together. The atmosphere seemed increasingly charged with excitement and anticipation.

6 February 1972 8:00 a.m.

The hunters returned with heavily laden canoes. Bundles of roasted/smoked fish, several roasted wild turkeys and wild chickens, pots of honey, and some salt traded for at a cattle ranch far upriver were all carried up to the boy's house and soon distributed to kinsmen in the other houses.

The Kayabi Indian who ran the nearby Indian post arrived with his Suyá wife, his children, another Kayabi married to a Suyá woman, and three young Kayabi men who were courting young Suyá women. They, too, were given food and sat to talk with the men.

Since 1959, when they were contacted by an expedition sent to make peace with them, the Suyá have been part of a complex social system consisting of some fifteen different native groups and two Indian posts. In the succeeding years, an unbalanced sex ratio, factional disputes, and the interaction of the groups resulted in a fairly large number of marriages with non-Suyá. Ceremonies now bring most of the scattered members back to the village (the exceptions live at the more distant Indian post, Posto Leonardo Villas Boas), as well as a non-participating audience of male affines. This group is sometimes, but not today, augmented by non-Indian visitors from the Indian post – nurses, doctors, casual visitors, and any others that wish to come. Ceremonies have become assertions of identity in a multi-ethnic social system, and it is common now for a few outsiders to be there to be witnesses.

The following discussion of the final day and night of the Mouse Ceremony is divided into several parts, each preceded by an indication of the time of day and a map indicating spatial movement. I will discuss the entire structure of the event following a description of the events on the morning of 7 February 1972.

6 February 3:00 p.m.

> 'Big mouse, cut my cape, I leap and sing. Te-te-te-te . . .'
> 'Red mouse, paint my cape, I put on my cape and leap and sing. Te-te-te-te . . .

> 'The reason my mother's brother Mawchi's baby is so big is that Mawchi screws his wife so much.'

Kaikwati enters Niokombedi's house, joking with its inhabitants by a reference to his mother's brother. Carrying a gourd with a stick protruding from it he picks his way among the hammocks followed by his youngest son and daughter. His son carries a gourd filled with sticky sap, and his daughter some red *urucum* and a glass bottle filled with piqui-nut oil. Since they are formal friends of many of the residents, the three of them have rarely entered the house. They are making an exceptional visit, and for a particular purpose.

'Let's begin,' Kaikwati declares.

One by one the burity capes belonging to Niokombedi, his brothers, and their children are taken down from where they hang, strikingly white against the smoke-blackened thatch and upright poles of the walls. Each is placed on a man or boy's head, and held there. Kaikwati gathers the fringe of fronds at ankle length and cuts it off evenly with a sharp knife. Then the cape is removed and hung up on the wall for painting. Blackening his hands with charcoal, Kaikwati paints wide horizontal black lines on some of them, thin vertical black lines on others, and leaves some untouched. Dripping some piqui-nut oil on her hands, then reddening them with the red plant dye *urucum*, his daughter rubs her hands along the bottom of all the burity palm capes, making an even red line. She paints three additional thin vertical red stripes on a single small cape by running her hands along a few of the thin fronds.

With a small stick, Kaikwati's son removes some of the white sticky sap from the gourd he carries and smears it on the tops of the capes. With another stick his father pulls white parrot

2. A boy's mask is cut by Kaikwati, his formal friend

down from his own gourd. With a shower of white feathers he powders the tops of the capes with down. Most of it sticks to the gooey sap. The rest falls unheeded on the floor – where parakeets and a naked-looking plucked parrot, whose down has been stripped for similar ornamentation, waddle around searching for maize kernels. After the initial joking, very little is said. The cutting and ornamenting is done virtually in silence, and the man, his son, and his daughter leave as soon as they are finished. In a few minutes, Niokombedi and one of his sisters walk to Kaikwati's house to cut, paint, and ornament dance capes for him and his sons.

The mouse cape (called *amto po*) is the most important ritual object in the Mouse Ceremony. It is made from the tender inner leaves of the bud of the burity palm frond, which is opened, the spines removed, and the fine leaves dried in the sun. The burity palm, abundant in certain swampy areas, is quite difficult to find in the region in which the Suyá now live, and considerable care is taken in preparing the fronds for weaving the capes. The palm is important in other ceremonies because the most important log races are run carrying heavy sections of its trunk.

To make the cape, a number of stems of approximately the right length are gathered into a bundle. A piece of flexible vine is formed into a circle for fitting the head. The stems of all the palm leaves are tied together, the fronds are woven to form a round 'hat' for the head. The rest of the strands are left loose, the cape hung high on a wall or in the thatch to keep it clean, and another one is started.

Each adult man should gather enough burity buds to make his own cape and that of his name receiver(s). Many men do not know how to make the capes (this has apparently always been the case), and they simply collect the burity palms and ask others to make them. The request is made formally: the man takes his name receiver by the hand and, carrying the fronds, walks with him to the house of the person who has agreed to make the capes. There they hang the fronds in the thatch and leave. After the capes are woven, the bottoms hang raggedly, and they are unpainted.

Cutting and painting the capes is a significant moment commemorated in many Mouse Ceremony shout songs. The importance of the act stems partly from the people who do it, the 'formal friends,' in Suyá *ñumbre krà ti* and *kràm ngedi*. While the Suyá resisted any attempts of mine to discover meanings in the terms, they evidently have something to do with being friends of a particular sort. The phrase *ñumbre krà ti* may be divided into the root *ñumbre* which is a term for companion, and *krà ti* which I cannot translate except for *ti* which is an augmentative. *Kràm* is another term for a friend, and *ngedi* is a term for mother's brother. 'Formal friend' is a convenient translation of the relationship because it is characterized by very formal etiquette. Formal friends are not supposed to have sexual relations with each other's sisters, or marry their formal friends of the opposite sex. They treat each other with the same deference (respect, or shame) as brothers-in-law. They do not look directly at each other, they never refer to each other by name, they do not often joke together, and they usually address each other quite obliquely. Although the formal friends prepare each other (and each other's children) for the name-based plaza activities of a number of ceremonies, the relationships are not passed with names, but rather from father to son. The sons of a father's formal friends will be his own son's formal friends. Exactly which of them will be responsible for the cutting, painting, and other ritual activities is formally established at the end of certain log racing ceremonies, and continues throughout the lives of the participants.

Before they are cut and painted by the formal friends, the Mouse Ceremony capes are simply artifacts. Once they are painted they are in a sense activated, and the final phase of the ceremony has begun. The capes are a kind of 'mouse skin' which the men wear. The formal friends who cut the capes paint them with the design of the particular formal friend's moiety and the sub-group within the moiety to which its wearer's name belongs. They paint a person's cape a certain way because his name giver's cape is or was painted that way, as are the capes of all the members of the group that share those names. Some capes have certain ornaments that are restricted to a single name group. The right to use certain paint styles and ornaments is called 'our ceremonial things,' *mē kini*. Some ceremonial things are very old and have been passed down for as long as people can remember; others were invented by historical figures, whose name receivers added them to the repertory of their ritual activities. While a fairly complex system of ceremonial things is one of the centerpieces of Northern Kayapo ritual organization, according to recent work by Vanessa Lea (1986) and Gustaaf Verswijver (1985), among the Suyá they are strictly associated with the name sets.

The Mouse Ceremony involves a pair of moieties, but they are not the *Ambàn* and *Kren* moieties that appear in log races, but rather the *Soikokambrigi/Soikodnto* moieties, whose membership cuts across the *Ambàn/Kren* membership. The total number of ceremonial groups is four, but divided into two halves. Each moiety has a small affiliated sub-group of masks painted with the same color. The *Soikokambrigi* are identifiable by the lack of black on their capes. Their capes have only a red bottom fringe, and in the case of the auxiliary group, three thin red vertical lines as well. The *Soikodnto* have either parallel horizontal bands or thin vertical bands of black.

Figure 6.1 gives an idea of the appearance of the capes, their parts, and their painting

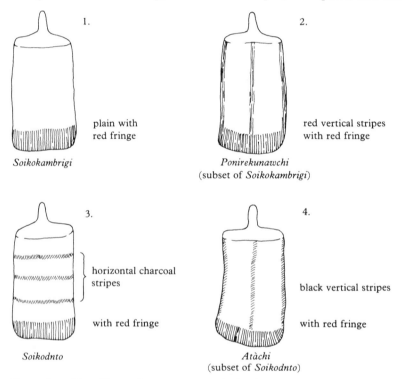

Figure 6.1   Four Mouse Ceremony capes indicating group membership

styles. Cape number 1 is left unpainted except for a red stripe at the bottom, and is worn by most of the members of the *Soikokambrigi* moiety. *Kambrigi* means 'red' and the name for this cape probably refers to the redness of the dance ornaments which are used by this group, including their capes. Cape number 2 is worn by only a few members of the *Soikokambrigi* moiety, and consists of a red fringe and an additional three thin vertical red lines. The design is called the 'capes with red painted side lines' (*Ponirekunawchi*). Cape 3 has three or four horizontal black stripes (the number depends on the length of the cape), in addition to the red fringe. It and the *Atàchi* design of cape 4 (worn by the members of two name sets, one from the *Ambàn* moiety and one from the *Kren* moiety found in the log races) are both of the *Soikodnto* moiety in this ceremony.

Throughout the village ritual relations are cutting and painting each other's capes. The whole afternoon suddenly takes on the appearance of an amateur theater production. People rush back and forth with paint, charcoal, water, knives, and burity fronds. In every corner a man is painting himself, a woman is painting her sons, or a cape is being fitted and cut. Some capes are in the wrong houses. 'Where's some charcoal?' people cry from various houses.

As they paint themselves, the men are visually transformed. Their individual features disappear behind designs of black and red paint, and their similarities are enhanced by their similar ornaments.

Just as each moiety has a cape design, they also have distinctive body painting designs. The *Soikokambrigi* paint themselves red from foot to calf, then black over the rest of their bodies. Their faces are painted red except for a black triangle around the nose (see name set pictured in Illustration 3). This is distinct from the members of the *Soikodnto*, who paint themselves red to the calf, then in wide horizontal black stripes to the neck. The face is also painted red with a black triangle (see Illustration 4). The members of two name sets called the *Atàchi*

3.　A name set sings in the plaza before leaving for the forest camp. It is a member of the *Soikokambrigi* moiety, with the right to leave the houses before the other moiety

4. A group of men sing in the forest camp. Note their different mask and body paint designs, indicating different name sets and moieties

5. Women strip the masks from one group of dancers while other wounded dancers continue to circle the plaza. The old man watching from the center of the plaza shouts in the falsetto style of the elderly

group paint their entire bodies black above the calves, including their faces. The members of one name set from this group paste a thin line of white parrot down on their noses and chins. Members of the other name set stick a thin white line of down extending down to their navels. This is a clear example of the level of ornamental detail that may be passed along with names from name giver to name receiver. In addition to the usual ear, lip, arm and leg ornaments, the men all wear woven burity sashes, arm and leg bands of burity palm frond, and pointed head ornaments on their foreheads (see Illustrations 3–6). When they have painted their bodies, most of the men pull their government-supplied shorts back on. To me they look incongruous against the body paint.

The painting of the capes, and then the painting of the bodies initiate a dramatic visual and conceptual transformation.

Late afternoon: the mouse singers leave the houses

'Big mouse, where are you going? We are going to put on our capes and leap and sing. Te-te-te-te . . .'

Fully painted and wearing his cape, each child goes to his name giver's house. Concerned about a towering thundercloud, Kaikwati performs an invocation to keep rain from falling on the ceremony. Members of each name set gather in the oldest member's house and begin to sing their shout songs. Standing side by side, they stamp back and forth, singing loudly. Singing can be heard from every house around the village from where I stand in the men's house, taking photographs, working the tape recorder, and taking notes, smudging everything with charcoal and greasy red dye.

Suddenly one group of singers squeezes through the doorway of a house, then turns to sing facing the door. Being the first to 'come out' (kataw) is the prerogative of a certain Soikokambrigi name set. For a minute or more they sing facing the house, then turn and circle the center of the plaza twice. As they circle the plaza another group, member of the same moiety, leaves a different house and begins to sing facing it. The first group comes to the men's house and sings there for a short time. Their white capes with red fringes are in constant movement as they roll sideways at each stamp. They sing loudly for a while, then march off to the trail leading to the 'forest camp' on the way to the gardens. A second group of dancers replaces the first at the men's house, its members shouting at the top of their voices with the exception of a red-painted, capeless, young woman who stands silently with her eyes downcast. Another group has begun to sing in front of one of the houses. Then the second group takes the path to the forest camp and the third sings before the men's house. Shout songs are everywhere: in the houses, in front of the houses, in the plaza, at the men's house, in the gardens (Example 6.1 on the cassette).

As soon as each group disappears down the path to the forest camp, women hurry out after it, carrying pots of drink or woven mats piled high with pounded meat, fish, fowl, manioc or corn cakes.

A name set without an adult leaves a house. Its oldest member is about ten years old. Two old women, the grandmothers of the boys, help them, showing them where to turn and face the house and instructing them when to go on and sing in the plaza.

A name set with a very old man comes out of another house. The old man staggers as he marches, pulling the others off balance. He falls down. He gives a high shout. The onlookers laugh excitedly. Staggering and shouting, pulling his group around, he marches off with

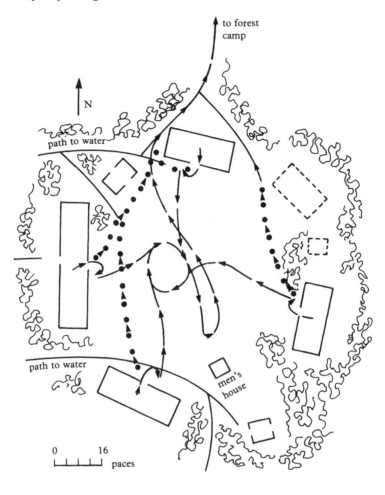

to forest
camp

N

path to water

path to water

men's
house

0   16
�
L L L L L   paces

→ ─ → = movements of name groups

● ● ● ► = movement of women carrying food

Figure 6.2   The mouse singers leave the houses

them toward the gardens. Eventually the last name set and the last of the women follow the others down the path toward the gardens.

The Suyá describe this part of the ceremony as the adult men taking the children out to the forest. The children's identity with their name set is established by the painting of their capes and their bodies, and their removal from the domain of the houses to the plaza and then to the gardens.

The removal of the boys to the gardens begins, and is in a sense made possible, by the cutting and painting of the dance capes by the formal friends. Once the capes have been prepared, the boys go to the house of the oldest member of their name set. Some houses have several name sets gathered inside them; others have only one. The name sets begin singing shout songs inside the houses, but soon leave them and sing in front of them. Every time a shout song begins inside a residence, its performer soon leaves the house for the plaza.

Leaving a house is usually elaborately undertaken in Suyá ceremonies. A man's removal from his natal household to live in the men's house and later in his wife's house is an important part of his life. A symbolic, or temporary, removal is an important part of most initiation ceremonies, including the Mouse Ceremony. The men sing inside the house in front of the public (plaza side) door. Then they exit and sing facing the house. Only after that emphasis on the act of leaving, do they circle the plaza and sing in front of the men's house. Then they go off to the gardens. Every adult male is removed, or removes himself, from his natal household during the late afternoon of the final day of the Mouse Ceremony and sings shout songs for his sisters and mothers, while the mother of each boy takes food to him in the forest camp.

Example 6.1 on the cassette gives an idea of the cumulative sound built up through the addition of more and more simultaneous songs. This accumulation of sounds through their simultaneous performance is an essential feature of what might be called the 'development' of a Suyá musical event. In the finale, the parts that had been sung separately are performed simultaneously. When everyone participates, true euphoria reigns. The effect resembles the finale of the Bee Ceremony.

There is a mixture of humor with drama in this part of the ceremony as well. When the old man staggered out of the house I was shocked at how spastic he had suddenly become (he had been ill recently), and at how cruel it seemed to laugh at him, as everyone made fun of his erratic movements. When my understanding of the ceremonial role of old people improved, I realized that he was just as much doing his part for the ceremony by staggering around and exaggerating his infirmity as the younger men were doing theirs by stamping hard, marching in a straight line, exaggerating their strength and shouting their songs. He was a member of the old people's 'clown' age grade. The Suyá say a ceremony without clowns would not be as much fun, and would not make people as euphoric.

Dusk: a meal and a transformation in the forest camp

'Niati mouse, will you eat corn? Te-te-te-te'

When the members of a name set reach the clearing in the gardens, they turn to face the village, and continue singing. The women place pots and mats piled with food in front of a name group, then stand off to one side. As more name sets arrive, the singing gets louder and louder, and more and more food arrives, and with it the evening. The mosquitoes are vicious. A few women wave manioc leaves around their small children to keep the mosquitoes off them as they continue to sing their shout songs.

A few minutes after the last group has arrived, everyone stops. Kaikwati, the ritual specialist, announces it is dusk. Everyone takes off his cape, hangs it up, and starts eating. Any man or boy can eat from any pile, and people walk around sampling different food and pots of drink. The flesh of fish and game birds, hardened by successive nights on a roasting rack during the hunting trip (necessary for preserving it), has been pounded with pepper and special manioc. Each species of fish and game has a different taste. Large corn cakes lie before almost every name set, and pots of corn gruel mixed with honey are being consumed enthusiastically. The Kayabi and Juruna guests are offered food from a very large pile in front of Niokombedi and his name set. Some of the men give women food as well, but these do not help themselves from the piles. The meal is a somewhat rushed affair, but a gourmet one nonetheless. One or two men learn new shout songs from Kaikwati as the rest finish eating, in order to have something new to sing during the night ahead.

As soon as the meal is over, the women and guests return to the village. The men replace their capes and line up in a different order. Instead of reassembling by name group, they form a line two abreast. Now friends in the same moiety can dance and sing together, elbows linked. A man can dance with anyone as long as the two have the same dance cape design. The older men are in the front of the line, and the children bring up the rear. A new phase is about to start.

The Suyá not only eat a lot in their ceremonies, the provenance of the food, and the way it is provided are quite different from everyday life. The food is special food, roasted and pounded rather than boiled. Corn figures prominently in the meal. It is Suyá cuisine at its most formal and elaborate. The Mouse Ceremony meal has parallels both with the roast goose of traditional Christmas dinners and with the Catholic mass. It is 'holiday' (special) food and somewhat 'holy' (described in the myth) food. It is specially prepared by certain women and given to their sons and brothers. On a number of different levels the meal in the forest camp is different from everyday meals in the village.

Women usually prepare food for their husbands and children. But in this ceremony (and a number of others) the mothers and sisters of a man prepare food. A man's real and classificatory sisters and mothers form a group called the *whai wi yeni*, and the food they bring is called the *yeni*. These women perform a number of special tasks in ceremonies, from holding a man's bow and arrow while he races to providing food on several occasions. The provision of food in the Mouse Ceremony reverses the usual food relationship, where a woman provides cooked food primarily to her husband. In the Mouse Ceremony a boy's mother brings out the food. If he has none, a mother's sister or sister will carry it to the forest camp.

Corn is an important part of the Mouse Ceremony meal. The mouse gave corn to the Suyá, and the Mouse Ceremony is performed about the time of the corn harvest. There are always several kinds of corn cakes to eat, and corn gruel to drink. Mice are also known to like maize today – they come into the houses, run along the rafters, and chew on the ears hanging from the rafters for next year's seeds. The ceremonial meal in the forest camp refers back to the myth and to the relationships around which the myth revolves.

The meal also resembles an important moment in the myth of the origin of maize. In the myth, the woman who learned of maize from the mouse addresses her young son by his name for the first time and gives him a corn cake. She tells him to take it to his *ngedi* (mother's brother(s)) in the men's house. The boy carries it to the plaza and shares it with members of both moieties, who address him as 'our name receiver.' In the ceremony, women prepare food and carry it out to the forest after their sons have gone there, and put it down in front of their sons. There it is shared by his name givers and the adult men of both moieties. No women were in the men's house in the myth; no women help themselves from the piles of food in the ceremony. As in the myth, food is given to the child for the collective men's groups.

The provision of food for their sons and indirectly to their brothers (their sons' name givers) parallels the way the men sing shout songs for their sisters, and perhaps reciprocates for it. The men sing (a verbal projection) for their sisters; the women provide food (an oral incorporation) for their brothers through their sons. The re-establishment of ties between brother and sister that is characteristic of many Suyá ceremonies is reciprocal, but they reciprocate with different modalities – the gustatory and the vocal. This part of the Mouse Ceremony combines food and sound in a single moment of elaborate exchange.

Night: of mice and men

'Black mouse, we go to our name receivers and leap and sing. Te-te-te-te . . .'

With their capes on again, in a double line, the men sing as they have been doing in the village every afternoon, but this time they are in the forest camp. They sing the first halves of their shout songs facing the village, then fall silent when they have completed their verses, trot around in a small circle, and sing the second halves. With a stamp and a shake of the rattles the second parts are concluded. The caped figures become still and silent. Silently they walk down the path toward the village by the last light in the western sky.

When they reach the village the line of men and boys avoids the plaza. They sneak around in back of the houses, and enter the house of Hwinkradi's sister through a small opening broken through the rear wall of the house. Inside it is completely dark. The caped singers form a rough U-shape around the center of the house, with the name giving group in the very center facing the door. There are three figures in the group, and the middle one – Hwinkradi, whose song began the ceremony two weeks before – stands astride the stretched out legs of his name receiver's maternal grandmother, who holds her four-year-old grandchild in her lap. (So dark was it, and so perfunctory were the Suyá descriptions, that I only really discovered what happened when I was a member of a name-giving group in the 1976 performance of the Mouse Ceremony. The description of what the name givers do is thus partly a reconstruction made after the 1976 performance.)

The singers begin to shake their rattles, stamp their feet, and hum their shout songs. Inside the confines of the house the sound of the unison rattles is overwhelming. The stamping raises choking dust, and mosquitoes feast on the unprotected flesh. The whole house resonates with the humming of every man and boy over five years of age in the village (Example 6.2 on the cassette).

As the men hum, the boy's relatives carry more food to the doorway of the house – a pile of roasted fish, some manioc pancakes, and a huge clay pot full of corn pudding. This food is for the name-givers, the specific men humming over the boy. There is whispered commentary and discussion between the women and Hwinkradi about who should receive some. The men keep singing. The silhouette of the doorway – formed by the evening sky – disappears completely with the ensuing darkness of a cloudy night. The men become still and silent again, then file out through the back wall. Except for one name set, that whistles later, the men silently circle around the village to reform on a garden path that enters the village from the South. Hwinkradi takes his sister's son with him. The red fringed capes take the lead, followed by the vertical red stripes, then the vertical black stripes, and last the horizontal black stripes. Clouds have covered the moon; it is completely dark. Neither moon nor stars illuminate the village.

The capes the men and boys wear are Mouse capes. The songs are Mouse songs. In the clearing, with the coming dusk, a subtle transformation takes place. The dancers become

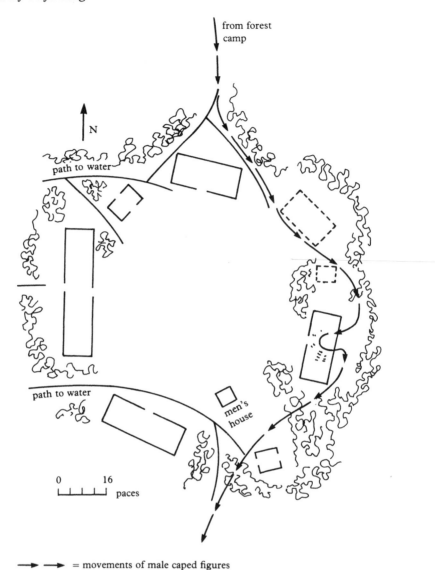

from forest
camp

N

path to water

path to water

men's
house

0   16
⊢┴┴┴┴┤ paces

➤ ➤ = movements of male caped figures

Figure 6.3   The mouse singers return to the village

more than just men; they become a combination of men and mice. As such, they come from the forest, sneak like mice through the rear wall of the house, sing over the child, then sneak out again.

I asked several men whether the singers were transformed into mice in the Mouse Ceremony, and they all replied that they were. They are all mice (and also men) during the night. This transformation is one of the highpoints of the entire ceremony. It is established partly in the singing after the meal. The forest camp is treated as though it were a village plaza. Then as animals they leave their 'forest village' for the human village. The silent entry into the house by the rear wall is like that of a mouse, and the humming may well mark the crucial moment of the transformation, for at that point they do not even sing the words to their songs.

What does it mean to become an animal? J. Christopher Crocker has addressed this for a nearby Brazilian group, the Bororo, whose stout insistence that they were parrots contributed to Lucien Lévy-Bruhl's idea of totemic participation. Crocker writes:

My conclusion shall be that neither a totemic framework nor one reflecting metaphysical beliefs nor yet one based on Bororo taxonomic classificatory principles is sufficient grounds for understanding the postulated identity between a certain animal species and human kind. Rather, it is an example of paradigmatic association in terms of the structural equivalence of men and macaws in several distinct relational contexts. Its meaning and logical character cannot be understood without an appreciation of the particular social situation in which it is utilized, as a strategy for expressing the ambiguous character of the actors in that context.

(Crocker 1977: 164)

The Suyá are mice as the Bororo are parrots: in a certain context and as an expression of ambiguity. Outside of the Mouse Ceremony the question 'Are you a man or are you a mouse?' makes no sense at all; in the ceremonial context the answer is 'Yes.'

The way to understand the importance of the mouse in the evening's proceedings is to return to the myth of the origin of maize. After the boy has grown old enough to walk, the mouse instructs the boy's mother to make a large maize cake, and send him into the plaza with part of it to give to the adult men. This act not only introduces maize to the men, but dramatically injects the boy into the midst of the collective men's house activities. He becomes a participant in, and a contributor to (through the food he brings) the name-based men's moieties. Just as the mouse's instructions introduce the boy to the men, so the dancing over the child held between his maternal grandmother's legs and then taking him with them when they dance during the night make Hwinkradi's sister's son a part of the male collective activity of the village.

When the men become both men and mice they remove themselves spatially and temporally from everyday activity. Their identity refers back to the time of the myth itself, and 'encapsulates a paradox' (in the sense of Herzfeld 1979) in that they are at once creatures of the plaza and creatures of the periphery. This is the kind of radical juxtaposition of different times and different spaces that gives such moments their conceptual and emotional power. The evening transformation of the men into mice/men has parallels in rites of passage around the world. In the classic formulation of Arnold Van Gennep, later elaborated by Victor Turner, the final night of the Mouse Ceremony is a marginal period. But it is not only the boy on his grandmother's lap who is 'at once no longer classified and not yet classified' (Turner 1967: 102), but the entire male population of the village.

Turner suggests that an important part of rites of passage is the communication of the *sacra* that he calls the heart of the liminal matter. The things he mentions are evocative instruments or sacred articles, the 'real' names of spirits or deities, and instruction in the theogony. With the exception of the mouse/men's capes, not much of the Mouse Ceremony has visual *sacra* or formalized instruction. Suyá *sacra*, I believe, are aural – the sounds of speeches and shout songs, the tremendous resonant humming of the stamping and rattling of the dancers in the house, and the unison singing yet to come. The singing, with its combination of individual and collective perspectives, the text with its animal names and first and third person verbs, and the leaping movement are all just the kind of exaggeration or combination that makes relationships an object of reflection (Turner 1967: 103). The small boy, sitting in his grandmother's lap as the caped dancers sneak into the house and begin to stamp over him, sees and feels the power of the adult men/animals. In the acoustically transparent village, the sounds reach through the darkness to the entire Suyá population, and the visitors. The entrance of the mice/men into the village is an object of reflection for the entire village, not just for the small boy.

The sound at this point in the night is different from any other moment. The singers only stamp and hum. It may be significant that at this moment the assembled men are above all representing the collective men's groups, and may be at a particularly powerful moment of their transformation, for they do not sing their individual songs in an individualizing way, but stamp and hum them producing a definitely unison sound composed of fairly quiet individual melodies and a regular, loud, unison stamping rhythm.

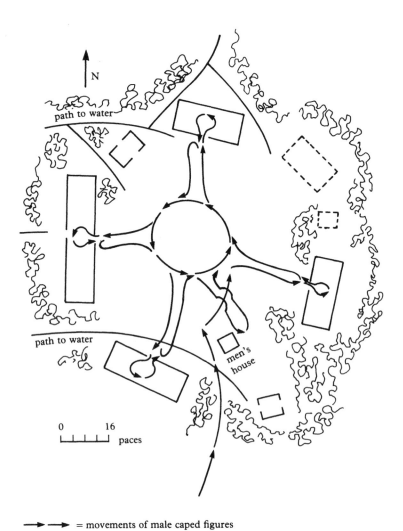

→ → = movements of male caped figures

Figure 6.4   The mouse singers leap and sing

Leaping and singing

'Become the big mouse, I put on my cape and leap and sing; we leap and sing. Te-te-te-te . . .'

What happens next can be heard on Example 6.3 on the cassette. A whistle comes from the plaza, and there is an answering one from the line. Then the whole group rushes toward the center of the village shouting 'huuuuuuuuuuuuuuuuu' and begins to sing. We enter leaping and singing. Giving a hop on the left foot, a stamp with the right foot, and a slight toss to the head to give the cape a swaying movement, we surge into the plaza. Women throw dried thatch on a small fire in the center of the plaza and the blaze illuminates the capes with their tall feathers, their white, red, and black markings, their fringed ends whipping and swaying with the movements of the dancers. It is a strenuous dance, around and around the plaza. Then we hop and march out from the center in straight lines to each of the houses. We sing for a moment in front of a house, then return to the center, where we go around some more and then out to another house.

After singing in front of every residence, the caped dancers sing in front of the men's house. Brothers in opposite moieties begin a special shout toward each other 'Hu-a, hu-a hu hu hu.' A male relative of the boy who was sung over brings the name group's food to the men's house where Hwinkradi gives some of it away and tucks a dried fish into the men's house thatch for later.

Instead of reforming a line, friends march together in small groups around the plaza, up to the houses, and back, singing constantly. Ceremonies are also a time when companions sing together and both establish and reaffirm their friendship and mutual support. This kind of companionship is the opposite of the relations between formal friends: companions eat together, joke together, hunt together, and sing together without regard to their moiety or name set membership.

After a while the women retire to their houses and their hammocks. They may sleep, but it is hard not to hear the sounds of the men shouting right outside the houses. The fire in the plaza dies down. While most of the men keep singing, a few sit near the embers and rest, smoke, and talk for a while, then get up to sing some more.

At about 10.30 p.m. the men reconvene in the center of the plaza. Once again in a line two abreast, ordered by moiety membership, they march around the plaza and then up to the door of the westernmost house. Backing off, going forward, backing off, going forward they suddenly charge into the house and form a circle around the center of the house. Each man falls silent when his verse comes to an end, and for a moment they just stamp and shake their rattles in the dark.

Then they begin to sing one of the unison Mouse Songs, or *amto ngére*. For the first time that day their voices blend in a low unison chorus, boys singing in an octave (or in one case nearly a monotone). (Example 6.4 on the cassette.)

Bawchi   te kaw tügü, mana niu mu
Savannah deer leg skin black, I see it

Te kaw wi   katàdà
Leg skin become cotton

(Repeat lines 1 and 2)

Na po daw sarĩ ne ta   taw ta
Cape with leap and sing stand there

(Repeat whole song once)

Hu-a, Honiiiiiiiiiiiiii
Hu-a, it is finished

Free translation:

'The black leg of the savannah deer becomes white cotton. It leaps with its cape and sings, and stands there'

As soon as the unison song is concluded the men begin to sing their shout songs and rush toward the door of the house. As is so often the case, the apparently free-for-all rush toward the door by the shouting singers has a particular order, determined by name set and moiety membership. I only discover this when I drag my somewhat reluctant partner to the door and get to it before the rest. He pulls me back and explains that our name set should never leave the house first, but instead should be among the last to leave. Once outside, we re-form our line, circle the plaza twice, and then march out to the easternmost house on the periphery and sing the same unison song inside in the same way. The rush is repeated, and we sing in the two other large houses on the periphery.

Again the line breaks up and groups of friends go around singing together in front of the houses. The hours pass slowly. The moon rises at about midnight, which helps estimate when it will be day. At times many of the singers are sitting around the fire resting, with only a few dancing around the village. The older children are enthusiastic participants. The younger children have gone to bed, and their name givers wear the children's capes hung over the points of their own capes. In the dark I think they have red bulls-eyes on their capes, but these are just the small capes hanging in the middle of their backs. We seem to reach a low point of activity at about 11.30 p.m. At about 3.00 we sing a second unison song (see below) with the same structure but different words (Example 6.5 on the cassette), and at 4.30 a.m. there is another low point. Most of the exhausted singers are gathered in the men's house, shouting hoarsely from time to time.

> *Po keingoro, po keingoro*
> Cape striped cape striped
>
> *Kukeni da pokeingoro daw   sarī ne ta   nē*
> Kukeni mouse cape striped with leaps and sing standing thus
> (Repeat lines 1 and 2)
>
> *Po keingoro, po keingoro*
> Cape striped cape striped
>
> *Imoi po keingoro taw iarī ne, ta*
> My cape striped with I leap and sing thus, standing
> (Repeat whole song)
>
> *Hu-a, honiiiiiiiiiiii*
> Hu-a, it is finished

In free translation:

'Striped cape, striped cape, the kukeni mouse leaps and sings with its striped cape, standing there this way. With my striped cape I leap and sing thus. Hu-a, it is over.'

These songs have not been sung since the last time the Mouse Ceremony was performed. Kaikwati insists on holding a note by himself, to indicate how it should be done (Example 6.5 on the cassette). The singers make some mistakes, corrected in the next house. As soon as the drawn-out coda is through, men start to sing their shout songs and rush for the door.

The grand entrance into the village is a mixture of the stealthy and the triumphant. One name set has the right (or privilege) of going to the west side of the dark plaza and whistling. Another name set has the right to whistle back. After the two whistles, all of the men shout huuuuuu and rush into the village in their first appearance as a body of painted and caped dancers within the village limits (they have only sung as a group in the forest camp). There they take possession of the plaza, and sing in front of all the houses. It is the supreme moment of shout song performance, expressed by a particular dance style (leaping) that is most consistently performed at that point. While the mice/men entered the boy's house stealthily, through the back door, they enter the village plaza huuing, singing, and leaping. They seize the plaza, and retain it through the next morning.

When the men sing inside the houses there is a striking contrast between the performance of shout songs and unison singing. There is a tremendous difference between the shouts of the plaza and spaces in front of the houses and the unison songs inside them. The men are individuals in the shouting; they are a solidary group in the houses. Re-formed according to moiety membership, they enter and leave in a strict order, and sing strictly unison songs inside the house. It is the transition from a male collectivity to individuals that is most dramatic in the singing. As soon as the group ends a unison song, the men begin their shout songs and rush to the door. Shout songs are for the plaza; propelled by their singing the dancers rush out the door.

The two song texts stress transformation, and are an example of a text the Suyá could translate but not explain: 'The black leg skin of the savannah deer becomes cotton, it leaps and sings.' White cotton forearm ornaments were an important part of body ornamentation for some Suyá ceremonies that are no longer performed. Suyá could not explain what the song was about beyond translation, which indicates that the savannah deer becomes like a human dancer, with its forelegs covered with the cotton ornaments. Standing (like a human dancer) the deer leaps and sings. The unison song refers to one partial transformation, and is sung by men/mice in the midst of another. The second song is much the same. 'The kukeni mouse [I believe this is a small striped rodent whose stripes are likened to the black stripes on the dance masks] dances and sings with its striped cape, standing, thus. With my cape I dance and sing, standing.' Song texts that stress body ornaments are quite common, and generally reflect parallels with the dancers themselves. I suspect there was a time when the white forearm ornaments were worn by one of the name-based groups, just as the striped masks are worn by the *Soikodnto* today.

The way the adult men wore the capes of their young name receivers after those have gone to bed is perhaps related to the terms in which the relationship is described. Name givers refer to those younger than them that have the same name set as *krā ndu*, which directly translated means 'new head.' They are addressed in return as *krā tumu* or 'old head.' The word 'head' has more than an anatomical reference: sweet potatoes and tubers are called 'heads' as well. During the night of the Mouse Ceremony, the masks of the young name receivers are suspended from the heads of the masks of their name givers by their chin loops, and the two ornaments remain together during the entire night, even while the young children are asleep. It is indeed the conjunction of 'old' and 'new' heads.

This singing and leaping takes considerable stamina. It is considered a positive attribute to be strong, able to dance energetically and sing loudly for long periods of time. During the long hours between the entry of the dancers into the village and dawn, women listen to the men from their hammocks, and evaluate their singing.

Dawn: killing the mice and concluding the ceremony

'Too bad, our ceremony is over'   (Hwinkradi)

The women and children begin to rise at about 5:00 a.m. Children who went to sleep are brought to the plaza, put on their capes again, and start to sing. The women light small fires in front of the houses and provide an audience once more. The line of friends is re-formed and marches around the village and up to each house, singing. In the misty light of dawn the men are at last visible. Their capes still sway, the charcoal of the black stripes smudged. They sound hoarse. They have been singing for over twelve hours. One man sings a special solo, belonging to his name set and learned from his deceased mother's brother.

When it is light, but still some time before sunrise, the men stop dancing. What happens now would usually occur in the western men's house, but since the only one built at the time is in the east, the men squeeze into and gather around the eastern men's house. Women rush up with hunting arrows and wound the mice/men by pushing hunting arrows through the woven crowns of their capes as the men sing. Earlier the women have decided which brother each will wound. Each dancer must be wounded by a sister, and every mask must be pierced. Although I have been reluctant to be included in any kinship network (because of factional

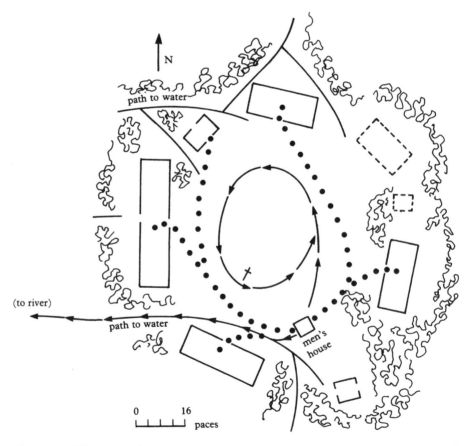

Figure 6.5   The mouse singers are wounded and die

disputes), I have a 'sister for ceremonies.' An Upper Xingu Indian, she is a foreigner like myself. It is not a solemn moment, and some women have trouble pushing the arrow through the woven headdress. I, for example, am too tall. At last she pierces my cape, and the arrow pulls it heavily to one side.

When every cape has been pierced, the men leave the men's house according to friendship, size, and dance cape designs. The men sing and march around with the arrows hanging from the crowns of their capes. After a while they return to the men's house, and continue to sing, but begin to re-form in name-set groups. A *Soikokambrigi* name-set group leaves the men's house in a line across with elbows linked. Another follows it, then another. The dancers leave the men's house in name-set groups as they had left the residential houses the afternoon before. Suddenly the first group to leave the men's house stops singing, bends over and remains motionless. This is called 'dying' or becoming dead. The women who pierced their capes come running up and strip off the capes. Running with them back to their houses, they return with gourds of water, chilled by the cold night air, that they splash over the man whose cape they have taken (Illustration 6). Shivering and spluttering the men return to the men's house to watch the other groups die. One after another, the name groups fall silent and still, stooping over. Women rush back and forth with masks and gourds. The group gathered in the men's house swells with silent watching men.

The old clown, instead of dying in a stylized way by stooping over, rolls on the ground shrieking and groaning as if in agony. He kicks his feet in the air and rolls in the dust. Several women rush up to him and tickle his genitals with sticks. There is a great deal of laughter as he shouts louder and intensifies his animal-like death throes. He is soon drenched with water.

Finally only a single group of men marches around and around the plaza. It is a black-striped group, member of the *Soikodnto* moiety, and one of its ritual obligations is to keep going long after the rest have stopped. I am a member of it. Our steps drag, our voices crack. The oldest name holder insists that we do not stop. Finally, though, he says 'Now!' and we all stoop over. We die and are stripped of our capes. The cold water is a sudden shock. As I walk to the men's house I hear Hwinkradi's voice – the man whose song had started the whole ceremony and whose name receiver had been sung over. He says 'Too bad, our ceremony is over.' Fifteen hours of shouting and singing, leaping and dancing, and yet he and the others were sad to see it end.

The men are externally men again, their mouse capes removed and their bodies publicly bathed in the village plaza. But there are still some things to conclude before everyone can return to his house and perhaps sleep a few hours. The old man who had died with such drama collects the arrows from all the capes. This is a prerogative of the old clowns – the *wikenyi*. Arrows, even older ones, are valuable possessions and these will be used by his relatives. Women pluck the long feathers from the stems of the capes. These will be stored for future ceremonies.

As the sun breaks through the morning mist the men walk to the river. There we strip off our burity sashes, our arm bands, and our head bands, and throw them far out into the current. The river is dotted with these ornaments, carried along on its swift current. As they throw them, some men mutter 'go, go back to the river of food.'

Then we all jump in the water, which feels warm compared to the chill air. A few hot fires of dry palm fronds are lit on the banks. Shivering, we dry ourselves, then walk back to the village. The ceremony is really over.

6. A man drips and shouts he is cold as his sister runs back to her house after pouring cold water over him next to the men's house at the conclusion of the Mouse Ceremony

Only the children continue to sing. Repossessing their capes they play in back of the houses and down by the river. But the men never put them on again. Inside their sisters' houses capes hang from the thatch for a time and are eventually used as mats for manioc cakes, or woven into something else and eventually discarded. One became part of an anthropological collection.

The humanness and the mouseness are separated in the dawn, just as they were conjoined at dusk the night before. The dancers' sisters pierce their mouse capes with arrows. Wounded, the men continue to march around the plaza until, name group after name group, they 'die.' Sisters rush to strip the mouse capes off them, then return with water to douse them with in the men's house, where they gather to watch the remaining name groups die. The wounding, dying, and bathing are all part of a reintegrative process that occurs in most rites of passage. If the dancers become powerful through the conjunction of animal and human, their return to everyday life requires the disjunction of those two aspects of the dancers.

The coming of day requires a return to order and a re-humanizing of the dancers. The preservation of social order in myths and a great deal of social action is the responsibility of the adult men. Yet all the adult men, and the boys as well, have become animals. One might expect those other mediators, the formal friends, to effect the transformation; but they, too, are all wearing mouse capes and dancing. It is instead the dancers' sisters who help return them to their human and social guise. The ritual roles of siblings to each other once again come to the fore. If men sing shout songs for their sisters, their sisters are the ones who wound the dancers, strip them of their capes, bathe them, and humanize them.

Public bathing in the plaza (as distinct from behind the house or in the river) is an important kind of public purification in Suyá life, and reintegrates a person into all of his or her social roles. The bath usually consists of a relatively small amount of water being poured so that it wets the person from the neck down. It is not the amount of water, but that certain people pour it and certain others receive it that makes the ritual bath so important. I witnessed one other important plaza bathing ritual, the declaration of the end of a period of mourning. One of the hereditary political leaders invited each Suyá individually to come to the center of the plaza to be bathed at dawn. After bathing, the members of the village all painted themselves again, and initiated the first ceremony after a burial. All the mourners, including close kinsmen of the deceased, were bathed, painted, and reintegrated into social life once again. The plaza bath marked the end of individualized mourning and the renewal of public life. The other major bathing (that I never saw) occurred in the Wild Pig Ceremony, which involved a night long series of plaza baths for boys at the end of a period of seclusion. There, too, the baths reintegrated the boys and marked the end of a liminal period.

While the 1972 ceremony drew smoothly to a close, there is always a possibility that the men will not return to their human form. Such an ending is recounted in several myths. In the story of a man who became a savannah deer referred to in an earlier chapter, a man's savannah deer cape grows onto his body during the night so that he cannot take it off. At dawn the dancers all 'die' but he keeps on singing, walking around and around the plaza. The men wait and wonder what has happened. The sun climbs high, but the ceremony does not end because the lone singer continues singing around and around the plaza. At last he runs off down a path deep into the forest where his transformation is completed. He is still there today, according to a Suyá who saw him, but he walks on all fours. While the Suyá do not expect one of their companions to actually become a mouse, the myths stress the possibility, and emphasize the importance of performing all parts of the ceremony correctly. The exact ending is still unpredictable: a certain name set has the right to keep going long after the others have stopped.

When Hwinkradi says 'Too bad, our ceremony is finished' his statement is performative. As the man whose request to his sister began the whole event two weeks previously, when he says the ceremony is over, it is indeed over. His statement indicates regret as well. Like Christmas to a child, the ceremony generates a tremendous amount of energy and interest, and its conclusion leaves everyone tired, and facing the everyday round once again.

When the last wounded name set dies, silence falls on the village and the sounds of everyday life return to it. Once the last man has been bathed by his sister, the men take the final step to dissociate themselves from their mouse identity. They walk to the river where they strip off their burity body ornaments and throw them into the water with the injunction that they are to return to the river of food. The reason for doing this is because they have not only taken on the physical aspects of mice during the night, they have also absorbed the spirit (*mēgaron*) of a mouse: they have been a single (human) body with a mouse skin and body paint, but with two spirits. When the men return to a human physical state, they must still rid themselves of the mouse spirit. The injunction for the mouse spirits to return to their own river (where the mouse originally gave maize to the mother of the crying child) dispatches the mouse spirit. The sisters strip off the physical appearance; the men's body ornaments carry the 'spiritual' or non-substantial mousiness back to the place where the mouse jumped on the woman's shoulder and told her about corn (the Suyá identify the river of food as the Rio Fresco, an affluent to the Xingu where they say they once lived).

Finally, the men bathe in the river. This bath, unlike the plaza bath, actually removes some of the physical signs of their ritual identity. In 1972 the young men used soap to take off the greasy red *urucum* and the black charcoal. Bird-down doesn't come off as easily, and sticks for a few days. This bath removes some of the last vestiges of the alternate, ritual identity which they donned the afternoon before. Walking back to the village they return to the houses where they live with their wives and children, or their mothers, and to daily life.

Hwinkradi's statement about the ceremony being over is significant because he started it. Suyá ceremonies, myths, and songs are very clear about beginnings and endings. The myth of the origin of maize ends with the words 'It was thus', which is always used to indicate a story is over. The second unison song ends with the same word '*honi*' meaning it is ended. Hwinkradi marks the end of the ceremony in the same way: it is over. Our ceremony is finished. Although the last vestiges of the mouse identity were yet to be removed from each dancer, the end of the collective part was clearly marked.

Conclusion

Between the opening and the closing of this ceremony the men sang during fourteen days. The whole ceremonial period, when compared with the daily life of the village, was one of heightened activity and heightened awareness of certain values and structures. Village spaces were cleared, a forest camp established, time was marked by song. Children were instructed in ritual life, women were excited as they prepared the food for their children, listened to the music during the long final night, and prepared to pierce the capes of their brothers. On the final night space was used in new ways, the use of time was altered (singing all night), and the very nature of the participants was dramatically altered at dusk and at dawn. The entire population of the village was involved in the event. The degree of excitement, the realignment of social relations, and the different forms of cooperation in the preparation and consumption of food, as well as the singing of songs re-animated important parts of Suyá life.

On the final day, in the interval between dusk and dawn, the highest masculine values were honored. Song, strength, self-assertion through shout songs and leaping expressed and reaffirmed masculine values. And yet in the overall structure of the ceremony, many other values were also activated. Relationships between men and their mothers and sisters were reaffirmed, relationships between men and the animal world were revived through the introduction of songs and through metamorphosis. The present and the past were brought together through the parallels between the Mouse Ceremony and the origin of maize so many generations ago, as well as through the continuity of the name-set groups. Euphoria was experienced and expressed in the songs, the shouts, and the laughter, for the event expressed the complex relationship between men and animals, and was part of the shifting relationships between a man and his sisters or a man and his wife and affines.

Through the fourteen days of the ceremony, and the fifteen hours or so of singing on the final day and night, music helped express and create the euphoria that should characterize Suyá ceremonies. It did so in particular ways, and resulted in the successful transformation of men into men/mice, an infant into a boy with names, and the men/mice back into men again.

Space, time, human relationships, and many of the musical genres discussed above were employed in the final night of the Mouse Ceremony. An invocation kept rain away; men and boys sang shout songs individually for a short time in the houses, in the plaza, in the forest, and in the plaza again. Strongly contrasted unison songs were performed in the houses. The importance of the use of different spaces, and the transformations of dusk and dawn appeared. Metamorphosis was central to the ceremony itself, and to the songs, their texts, and the singers. In this final night, much of what was discussed in earlier chapters was illustrated in its actual performance. Now we can return to the question of why Suyá sing.

7 *Why Suyá sing*

This book opened with the observation that music is important in the lives of the South American Indians. We are now in a position to assess the nature of that importance, and to respond to the question we posed at the outset: why did the Suyá sing? What was it about music, specifically song, that made it such a frequent and valued social activity?

I have shown that Suyá song was a verbal art form characterized by the priority of melody over text, the fixed length of its phrases, the relatively fixed relations among pitches, the degree of repetition, and the unimpeachable authority of its entirely fixed texts that often played on the ambiguity of human and animal identity. Unlike other verbal art forms, songs all came from outside – from animals, transformed Suyá, and other human communities. All songs were part of collective rituals; there were seasonal songs, songs of specific ceremonies, and individual shout songs performed as part of ceremonial activity, but no love songs, protest songs, or lullabies. Suyá singing was an essential part of social production and reproduction. It re-established the clarity of spatial domains, temporal durations, and certain forms of human relationships. Singing enabled individuals to create and express certain aspects of self, it established and sustained a feeling of euphoria characteristic of ceremonies, and it related the present to the powerful and transformative past. The Suyá would sing because through song they could both re-establish the good and beautiful in the world and also relate themselves to it.

Suyá would sing because through singing they could restore certain kinds of order in their world, and also create new kinds of order in it. Singing was an experience of the body and of the social person, and a means for reproducing society. Singing was also intimately linked to material production and social identity. Suyá sang because singing was an essential way of articulating the experiences of their lives with the processes of their society.

Singing and the self

The physiology of song

The body was the song's instrument, as described in Chapter 4. The long hours of singing and dancing certainly had an effect on the body itself. Some of the sentiments characteristic of Suyá ceremony were probably the result of the physiological effects of exertion and consecutive singing. Other feelings were produced by context (we are in a ceremony therefore we must be euphoric), by transformation (I am not only myself, I am also an animal), and by memory (a certain deceased relative was always happy in this ceremony, I miss him and cry). Most of the Gê-speaking groups were somewhat unusual among South American Indians in that they apparently never used any form of hallucinogen or drank fermented beverages as central parts of their ceremonies. Although the Suyá had adopted tobacco use and manioc

128

beer from other groups in the past hundred years, these had not become focal points of their ritual or musical processes. Their visions accompanied fevers rather than drugs; their euphoria was produced by song, collective activity, and food, rather than alcohol, hallucinogens, and narcotics. Suyá sang and their 'high' was euphoria (*kin*). Singing made men euphoric; listening to their brothers made women euphoric; old people's clowning indicated their euphoria and made the village euphoric. Singing and dancing for long periods of time was a physiological experience that probably altered perception.

We know little about the ways music and dance may affect the body, outside of some work on trance. Yet there is an undeniable physical component to performance arts that we ignore at our peril. Suyá song was a physical as well as social experience, something to be done in a tough and exhausting way that resulted in an out-of-the-ordinary experience. The experience itself, however, was experienced by them as social beings, not as purely physiological entities.

Song and the person

The Suyá concept of person involved three distinct components, described at length in Chapter 3. One of these was the physical body, which was formed by the father's semen and nurtured by the mother and whose permanence was expressed partly through dietary restrictions when a close kinsman was ill. The second was the social identity that was passed with a set of names from a mother's brother to his sister's son (or from a father's sister to her brother's daughter), which did not involve a physical bond but a social one, expressed through body painting, singing, and participation in ceremonies. The third component of the person was the spirit, unique to every physical object – persons, animals, plants and things. The spirit was essential to human life: without it a person sickened and died.

A person's bond with parents and children was physical. Among other restrictions, a person avoided certain foods when his or her parents or children were sick because if they were ingested, the properties of the animal or plant could harm the sick person. These restrictions were common among the Northern Gê, and I have called the group formed by people who observe such mutual dietary and activity restrictions a 'corporeal' group – as distinct from a 'corporate' group (Seeger 1980b: 127–135) – because they shared some internal bodily identity. The bond with name sharers was not internal but was worn on the skin. Name givers and their name receivers painted their bodies alike, wore the same ornaments, and sang the same songs. This dual aspect of the body was an essential feature of the contrast between the kinship-based social groups on the periphery of the plaza and the name-based ceremonial groups in the center of the village. It has been noted by a number of writers, including Melatti (1976), Da Matta (1982) and Seeger (1980b: 127–135). Spirit and songs were also intimately related: a teacher of songs was a person whose spirit was outside his or her body, and in direct communication with the spirits of animals, plants, or bees.

One or more song genres were associated with each aspect of the person. Invocations and weeping were associated with the physical body and close relatives. Invocations acted on the body itself. Women usually wept for close kinsmen. Unison songs were usually associated with one or another name-based plaza group, and many solo performances were determined by name-set membership. The shout songs were as individualized as the spirit. Each person had his own for each ceremony, of a style more or less appropriate to his age. Even though they were learned from someone else, shout songs were remembered not by who taught them but by who sang them for the first time. A man would be remembered by some of the shout songs he sang, which might be sung after he was dead and his voice stilled.

Every Suyá could sing songs in public (at the appropriate times). Not everyone could employ the other verbal forms. Most oratory was restricted to a few older men; young men, women, and children were supposed to listen. Direct verbal confrontation between men in a public arena was rare. All men sang, however, and through their performance they publicly displayed their anger, sadness, or euphoria. A person in mourning would not sing; an angry person would not sing; a person who in the middle of a political dispute might only sing for a very short time then return to his house, revealing his discontent and lack of euphoria. Ceremonies were moments when expectations were particularly clear, and when individuals aligned and realigned themselves with those expectations at each performance. Unlike dreams, fantasies, and private speech, which also reveal attitudes and feelings, singing was done in front of everyone, for everyone to hear. To a certain extent Suyá could sing who they were, what they would like to be, and how they felt.

Music and society

Singing was part of social reproduction. It was an integral part of the series of rites of passage that ordered a person's life. Ceremonies ordered production and through their performative nature were a way the Suyá created and re-created their village and themselves. As Roy Rappaport has argued 'the performance does more than *remind* individuals of an underlying order. It *establishes* that order' (1979: 197, emphasis in the original). The order established could be visible and tangible – as in the clearing of the village and its public paths – or invisible, as in the conjunction of men and animals in the dark of night. Indeed, without collective rituals there might not have been villages at all.

Gê villages were unusually large compared to other lowland South American groups. Several authors, for widely varying reasons, have suggested that Gê ceremonial groups enabled the Gê to live in larger villages than many other groups (Gross 1979, Lave 1979, Turner 1979b, Rivière 1984:87ff). While most forest Indian villages averaged twenty to sixty inhabitants, Gê communities of several hundred were common, and settlements of as many as two thousand were reported by early explorers and supported by oral history. The authors differ on the reasons for the small size of the Amazonian groups, with Gross suggesting a lack of protein and Rivière suggesting a lack of social and political structure. It is clear, however, that the nuclear family was the basic subsistence unit, and that each house or group of houses in a Gê village could conceivably survive as a separate settlement except that *social* reproduction would be impossible. Men could not be initiated, and ceremonies could not be performed. Small numbers of people were associated with silence and sadness; it took the entire population to create euphoria and transformation.

Ceremonial activity was one of the main justifications for village residence. Suyá families spent a good deal of time away from the village. Before the introduction of steel tools and an Indian post that dispensed medicines they probably spent considerably more time away from the village, as did other Northern Gê. They would return to the village and either continue a ceremony that had been opened months before, or begin a new one. Collective life was essentially ceremonial life. Suyá unison song, with all its permutations of who sings what when and with whom, was the way those non-kinship groups were formed and expressed.

The importance of the entire group participating in a ceremony was reflected in the evaluation of how beautiful a performance was said to have been. That was the importance of the return of the women married into other groups. When everyone participated in a way appropriate to sex and age, the performance was beautiful and people were euphoric. When many remained silent or did not appear, it was considered ugly and emotionless.

Daniel Gross suggests that the large villages and long ceremonies of the central Brazilian groups (as contrasted with forest dwelling ones) are a specific ecological adaptation to low protein density. The lack of protein is still far from proven. But the central Brazilians may have had a particular social form that thrived in the ecosystem of the savannah and gallery forests of most of the Gê homelands. It is not clear why there was any impulse toward large villages at all (Gross has not demonstrated any ethnohistorical support for his suggestion that they were a response to attacks from powerful riverine groups), yet the Gê cling tenaciously to their large villages in the face of Brazilian domination and transformed socio-economic circumstances.

In some ways Gê ritual resembles some of the communal rituals of the Australian Aborigines and other societies whose local groups congregated occasionally in large seasonal camps for ceremonies associated with collective participation and euphoria. Perhaps the description of Suyá euphoria resembles Durkheim's 'effervescence' (Durkheim 1965) precisely because of the similarity in social forms between the Aborigines and the Gê. In both cases singing and ceremonies brought groups together in a collective endeavor, made a village beautiful, and a person euphoric.

The economic features of ceremonial life cannot be divorced from musical performances; social reproduction and economic production are indissolubly linked. Suyá ceremonies were not divorced from economic life, but rather organized many aspects of it, including the coordination of production and the distribution of food. The description of the Mouse Ceremony showed repeatedly that food and singing were parts of the same event. An old man was given food after singing and clowning; men's house meals were frequent; the final night of singing was preceded by a forest feast; and the name group was given food after it sang over the child. Groups of men and women were repeatedly mobilized for hunting, fishing, and preparing food for the village as a whole or for particular relatives. Clearly production was being coordinated by the ceremony. Collective hunts were usually associated with ceremonies. One moiety hunted and fished for the other; the relatives of a man hunted and fished for the people singing; children sometimes provided tiny fish as food for the adult men involved in a collective activity associated with a ceremony.

Some parts of Suyá production were exclusively for collective activities. Certain gardens were cut, burned, planted, and harvested to provide food exclusively for ceremonies. Surplus was purposely produced for ceremonies, not simply used in them. Food was also constantly redistributed throughout the village in ceremonial periods. Ceremony distributions tended to be collective, and oriented toward specific age, sex, and ceremonial groups rather than oriented toward domestic groups or kinsmen, which was the 'everyday' form of distribution. Many gifts of food were specifically said to be food for a group that had just sung. The morning pots of manioc and corn drink, the distribution of game by a hereditary leader who attempted to forget no one, and the collective men's house meals all distributed food in entirely different ways than was done within the domestic group.

Some instructive things happen when the ritual cycle falls into abeyance among Gê-speaking groups. Among the Gavião in Pará, the National Indian Foundation (FUNAI) discouraged some rituals because they interfered with the Indians' collection of Brazil nuts, which were collected by the Gavião, and sold by FUNAI, which gave credit to each family according to what it produced. When, through a brilliant maneuver, motivated by the vision of a powerful Gavião leader and described by Iara Ferraz (1983), the Gavião managed to get control over their own Brazil nut groves, they began to perform their ceremonies again. The groups that collected the nuts were based on age and sex rather than the nuclear family, and the distribution of credit changed. In a similar vein, J. C. Melatti reports that during his fieldwork the Kraho Indians were not planting enough to feed themselves, partly because of their abandonment of the ritual system that provided the symbolic underpinnings of economic activities (Melatti 1970). Here are two cases where it was not the economic system that created the ritual, but the ritual that made possible the mobilization of men, women, and children fundamental to the economic system itself. The Suyá said 'When we sing we eat.' In some cases the corollary was 'When we do not sing, we go hungry.' Singing, production, and distribution were intertwined in the social processes of Suyá ceremonial life.

Cosmology

Suyá cosmology was expressed with special clarity in the design of the village, the use of space, and the ornamentation and use of the body. I have argued that Suyá created space, time, and the person, as well as introduced and controlled the power of transformations through their singing. Song was thus an important way of (re-)establishing the cosmos in its 'correct' order. Singing and ceremonies brought many aspects of the cosmos into direct personal experience. Songs attested to the continued interaction of humans and animals through specialists who heard natural species sing and could teach people their songs. Songs made the events recounted in the myths real to every member of the society. Myths described transformations; in ceremonies people experienced them.

The socio-political context of singing

Suyá performances were not only imbedded in the context of their social definitions of space, time, and person, they were imbedded in the context of their understanding of their history and their strategies for the present. They were residing in the Xingu National Park, which they shared somewhat uneasily with other Indian groups. The possible loss of their lands to ranchers joined eclipses and raids as major threats to their society. This had an effect on their singing and the weight they gave to different song traditions. During the 1970s, Suyá ceremonies were largely performed for internal consumption. In the complex social and political arena of an Indian reservation in the heart of a developing country, however, Suyá singing took on an added dimension – that of the interethnic context in which they were (and continue to be) struggling to survive.

Before about 1915, when some Juruna Indians and their firearm-carrying rubber tapper allies attacked the Suyá village and burned it to the ground, initiating a new and bloodier phase of inter-group hostility, Suyá life was rich in ceremonies identifiable from the ethnography of the other Northern Gê groups. After that attack and a few others, the Suyá raided the Upper Xingu for women. Later some of them sought refuge in Upper Xingu villages for a time, and many aspects of their lives underwent profound changes. One of these was that many of the women were outsiders, who brought with them a technology for making pots and processing food in them, and an entirely new ceremony, Iamuricumã, which they taught the other women and which superseded virtually all the traditional Suyá women's singing (a short excerpt is given as Example 7.4 on the cassette). Suyá women adopted Upper Xingu body ornamentation and hair styles, and by 1959, when they were contacted by representatives of the Brazilian government, the Suyá had the material culture and appearance of a sexually divided village: the men looked like Gê and sang Gê songs, the women looked like Upper Xingu women, and sang Upper Xingu songs.

Amadeu Lanna, a Brazilian anthropologist who visited the Suyá in 1962, characterized them as an impoverished version of the Upper Xingu societies, and as a society in ruins (Lanna 1967). He did not, however, have the chance to learn their language or to see name-based rituals being performed, since his visits were brief and during the dry season. He only observed the Upper Xingu technology adopted by the Suyá – which was devoid of Upper Xingu cosmological significance and consequently used without much attention to other than utilitarian ends.

In addition, the Suyá were rapidly adapting to their new situation in the Xingu park. When they moved back down from the headwaters of the small river where they had sought refuge from rifle-carrying enemies, into the lower reaches of the Suiá-missu, they encountered their former enemies – Juruna, Txukahamae, and Trumai – living there already as well as another group being brought into the area, the Kayabi. Women from one of the Suyá political factions married into the Trumai group. The two small villages, made up of shattered Suyá and Trumai populations, lived close to each other and celebrated rituals, married, and shared food together. The ceremonies they performed were largely Upper Xingu ceremonies (Examples 7.3 and 7.4 on the cassette). Sometimes they sang the songs of other groups in conjunction with ceremonies learned from them (Example 7.1 on the cassette).

Amadeu Lanna was right about the apparent pale reflection of the Upper Xingu he found among the Suyá in the early 1960s. In the years immediately following their move to the Xingu the Suyá became more like the Upper Xingu and their Trumai affines. But the close alliance between the Suyá and Trumai groups ended when a Kayabi man killed a Trumai who was married to two Suyá women, and the rest of the Trumai moved over a hundred miles upriver. Soon after, the Suyá built a village without either a circle of houses or a men's house – abandoning two central spatial features of a traditional Gê village. But the social disarray indicated by their changed village plan was not permanent.

In 1970 forty-one survivors of the Beiços de Pau, or Tapayuna, communities in Mato Grosso were transferred from the Arinos River to the Xingu National Park to live with the Suyá. These Indians looked, talked, lived and sang just like the Suyá ancestors were said to have done. They even sang the same songs for many of the older Suyá ceremonies. They were apparently descendants of a Suyá group that had not moved east from the Tapajos to the Xingu river in the nineteenth century. The new group knew none of the Upper Xingu traditions at all. At the time there was also hope that more survivors would be brought to the Xingu, and that the Suyá community would be large again.

The arrival of the new group set off a Suyá cultural renaissance. The two groups investigated each other's common ceremonies, and shared experiences, songs and ideas. Shortly after this we arrived, extensively trained in Gê ethnography and expecting to find Gê forms of social organization and ritual. They were duly found. The Suyá and Tapayuna had just built a large circular village, with a cleared plaza and a thatched men's house. The Suyá were interested in telling me about how the two groups were related, and in January 1972 I saw my first Mouse Ceremony. I probably watched for the Gê features of their life more carefully because of the comparative nature of my research.

My impression of the Suyá and Lanna's characterization of them could not have been more different. He saw a pale reflection of Upper Xingu societies; I saw a weakened picture of a Gê society. Although apparently a clear example of observer bias and the apparent unreliability of anthropological description, in fact we were both probably correct. What it meant to be Suyá at the times of our visits was quite different. The songs they were singing, the groups they were mobilizing for their ceremonies, and even the technologies they were employing, were very different (Upper Xingu ceremonies were largely based on groups defined by age and sex rather than names). In 1971–3 the Suyá performed a lot of Gê ceremonies, recounted exploits of their common Gê history, and emphasized traits shared by the two related groups. Neither Lanna nor I were wrong; we were simply reporting what we saw. This experience can be extended to other debates over which the ethnographer is observing and describing 'the ethnographic truth' in other regions. A few years can make a big difference not only in what the ethnographer sees, but in what the members of the community have an interest in his or her (and the neighboring communities) knowing about them.

In my later visits, some of the other Upper Xingu ceremonies were performed more fully than they had been in 1971–3. In 1980 the Tapayuna built their own village some distance from the rest of the Suyá, and in 1985 relations between them were severed over witchcraft accusations and assassinations. The Suyá village itself fissioned in 1984, and one of the reasons given for a faction leaving the main Suyá village was a difference of opinion over which ceremonies should be performed. (I am grateful to Tânia Stoltze Lima [personal communication] for recent information about the Suyá.) The strong emphasis on Gê traits may have been unique to the two years of my most intensive work with the Suyá, yet since what I have published is based on just a few years with them, that would have been their anthropological identity if I had not returned regularly over a period of eleven years.

Throughout their history the Suyá have learned the songs of powerful strangers. In the distant past recounted in myths they learned songs from jaguars, mice, and enemies who lived under ground, as well as from Suyá in the throes of permanent transformation into animals. More recently they learned them from the Indians and non-Indians whom they met. But regardless of whether they were dealing with singing jaguars or guitar strumming rock stars, the process was much the same. The songs were incorporated into the collective village life, and performed in the plaza itself. The Suyá treated their contemporaries in the Xingu, and the non-Indians, very much as they treated monsters in the past – they learned their songs and incorporated their material benefits into Suyá society. They sang the songs of the mouse and ate his maize (in the Mouse Ceremony). They sang the songs of the Juruna Indians as they drank the fermented manioc and maize beer they learned to prepare from them (Example 7.1 on the cassette). They sang songs of groups with whom they warred and captured women and children over 200 years ago (Example 7.2), and more recently (7.3, 7.4). They sang songs they have learned from visiting anthropologists (1.5). While the mixture of the various styles produced an apparent musical hodgepodge, the various styles were unified by a common conception of the origin of music and the common processes of its incorporation and performance.

Changes in Suyá identity have been rapid and often based on external events. In a very small community such as theirs, decisions of a few can have tremendous effects on the attitudes of the rest. It may be that someday the Suyá will sing Upper Xingu songs to emphasize their identity as Indians from Mato Grosso. It may be that they will transform themselves into Brazilians – something they might do by wearing Brazilian clothes, refusing to wear body ornaments, and abandoning the village and its collective ritual life. No one had done so yet, but it was an ever present concern during my stay – put into words by Kaikwati in his speech about the young men's abandonment of body ornaments.

Inside the Xingu National Park reserve, each group performed its own rituals, and established its own identity. Even when they shared a ceremony, there were sometimes differences of interpretation. In the Upper Xingu area, roughly one hundred miles upriver, ceremonies were public occasions providing especially good opportunities for visiting other groups. The different communities took turns convening at each others' villages for days of singing, trading, establishing social relationships of various kinds (described in Basso 1973 and Gregor 1977). The Suyá occasionally participated in the Upper Xingu ceremonies, one of the most recent being a pan-Xingu Jawari ceremony in 1978. After weeks of preparation they traveled upriver to sing and dance with the members of Upper Xingu groups. I saw photographs of the widely publicized event in a glossy magazine with the title 'United Nations of the Xingu Make Music Not War' or something to that effect, and recognized the Suyá painted for the ceremony. When I asked the Suyá later how it went, they said they were disgusted. The Upper Xingu Indians sang the songs wrong, and stopped the lance throwing when the Suyá began to get the better of them. They said that it was clear that only the Suyá preserved the traditions correctly, and there was no indication that they would invite the other group down to their village for a reciprocal ceremony.

Although there was considerable intermarriage in the Xingu National Park, no one forgot the origins of the different spouses, and mixed couples often attended ceremonies of both groups. This was particularly clear in the case of the Juruna who had married Suyá women. They would always return for a ceremony from wherever they were, and would take their families to Juruna beer drinking ceremonies whenever these were nearby. Every Indian could recognize a song from the Upper Xingu, the Juruna, the Kayabi, the Northern Kayapo, and the Suyá. Songs were markers of identity, and when people traveled they either carried tapes or went prepared to sing some of their own songs. The Suyá shout song was a form they claimed was not used by any other Indian group they had encountered, and along with their lip discs and ear discs it was described as a unique feature of Suyá society.

Ethnic identity is a process, not a state. Its concrete features depend on the relationships among the various groups in a social arena. In the Suyá case these included the way foreign women were incorporated into the group before 1959, inter-tribal marriage following 1959, and the general social arena in which they lived. Ethnic identity was sensitive to new events, such as the arrival of the Tapayuna. A society may present very different images of itself at relatively short intervals. The songs the Suyá sang and some of the groups they mobilized to perform their ceremonies changed from year to year and from audience to audience, but the emphasis and most of the relationships remained the same over very long periods of time.

Singing for survival

The survival of native societies in Brazil today depends a great deal on the way the groups can mobilize public opinion to help resolve the severe problems they face – the most serious of which is the expropriation of their lands. In order to protect their lands, the many different native groups may adopt the symbols of the 'Indian' that the Brazilians have invented – a generic Indian that does not exist, for example, in the details of the Suyá, the Kayabi, the Tenetehara, or the Munduruku.

The characteristics of the Brazilians' 'Indian' (not to be confused with the Brazilian Indians) varied somewhat according to the Brazilians involved. For the Church the Indians were heathens, but with a primitive purity and virtue that was to be admired and emulated. For the Government the Indians were untutored and economically backward (as one Brazilian general phrased it, Indians were a kind of 'ethnic cyst in the body politic'). For the vast majority of Brazilians, the Indians were either like wild animals or approximated the romantic ideal of the noble savage. Indians were 'people of the forest' who wore feathers, few if any clothes (nudity was an important symbol) and sang and danced. This 'Indian,' perhaps more reminiscent of carnival parades than any true society, was a powerful symbol. In many Brazilians' eyes, an individual who did not go naked, wear feathers, sing, and dance could not be an Indian. This was something a number of groups had to deal with in very concrete ways.

In 1976 the President of the Brazilian National Indian Foundation (FUNAI) visited the Terena, an Indian group he was considering declaring 'non-Indians,' which would have resulted in the loss of their collective title to their lands and made it possible to dispossess them individually. In response to his threat, they plucked some chickens, made some instruments, and sang and danced traditional Terena songs for him. It seemed clear that they were saying 'We are Indians. We wear feathers, we sing our own songs, and we are not to be confused with the rural population. We demand [in our symbolic way] recognition as Indians, or at least as the Brazilians' Indians.' Song and dance was used as a marker not only of a particular identity, but of a generic, Indian, identity. The Terena were successful, at least that time. Their own actions, and considerable pressure from many groups within Brazilian society as well as from abroad, resulted in a temporary withdrawal of the arbitrary disenfranchisement of the Indians by decreeing them non-Indians. The Brazilian Indian movement has grown considerably in numbers and voice during the past decade, which is a hopeful sign for their involvement in political solutions to the pressures on their lands.

In a related example, when the Kiriri Indians of the interior of the state of Bahia in 1982 daringly repossessed lands that had been taken from them, they cleared the very top of a tall hill for a communal garden. On the very top they erected a shelter for the performance of a native ceremony, which they took care to perform at night when their fires and the collective ritual activity could be seen for miles around. The ceremony in question had not been theirs for long; members of the community had learned it from another native group in the Northeast of Brazil. It became, however, a marker of 'Indianness' and of being Kiriri in opposition to non-Indians. It also gave the takeover a religious as well as purely political and economic complexion, and helped maintain, for a time, an active mobilization of their own population.

Body ornamentation – especially feathers on a largely naked body – and singing were traits of 'Indianness' for Brazilians as well as for the Suyá. These naked, feathered, singing people were the Indians of the early explorers and of the carnival parades. Thus it is quite likely that for as long as there is any advantage to be gained from being an 'Indian' rather than a peasant, feathers and singing will be parts of the political strategy for Indian survival. The Suyá may someday sing to survive as the Terena and Kiriri have done, even when the complex interaction of song structure, social groups, and spatial organization outlined in this book has ceased to exist, as it already has for many other native Brazilian groups.

On the other hand, Indian groups can adopt a new musical system altogether. Brian Burkhalter paints a bleak picture of traditional myth and music among the Munduruku Indians, enriched by panning gold and able to buy batteries, phonographs, and records:

> The arrow has no meaning to men who stalk the jaguar, the tapir, the peccary, the deer with rifles; myths make no sense to children clustered about the transistor radio. The sacred flutes gather dust, their reeds rotten and their tunes almost wholly forgotten, and pose no challenge to the phonograph.
> (Burkhalter 1982: 203)

Yet there is nothing to guarantee that the Munduruku will not suddenly use their flutes again in new situations unanticipated by anthropologists, but visible in powerful movements based on ethnic group and a reversion to traditional religion around the world.

The Suyá may choose a middle course, found among some of the Northern Gê groups such as the Krahó and Canela, where traditional ceremonies are interspersed with regional dances using hired bands or phonographs, where the body ornamentation includes new shirts and dresses and the dance style includes couple dances.

Music can be an especially useful tool for establishing a group identity, along with costume and speech styles. Even when lifestyles are changed, village form is abandoned, the birds whose feathers were needed for ornaments are extinct, clothes are worn, and native language forgotten, members of a group may employ song and dance to indicate what they would like themselves to be on a given occasion and to re-establish a continuity with their past. Perhaps that is why so many fragmented groups cling to their musical traditions with a tenacity they show toward little else.

The Suyá may someday sing to let the people know they are Indians. This study has shown, however, that their music has done and continues to do far more than that. It is important to register what music does and can do in societies such as this one, because it demonstrates the close interrelationship between music and social processes in a society where music is not an option but an obligation, where everyone sings but only a few people speak in public, where song structure and social groups replicate each other and are further reproduced in performance. The description of the Mouse Ceremony has been purposefully written in the present tense: in 1972 (and 1976) the Suyá became mice, sang for fifteen hours, and became men again in a vivid experience. Regardless of what may happen in the future, music then had important roles to play in their lives. They valued their songs and they recorded them knowing they would be preserved in an archive. They were proud of their music and wanted the happiness and euphoria characteristic of its performance to continue to be a part of their lives and knowledge of it to be a part of ours.

Implications

An anthropological ethnomusicology

This book is not only about a small group in Mato Grosso, Brazil; it is also about the study of music as an approach to the study of social processes in general. Observations have been made about fieldwork, the anthropological study of music, and the musical study of society. The following points should be stressed:

1. Fieldwork should not be separated from the analytic process and academic presentation. It is argued that fieldwork is fundamentally an interaction with living subjects, not abstracted objects. Under these conditions, researchers must respond to the desires, or demands, of the group with whom they are doing research. Field research is embedded in larger social and political processes which need to be understood from a general, not a personal, perspective. Part of a general move toward a more reflexive anthropology (Boon 1982; Rabinow 1977; Fabian 1983), this book is unusual in the way the field research is built into the argument itself.

2. Ethnomusicologists should not study only those forms that resemble what our society calls music. They should examine the entire speech–music continuum, and in some cases the interrelationship of different performing arts such as music and movement, or movement and sculpture, in order to see what, if anything, makes music different from non-music for its practitioners and its audience. In any society music must be considered as part of, or contrasted with, a number of other ways of structuring time, tone, amplitude, and (in the case of song) language. Music is not only defined by what it is, but also by what it is not. It should be contrasted to silence, to speech, to gesture, and – when present – to writing. The systematic relationships among performing arts may often provide a kind of native musicology, and supplies information about what is important in the different genres. By considering the genres as a system, some of the boundaries isolating not only the performances but the specialists who study them can be lowered and our studies benefited. This work has been begun by a number of authors, but much remains to be done.

3. Attention must be paid to ideas or stories about the origin of music, composition, and the introduction of new musical forms. These concepts are part of what music is, and they are involved in any musical event. It was shown that the ideas about music found among the Suyá, Kaluli, Ancient Greeks and American conservatory musicians could be quite instructive.

4. Musical performances are not only sounds but the contexts of which those sounds are a part. Musical performances are embedded in other events, to which they lend salience and emotional force, and from which they also receive them. Performances cannot be studied without attention to these contexts. Various ways of incorporating the contextual aspects of musical performances into analysis have been suggested.

5. Considerable care should be taken to avoid pre-determining what is music and what is not through recording technique. When the Suyá did not like a recording that omitted their shouts and cries because it was 'too sad,' they were in fact not only criticizing the recording technique employed, but the implicit idea of what music was all about. Some features of Suyá song were nearly impossible to record – for example the cumulative effect of many

people simultaneously singing different things, crying, whooping, laughing, and making other noises in several different parts of the village. We must be on our guard against defining music through our recordings of events.

6. Musical performances are best studied using a variety of approaches. The discussion of rising pitch showed that musical participation, interviewing, recording, archival work, and laboratory work contributed to each other and led to a better understanding of musical performance. Musical transcription, for a long time the starting point of analysis and later revealed to be very problematic, has been shown to be a useful tool for raising questions, but not for providing answers, about musical traditions. When combined with other techniques, transcription can contribute to analysis but should not be confused with it.

7. A time dimension must be incorporated into the analysis. The tendency to confuse what we see with what was, is, and always shall be is widespread. Yet I have shown that the Suyá not only do not sing the same thing all the time, what they do through their song varies with the genre and the ceremony in which it is embedded. Suyá learned other people's songs, sang them, and in a sense became them. The Suyá might be Upper Xingu Indians at one time, their own ancestors at another, and an American anthropologist or a Brazilian peasant through their song and movements at yet other times.

The anthropology of music has often involved the application of anthropological techniques to musical phenomena. This is certainly valid, for music is part of social life. Alan Merriam's *The Anthropology of Music* is – even after twenty years – one of the most important statements of what such an anthropology would be.

There *is* an anthropology of music, and it *is* within the grasp of both the musicologist and the anthropologist. For the former it provides the baseline from which all music sounds are produced and the framework within which those sounds and processes of sounds are fully understood. For the latter it contributes further understanding both of the products and the processes of man's life, precisely because music is simply another element in the complexity of man's learned behavior. Without people thinking, acting, and creating, music sound cannot exist; we understand the sound much better than we understand the total organization of its production.   (1964: viii)

This book has discussed the total organization of the production of Suyá song, from its relationship to other verbal genres to its integral association with economic production and social reproduction. The study of musical performance contributes to anthropology an understanding of performative processes in general. Music is a performance genre, and the anthropological study of music emphasizes the importance of social process as performed, constantly reformulated in creative yet patterned ways. Musical performance is a *structuring* of time, tone, and amplitude in a given way by a given group of people, who may structure their own interactions using very similar organizing principles. Musical events are always different each time they are performed. The Mouse Ceremony will never be exactly the same twice, as the actors change and their intentions differ. There was creativity, fun, and also pattern and continuity to Suyá musical performances. Anthropological theory in the 1980s has seen a convergence of thinking with respect to processes through which societies perpetuate themselves. If societies used to be thought of as constructed of rules, laws, contracts, and social groups, in the 1980s more credence is given to visions of social life as the result of negotiations, practice, production, performance, and 'structuration' (see Ortner 1984; Bourdieu 1977; and Giddens 1979). This literature is paralleled by an increased interest in the performance of language, music, and dance. A musical anthropology is an anthropology attentive to social processes as intentional performances, 'structurations,' and creative solutions within a range of patterns and within certain perceived historical situations.

Suyá society was an orchestra, its village was a concert hall, and its year a song. Their singing created a certain kind of settlement, in which sounds revealed what vision could not penetrate. Singing coordinated collective labor in certain ways, and encouraged certain forms of group distribution. Which collective groups were activated depended on what songs were sung, which depended on the season of the year and the social and political context. Through their singing, the Suyá – and I suspect many other native South American communities – incorporated the power of the outside world into their social reproduction and simultaneously established the changing, growing self-ness of themselves as members of a community and re-established the form and existence of the community itself. Shouting new songs, leaping, dancing, stamping, and singing the Mouse Songs they participated in a creative act that far transcended the sounds alone, but was a part of many aspects of their lives and the social processes and institutions of their society.

Afterword to the Illinois Paperback Edition

August 2003

The Suyá and I are delighted that the University of Illinois Press is reissuing *Why Suyá Sing* in a paperback edition. Tired of making copies of the recording and authorizing photocopying of parts of the book for course readers, I was sorry so few people had the opportunity to hold the book, play the recording, and see them as an integrated, multimedia argument. The Suyá are happy because they receive all the royalties from it, are proud of their music, and are fighting hard to protect the way of life described here in a rapidly-changing part of Brazil.

I have changed very little in the previous chapters for this edition—a date, a reference, and one audio example. *Why Suyá Sing* is a product of a certain time, written at a certain moment in my own intellectual development. While I would not necessarily write the same book today, and would certainly have given more attention to some issues now than I did then, further fieldwork between 1994 and 2003 has confirmed the accuracy of what I wrote, and many of the general points about the study of music remain relevant. In particular, a massive, energetic performance of the Mouse Ceremony in January 1996 was so basically similar to the performance described in these pages that I am quite content to leave the account unchanged.

I wrote this short book, with little jargon and very few musical transcriptions, because I wanted to reach an audience of non-musical anthropologists who might turn their attention to music and performance. Anthropology, however, has largely taken other directions, and musical performances are more often analyzed by writers in cultural studies, performance studies, and the growing field of ethnomusicology. If anthropology has not become more musical, those fields certainly have. To those readers this book offers a look at a set of ideas about and performances of music and dance that is almost totally removed from capitalist markets. When music is created by animals and performed only in essentially sacred events, many aspects of its significance are different than when it is a commodity. Yet, in spite of the differences, the Suyá enthusiasm for the euphoria attained through singing and dancing reveals some of the same motivation that turns people in advanced capitalism into musicians and fans.

If I were starting to write this book today, I would pay more attention to individual choice in performances and to the complex processes by which the members of the Suyá community decide which ceremony to perform. I would relate the work to some of the fine ethnographies of music that have been published in the past fifteen years in the United States, as well as to the critiques of the ethnographic enterprise. I would also discuss some of the superb writings about Indian music being written by Brazilian scholars today (among them Bastos 1990, 1995, and the works of his students, as yet largely unpublished; other works that relate to this one include Viveiros de Castro 1992 on cosmology and Toner 2001 on Australian Aborigines). There is one aspect of my research, however, I would not change at all. The most interesting question for me is still "why." Why do the Suyá sing and dance the way they do? Why do we? And where do we look for the answers to these questions?

Mato Grosso, 2003

While my ideas about Suyá music have not changed a great deal since 1982, the year of my last field trip before writing *Why Suyá Sing,* the lives of the Suyá have been transformed by some of the processes I mention in the final chapter—the encroaching frontier, their desire for trade goods, and the possibilities offered by new media. Somewhat to my surprise, the Suyá have been very active participants in these processes and have shaped the way these things have affected them. Music has been a part of their interaction with local ranchers and national as well as international agencies, and it continues to be performed because it is "good" and makes participants "euphoric" while it also expresses solidarity, determination, and essential identity. By invitation of the Suyá, I was both a participant and an observer in their dramatic story, which I recount below.

An Appeal for Help

In 1993 faxes were still considered pretty high-tech. That was the basis of my surprise when a sheet of paper churned out at Smithsonian Folkways Recordings read, in translation from the Portuguese: "We are having difficulties with invasions of our land. Before we do anything drastic, we would like to talk with you. Could you please come to visit us? Kuiussi Suyá, Chief."

I had not visited the Suyá in twelve years, although Brazilian colleagues occasionally sent me word of them. I had decided my fieldwork phase was over after I had taken a number of questions to the field and accurately guessed in advance what the answers would be. If I had no questions I couldn't predict the answers to, and nothing had surprised me, I decided further fieldwork wasn't as important as sitting down and writing what I had learned. Even if the cause was a lack of imagination on my part rather than a lack of new things to learn, I seemed to have finished what I was capable of doing. I gave myself ten years to finish publishing that research; *Why Suyá Sing,* my third book, came out thirteen years after I received my Ph.D.

My wife and I still cared about the Suyá both as individuals and as a community. I sent royalties to them through third parties, but had no illusion that they needed us in any profound way—they were resourceful people. I continued to support efforts to demarcate Indian lands. Through Byzantine channels we occasionally sent each other tape recordings of our respective music (Seeger family concerts went south; Suyá ceremonies and commentary came north). I became deeply involved in issues of audiovisual archiving (as director of the Indiana University Archives of Traditional Music from 1982 until 1988) and record production (as director and curator of Smithsonian Folkways Recordings from 1988 through 2000), and like most researchers I had field notebooks filled with topics I had not yet addressed.

Then, in the fall of 1993 I received that fax. The message had clearly been dictated to someone and sent to the Smithsonian from Brasília. The appeal was totally unexpected—the Suyá had always thought themselves perfectly capable of handling their affairs and had never sought my advice before. They considered me "their White man," however, and they knew that I had been active in Indian rights issues when I was teaching in Brazil between 1975 and 1982.

I have always believed that researchers have an obligation to use their knowledge in the "real" world of social and political action. This is especially the case when that knowledge can be used to benefit the community from which it came. It was not a question of whether I would go but when and with whom. Good theory can be forged in the crucible of practice, and having shared Suyá food and fortunes for two years, I was ready to return even if I had no new questions. Much of what I embarked on after 1994 falls under the heading of "applied anthropology" or "applied ethnomusicology" because I was taking knowledge obtained for a scholarly purpose and using it to benefit the Suyá themselves.

My wife, Judy, and I decided to make it a family visit. We would take our two daughters, Elisa, seventeen, and Hiléia, fifteen, who had visited the Suyá thirteen years before and were accustomed to seeing baby pictures of themselves naked, painted, and surrounded by Suyá children. It took time to raise money and clear my schedule for a trip during the height of the dry season (July to August), when travel is usually easier, malaria less prevalent, and schools in the Northern Hemisphere have long summer vacations.

I wondered what I might do to help with the land conflict. It seemed to me the Suyá needed a way to find out who was entering their land and to obtain demonstrable proof of that illegal entry. Acting on a colleague's suggestion, I submitted an application to the Rex Foundation, established by the Grateful Dead, with a request for money to purchase an outboard motor and video equipment that ran on batteries charged by solar panels, as well as for some funds for training two Suyá in camera work and basic editing. I imagined the Suyá using the outboard motor to patrol their territory and the video camera to film the invaders, who could then be apprehended by government officials whose job was to protect the rights of the indigenous peoples. I thought this might reduce the possibility of violent encounters between the Suyá and those entering their land.

There was another reason to introduce video to the Suyá. I thought it was important for the Suyá to master the means of producing video materials before they became consumers of television programming. I was sure that parabolic antennae would eventually spring up in the Xingu region, and generator-powered televisions would become part of the daily life of the Suyá. Based on my observation of their use of audiocassette recorders to play their own music, I thought it would be helpful to give them an opportunity to create their own use of video before the advertising agencies created one for them. It was a good project, and we received the money and made our plans, unaware that the Suyá were not waiting for us to arrive before acting on their own.

We landed in Brasília in June 1994 to find that the Suyá had invaded a group of nearby ranches and had expelled all the Brazilians from them except for a few hostages, whom they held until the Ministry of Justice agreed to review their claim to the land the ranches had occupied. The immediate crisis was over, but the employees at the Indian Foundation in Brasília hoped we could help bring peace to the region. We were the only non-Suyá who spoke their language, and they had been asking for us. Never did my permission to enter the field come so quickly.

We arrived in the village after a grueling 30–hour bus ride to the small frontier settlement of São José do Xingu, known as "Bang Bang." Several Suyá met us in a pickup truck that had been given to them by a Suyá man living in another tribe who had been captured as a child. His community, the Gorotire Kayapó, had taken control of the gold mining on their land, and apparently had trucks to spare. We drove to the right bank of the Suiá Missu River, and after a short motorboat ride we arrived in their new village, called Rikó, at the very edge of what was then their territory. They slung our four hammocks in the same corner of the chief's house we had always used, gave us something to eat, and told us all about the raid, the hostages, and the singing that shaped the events. They recounted singing the song for raids (and eclipses) they had performed before leaving to take the captives, and listed the ceremonies they had performed since. They were euphoric—"when we are happy we sing," and our arrival was considered an additional strategic success of theirs. In their understanding, a tape they had sent had made us homesick to visit them again, and then their fax had made it official.

The next day they gave me a tour of the new village, which revealed some very traditional features—especially its large circular formation with a men's house near the center. All the houses were in their "correct" locations with respect to the sun and to each other, and trails led out to the surrounding gardens on three sides and to the river on the fourth. But instead of the seven houses of the earlier village, eighteen of them surrounded the very large plaza. Among the novelties were a schoolhouse, with bilingual Suyá teachers (see Temptxi Suyá et al. 1999), and a pharmacy with a Suyá technician. The teachers and the medical technician had been trained with funds from the Rain Forest Foundation set up by the popular musician Sting for the Kayapo and neighboring indigenous groups in the Xingu Indigenous Park. With my grant from the Rex Foundation, it seemed that popular musicians were having a strong impact on the lives of the Suyá and their neighbors, as were some Brazilian NGOs, among them the Instituto Socioambiental.

It soon became clear that the Suyá did not expect me to go hunting or fishing anymore. They had other ways they wanted me to be useful. The population of this village had grown, and there were plenty of young men to go fishing. We talked for hours about their land claim and the challenges ahead in making it legal. When my command of Suyá—decidedly rusty after twelve years—failed, most of the men now had no difficulty taking up the subject in Portuguese.

One of their biggest problems was entirely new since my previous visit—it was the quality of the water they traveled on, fished in, bathed in, and drank. The clear Suiá Missu River had been polluted by cattle and muddied by upstream agricultural runoff and wetlands drainage projects. The Suyá complained that the bass couldn't see the small fish to eat them and were thus small and without fat; moreover the Suyá themselves couldn't see the fish in the murky water, and had ceased using bows and arrows for fishing. They complained that the water was giving them dysentery. The headwaters of the river were far outside their territory and largely beyond their control. So they wanted to protect the headwaters of the last small affluent still unpolluted—the Wawi River, whose mouth marked the very edge of the Xingu Indigenous Park, and whose headwaters lay outside it. When a Suyá out fishing heard sounds of chainsaws near the river, they decided the time had come to act. They described with glee the fear of the vastly-outnumbered Brazilian ranchers surrounded by club-wielding, painted, feather-wearing men, and the fate of the hostages kept in a hole in the ground in back of one of the houses (where they were well fed and well treated, but terrified). They stressed to everyone they didn't want to kill anybody, but wanted the lands back on which they had lived in the 1950s—since then occupied by ranches.

My wife and daughters soon fit into the life of the village. Judy processed manioc and sang Upper Xingu songs with the women (like examples 7.1 and 7.4), and both men and women sang "Abiyoyo" with us (as in example 1.4). Our younger daughter taught the Suyá youth the Electric Slide, and gales of laughter reached the men's circle in the evening as the youth played on the periphery of the plaza—the traditional location for their games—learning the new dance and teaching our daughters their language. Suyá women, too, had assumed some new roles (or reassumed some old ones). Two women had learned new songs from "spirits" and introduced them to the community. Some were learning to read; others had mastered quite a lot of Portuguese; and the multiethnic cuisine of the Suyá had added some new dishes when the ingredients were available—coffee with sugar, rice and beans, fish fried in oil. Judy and I spent our days slowly learning to see the differences, and began to feel once again that we understood only a small fraction of what was before our eyes.

There was also a lot of new music to be heard in the village on cassette players and some

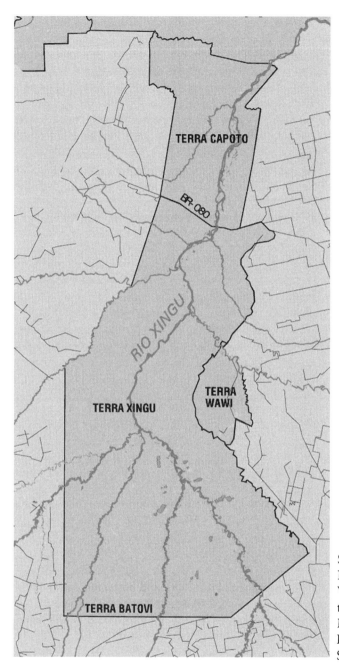

Small map of the Xingu
National Park showing
Wawi addition acquired by
the Suyá in the 1900s.
Map courtesy of the
Instituto Socioambiental,
São Paulo, Brazil.

radios. It was *música sertaneja*, a Brazilian popular music somewhat similar to U.S. country music, and popular throughout the interior of the country. Some young men had collections of tapes and proudly displayed them. Some nights the young men and women gathered in one of the residential houses to dance to *música sertaneja*, to the disapproval of some members of the older generation. I inventoried two cassette collections and tried to learn more about what they thought of it. Most of the recordings appeared to be pirate editions (commercially pirated, with color inserts). One of the important distinctions of this music from other genres is that no Suyá played or sang the songs; they just danced to them (Seeger 2003).

After a few days, the Suyá decided we should visit one of the ranches to discuss the future. The ousted Brazilians had been allowed back on their lands while the case was under review. We left all the women behind—this was clearly not a social visit—and traveled upriver in a fleet of canoes and a motorboat to a spot on the riverbank where an overgrown vehicle track terminated. The Suyá wore body paint and a variety of feather headdresses, and all of them carried weapons—guns, clubs, or bows and arrows. Was this elaborate theater? Or was this an armed party on a raid? It was both. The Suyá were very aware of the importance of presenting themselves as "wild" Indians to the surrounding population. It was a key to their ability to evict ranchers from their lands without bloodshed.

A ranch manager was waiting for us in his truck. He probably did not expect twenty armed Indians to attend the meeting; he certainly did not expect an American researcher to bring up the rear. He was reluctant to have me come along and said, "I don't like Americans very much." At that point, one of the biggest Suyá picked up his club and attacked a rotten stump next to the truck shouting (in Suyá) that people who did not like their friends might end up like the stump. The pieces of rotten wood that flew every which way as he smashed the stump into pulp needed no translation. The rancher clarified that while he did not like Americans as a group, the present company was certainly an exception and if they wanted me along I was welcome to come. I was even given a seat in the cab where I heard more about his anger at foreigners who were helping the Indians with their land claims. "Sting wouldn't last more than twenty minutes around here before he was in someone's gun sight," he assured me. Twenty armed Suyá in back made this easy to shrug off, and I was busy shaking the ants out of my clothes anyway, but the Suyá chief was listening carefully.

Driving through the forest was new to me. The land was totally flat, and the road completely straight. It was overhung with vines that tore the flesh and littered with trees that had fallen across it. The truck bounced unmercifully and the cab was hot and stuffy. Biting ants and other insects, flicked from the leaves by the passing truck, made the hot ride even more uncomfortable. I had enjoyed my months fishing with the Suyá on the rivers and hunting in the forest, but this mechanized travel was a totally new experience—and not one I preferred. After three hours or so we emerged suddenly from the forest onto a slightly better road flanked by huge pastures spotted with white Brahma cattle. Hardly a tree remained and the heat became even more oppressive—it was an amazing transformation. A few minutes more and we were sitting in the relative cool of the ranch-house veranda. The few ranch hands were vastly outnumbered by the Suyá, who had taken off their shirts, renewed their paint, and put on their headdresses toward the end of the ride.

I videotaped hours of discussion between the Suyá and the ranch manager, who was alternately blustering and conciliatory. Later, when I went to the bathroom I was surprised to be accompanied by four armed Suyá. When I went to bathe in the cool stream I was not alone—more Suyá just happened to want to come along. That night I slept surrounded by Suyá who assured me that they would not let me be killed like Chico Mendes in Acre or hanged as a priest had been in Altamira. Chico Mendes was shot taking a bath in back of the house where his bodyguards were sitting; the priest was hanged in his own church. The chief had been listening on the drive. Even though I had nothing to do with the Suyá decision to take back their land by force, they were probably right in thinking that I could be blamed for it.

Applied ethnomusicology can be dangerous. There is no telling who may get hurt if one makes a serious mistake. I always assumed the Suyá knew the local political situation better than I, and that my skill was with words and documents. The Suyá had summoned me down to watch, or maybe to help, them negotiate a very difficult transformation of lands from private property to federal property designated for their use. Land is an explosive issue throughout the country. I slept soundly; but I am not sure the Suyá did. We were all happy to return to the village the next day.

Judy, Elisa, Hiléia, and I left after a few weeks, profoundly changed by our new experiences. Our relations with the Suyá had been reestablished; our daughters had a whole new view of the world they lived in. There was a lot for me to learn about the relations between the Suyá and their neighbors. And there was a lot for me to do to demonstrate the legitimacy of the Suyá claim to the lands they had taken by force.

I wrote a detailed justification of their occupation of the lands surrounding the villages they occupied in the 1950s, based on my 1970s research, showing that the Suyá had continued to use certain resources found there after they were moved within the boundaries of the Xingu Indigenous Park. Many dedicated Brazilian scholars and lawyers also helped the Suyá regain their land, among them anthropologists Vanessa Lea (1997) and Mariana Kawall Leal Ferreira (1998), as well as people working for the Instituto Socioambiental in São Paulo (www.institutosocioambiental.org) and the Fundação Nacional do Indio (FUNAI) in Brasília.

I returned the next July, with a *Smithsonian* magazine photographer, a writer, and our older daughter, Elisa, to prepare a story for the magazine's issue on research undertaken by Smithsonian scholars as part of its celebration of the 150th anniversary of the founding of the Smithsonian Institution in 1846. The article, "The Suyá Sing and Dance and Fight for a Culture in Peril" (Roberts 1996), brought their struggle to the magazine's millions of readers.

On the 1995 visit I discovered that, instead of using the video cameras to document invasions of their land, they had turned the cameras on themselves and begun a massive documentation of their own traditions. They filmed house construction, collective gardens, fishing expeditions, and many, many ceremonies. The two young men who had been chosen for training in filming and editing were much less shy than I had been about getting into the middle of things. Since they knew the events better than I, they could position themselves well and used the camera well. Just as I had hoped, they were using video in an imaginative way. Even though they had a small collection of commercial videotapes, they did not as yet have a satellite antenna. They proudly showed us what they had done and I helped refurbish and replace missing equipment to keep the project going.

Our visits continued, at the request of the Suyá, usually for fairly short periods of time sandwiched between other obligations. I attended the Mouse Ceremony discussed in this afterword in 1996. My wife and I returned in 2001 to celebrate the thirtieth anniversary of our first trip. On that visit the Suyá gave me their video archive to copy and preserve (a wonderful store of tapes made between 1994 and 2000), and we replaced their camera and equipment.

In 2001 the Suyá had installed a television in the men's house, serviced by a parabolic antenna just outside it and powered by a generator some distance beyond the edge of the village, which they would start up at dusk so they could watch the news. I asked how they got the equipment, because it wasn't what I had given them. They said they had gone upriver to burn down the house of a rancher who refused to stop dredging his small river and muddying the river the Suyá lived on. According to their description, when they arrived in force at the ranch the person in charge said, "go ahead, take everything, burn it down." So they did—they took the television, the parabolic antenna, the generator, all the chairs they could carry, and set them up in the men's house, where women, too, were invited to watch. This pattern—a collective expedition that brings something back to benefit the whole village—has precedents in myths about the origin of agricultural products, body ornaments, and in many of their dealings with Europeans.

In early October 2001 the Suyá sent a member of the group out to a city to call us and ask if we were all right. They had seen the news about the World Trade Center and Pentagon and the coming war in Afghanistan. Honestly worried about our safety, they suggested that we come live with them in Mato Grosso. It was safer, they said. We were deeply moved by the invitation, and bemused by its inversion of commonly held stereotypes. When we went to Mato Grosso for the first time in 1971, we were leaving security and venturing into a dangerous jungle; today the inhabitants of the jungle were inviting us to join them for our safety.

The Suyá have not accomplished all this without tension and disagreement. Today there are four Suyá villages instead of one—three smaller ones and the new large one. There are challenges to the chief's leadership; some youth like to drink alcohol when they can; there are frustrations with the bilingual education program; the pharmacy is often without medical supplies. A few Suyá, including the Chief's son-in-law, spend a lot of time in Canarana, a fast-growing agricultural city inhabited largely by immigrants from southern states of Brazil, and send their children to school there. Food is still shared widely, but industrialized goods do not go as far. Some houses clearly have more material goods than others and that fosters jealousy and potential accusations of witchcraft.

These tensions may make the successful performance of ceremonies all the more important. A successful performance unites the village around a collective activity where participation depends on kinship and naming, not on belongings. The chief commented to me that some of the Indians in the region no longer paint themselves or sing and dance, and the residents of a village in another tribe all converted to Protestantism in exchange for support from a missionary organization. "But we sing. We are proud of who we are. When all the Indians get together, we are the ones who paint ourselves and sing."

The Mouse Ceremony, 1996

During my 1995 visit for the *Smithsonian* Magazine, the Suyá told me they planned to perform the Mouse Ceremony when the corn was ripe and asked if I wanted to participate. We talked about *Why Suyá Sing*, a copy of which I had sent down and the introduction to which someone had translated for them. They said they were happy with the book (although my attempts to discuss it in detail were unsuccessful). Their principal criticism was that they didn't like my choice of an example of "everyday speech"—it was too sexually explicit for people to hear. My assurances that no one but they and I could understand it made no difference, so I promised that I would replace it if the book were reissued. (That track is now a discussion of songs that were recorded by a Japanese researcher who visited them in the 1990s).

Another fax, this time in late December 1995: "The corn is ripe. If you want to be in the Mouse Ceremony, come now." I arrived in Brazil on January 3, 1996. I was a bit nervous about returning for the Mouse Ceremony. What would I do if I had gotten it all wrong? What if it was an irrelevant part of their lives today? What if I asked the same questions and got different answers? What if *Why Suyá Sing* were entirely believable but completely wrong? Would I recall the books and return the Kinkeldy Book Award?

The rainy season turns all the roads to slippery sloughs of mud. The Suyá had by then obtained a four-wheel-drive truck, but we barely made it to the bank of the swollen Suiá Missu River. The Suyá were disappointed to find I had come alone (as everyone else in the family was on an academic schedule and had to be in school), but they were happy to see me and enthusiastically told me all about the series of ceremonies they had been performing since I saw them in the dry season. The most recent of these, only four days before, had been an elaborate New Year's Eve ceremony they had invented that combined intoxicating Juruna manioc beer, Suyá singing, dancing to recordings of Brazilian country music, fireworks, and even documenting themselves on videotape imitating the "person in the street" style of the evening news (described in Seeger 2003). But by the time I had arrived, they were deep in the preparations for the first Mouse Ceremony in a number of years. This was clearly going to be a major performance.

Because the village had more than doubled in population since I had seen my last Mouse Ceremony, there were many more children than before. In fact, it was increasingly difficult for the Suyá to find available names for their children, since it was not good to have two living people using the same exact name. Almost every name in every name set had a living incumbent. Names that I had collected in my genealogies of the distant past were reappearing in young children as a result of the demographic explosion after decades with a fairly small population. This meant that every group of males holding the same name was larger than it had been in a long time. Many more dance capes, rattles, feather ornaments, and cotton wrappings were needed than ever before. A lot more food would have to be prepared by the parents of the child being sung over during the ceremony in order to feed the much larger number of celebrants.

This time the Chief's oldest daughter and her husband were the parents of the child to be danced over. The Chief's son-in-law was on the payroll of the Indian Foundation (FUNAI) as a motorist and had a small salary. In addition to their connections and resources, I was enlisted to provide ten kilos of sugar to sweeten the corn drink. The family produced a lot of food for the events. The opening shout song (*akia*) had been performed before I arrived, and children were learning *akia* and singing them in the afternoon. The days passed much as they are described in this book—eating corn, drying burity palm fronds for the dance capes, and going hunting and fishing. The older men were all teaching their sons how to make the capes— a clear attempt to be sure that the young men knew as many details as possible about the ceremony. I was besieged by requests for cassette tapes and batteries so the young men could use tape recorders to learn their new shout songs and also record the ceremony itself. There was almost always a flashing thunderhead in the sky somewhere, and heavy rains were common. As the days progressed, the intensity of the food preparation increased. More and more Suyá married to members of other tribes arrived with their families to participate. The excitement grew, and finally the last day arrived.

The actual order of events was virtually identical to that described in chapter six. The difference was that everything was larger, louder, and more elaborate. There was the same rush to complete the capes, to find all the right feathers and other ornaments, to cut them and paint them and get young children to put them on in the right houses. They leapt, danced, and sang from four in the afternoon until seven the next morning, performing the unison songs at about 10:00 P.M. and 2:00 A.M. After the name sets had all "died" and the dancers had been sprinkled with water in the plaza, they marched down to the riverbank in a single line and threw their ornaments into the water.

After the young men bathed and washed off some of the black ash and red urucum, they gathered in the men's house again, put on soccer uniforms, and began a lively game of soccer in the plaza where they had danced all night. I commented to one of the young men as he pulled on his soccer shoes, "Aren't you tired? You must be really tough." He replied, "The Suyá have always been tough," and dashed out into the plaza shouting "my name receiver, kick it over here!"

In 1976, most Suyá adults would have responded to my comment "our fathers and grandfathers were tough; we are few and weak." Clearly, a lot had changed. The Suyá were more numerous (at 250 total) than they had been in decades. They were newly victorious and they were tough.

The Bee Ceremony, 2003

In 2003 the Suyá invited us to visit them again to celebrate the completion of a new village built on the land finally officially returned to them. My wife, our younger daughter Hiléia, and I arrived in August to find them putting the finishing touches on the men's house in the west side of a huge circular village with 22 houses. It was erected on the very site of the village where many of the elders were living in 1957 when the Brazilians peacefully contacted them and moved them off their land. It is only about five kilometers from the ranch house where those tense discussions took place in 1994. That land now belongs to the Suyá.

The new village is huge. If the 1970 village was a concert hall, this new one is a stadium—literally, for there is a full-sized soccer field in the middle of it with a great deal of room to spare—and it somewhat dwarfs the groups of dancers. It is also accessible by truck, and the Suyá have begun trash pickup, and use radios (provided by another grant from the Rex Foundation) to communicate among their four villages. But in house design and layout this village is if anything more traditional than their last one. When we arrived the Suyá from all the villages congregated in the large new one and began the Bee Ceremony (aimendaupá), whose lovely songs are among my favorites. Euphoric, we commemorated their remarkable achievement.

How are the Suyá? As this afterword has shown, they are doing quite well. They are astute politicians; they are imposing opponents; they are aware that their collective performances of music and dance give them a particular authenticity in the eyes of Brazilians. But their singing is not only for outside audiences. They continue to introduce young children into the collective life of the plaza; they continue to become euphoric through singing; they continue to define many facets of time, space, social identity, and life by the singing and dancing that shape them. They are active shapers of their futures, whatever those may turn out to be.

As for us? While our contemporaries among the Suyá have spent the last 30 years hunting and fishing, canoeing and running, we have spent them in offices and automobiles. They are better able to hunt all day, or go to the gardens and process manioc, then dance all night and endure the hard traveling than my wife and I. As much as I liked my new shout song in 1996, taught to me by a man without his spirit, I think the day is coming when I will sit on the sidelines and give the falsetto shout I have been practicing, passing into another age grade and manner of musical participation altogether.

On another level, Judy and I feel privileged to have had the opportunity to live and learn from the Suyá for much of the past 32 years. I just wonder whether I have perhaps forgotten to ask the most important questions when they still knew the answers. What keeps me up at night is not what I have learned—some of which is presented in this book—but what I may never have thought to ask.

Additional Acknowledgements

Since the publication of this book in 1987 the Smithsonian Institution, the John Simon Guggenheim Memorial Foundation, and the University of California Los Angeles have supported my research among the Suyá. I am grateful to all of them, as well as to the Rex Foundation for funding Suyá projects and to the University of Illinois Press for publishing this new edition. Pete Reiniger at Smithsonian Folkways Recordings kindly remastered the audio tracks; the Instituto Socioambiental in Brazil generously granted permission to use one of their maps (others, and an online encyclopedia of Brazilian Indian societies, can be found on their outstanding website at (*www.socioambiental.org*); and to people too numerous to mention who have made suggestions and given encouragement over the years. When the Cambridge University Press editor read my dedication, she cautioned me about it, saying that authors are sometimes embarrassed by their dedications years later. I am happy to write that I am as comfortable with it now as I was then, and renew the dedication and acknowledgements to the first edition with enduring certainty and gratitude.

Selected Bibliography

Bastos, Rafael Jose de Menezes 1993. A Saga do Yawari: Mito, Música, e História no Alto Xingu. In Eduardo Viveiros de Castro and Manuela Carneiro da Cunha (eds.) *Amazônia: Etnologia e Historia Indigena*. Sao Paulo: Núcleo de História Indigena e Indigenismo da Universidade de São Paulo, 117–46.

——1995. A Festa da Jaguartirica: Uma Partitura Critico-Interpretativa. Ph.D. dissertation, Universidade de São Paulo.

——1995. Esboço de uma Teoria da Musica: Para Além de uma Antropologia se Música e de uma Musicologia sem Homem. *Anuario Antropologico* 93: 9–73.

——1997. Music in Lowland South America: A Review Essay. *World of Music* 39(2): 143–51.

——1999. *A Musicológica Kamayura*. 2nd Edition. Florianopolis: EDUFSC (Editora da Universidade Federal de Santa Catarina).

Ferreira, Mariana Kawall Leal 1998. Perícia Histórico-antropológica da AI Wawi dos índios Suya. Brasilia: Fundação Nacional do Indio (working paper).

Lea, Vanessa R. 1997. Parque Indígena do Xingu: Laudo antropológico. Campinas: Unicamp.

Roberts, David 1996. The Suyá Sing and Dance and Fight for a Culture in Peril. With photographs by Enrico Ferorelli. *Smithsonian* (May 1996): 62–75.

Seeger, Anthony 1974–2003. A complete list of the author's publications on the Suyá may be found at http://www.ethnomusic.ucla.edu/people/seegercv.htm.

——2003. Globalization from a Local Perspective in Brazil: The Suyá Indians and Música Sertaneja. In Steve Loza (ed.) *Musical Cultures of Latin America, Global Effects, Past and Present. Selected Reports in Ethnomusicology*, vol. 11. Los Angeles: UCLA Ethnomusicology Publications. Pp. 121–128.

Suyá, Temptxi et al. 1999. Kisêdjê Kapêrê: Livro Para Alfabetização na Língua Suyá. São Paulo: Instituto Socioambiental.

Toner, Peter 2001. When The Echoes Have Gone: A Yolngu Musical Anthropology. Ph.D. dissertation, Australian National University.

Viveiros de Castro, Eduardo B. 1992. *From the Enemy's Point of View: Humanity and Divinity in an Amazonian Society*. Chicago: University of Chicago Press.

Bibliography

Aytai, Desidério 1985. *O Mundo Sonoro Xavante*. Coleção Museu Paulista, *Etnologia*, vol. 5. São Paulo: Universidade de São Paulo.

Basso, Ellen B. 1973. *The Kalapalo Indians of Central Brazil*. New York: Holt, Rinehart & Winston, Inc.

1985. *A Musical View of the Universe*. Philadelphia: University of Pennsylvania Press

Bastos, Rafael J. de M. 1978. *A Musicológica Kamayurá: Para uma Antropologia de Comunicação no Alto Xingu*. Brasilia: Fundação Nacional do Índio

Bauman, Richard and Joel Sherzer (eds.) 1974. *Explorations in the Ethnography of Speaking*. Cambridge: Cambridge University Press

Beaudet, Jean-Michel 1982. Musiques d'Amérique tropicale: discographie analytique et critique des amérindiens de basses terres. *Journal de la Société des Américanistes* 68: 149–203

Béhague, Gerard (ed.) 1984. *Performance Practice: Ethnomusicological Perspectives*. Westport: Greenwood Press

Bergman, Roland W. 1980. *Amazonian Economics: The Simplicity of Shipibo Indian Wealth*. Syracuse: Syracuse University Press

Blacking, John 1967. *Venda Children's Songs: A Study in Ethnomusicological Analysis*. Johannesburg: Witwatersrand University Press

1973. *How Musical is Man?* Seattle: University of Washington Press

1982. The structure of musical discourse: the problem of the song text. *Yearbook for Traditional Music* 14: 15–24

Bloch, Maurice 1974. Symbols, song, dance and features of articulation: is religion an extreme form of traditional authority? *Archive of European Sociology* 15: 55–81

Boilès, Charles 1982. Process of musical semiosis. *Yearbook for Traditional Music* 14:24–45

Boon, James 1982. *Other Tribes and Other Scribes*. Cambridge: Cambridge University Press

Bourdieu, Pierre 1977. *Outline of a Theory of Practice*. Cambridge: Cambridge University Press

Bowra, C. M. 1962. *Primitive Song*. Cleveland: The World Publishing Co.

Burkhalter, Steve B. 1982. Amazon gold rush: markets and the Munduruku Indians. Ph.D. Dissertation, Columbia University

Cameu, Helza 1977. *Introdução ao Estudo da Música Indígena Brasileira*. Rio de Janeiro: Conselho Federal de Cultura e Departamento de Assuntos Culturais

Carneiro, Robert 1961. Slash and burn cultivation among the Kuikuro and its implications for cultural development in the Amazon basin. Antropologica Supplement no. 2: Wilbert, J. (editor) *The Evolution of Horticultural Systems in Native South America*. 47–67. Caracas

Crocker, J. Christopher 1977. My brother the parrot. In Sapir, J. David, and Christopher Crocker (eds.) *The Social Use of Metaphor*. Philadelphia: University of Pennsylvania Press. Pp. 164–193

Da Matta, Roberto 1982. *A Divided World: Apinaye Social Structure*. Cambridge: Harvard University Press

Densmore, Frances 1956. *Seminole Music*. Washington D.C.: Smithsonian Institution Bureau of Ethnology, Bulletin 161

Dobkin de Rios, Marlene and Fred Katz 1975. Some relationships between music and hallucinogenic ritual: the 'jungle gym' of consciousness. *Ethos* 3: 64–76

Durkheim, Emile, 1965. *The Elementary Forms of Religious Life*. J. W. Swain, Trans. New York: Free Press

Evans-Pritchard, E. E. 1940. *The Nuer*. London: Oxford University Press.

Fabian, Johannes 1983. *Time and the Other: How Anthropology Makes its Object*. New York: Columbia
    University Press
Feld, Steven 1982. *Sound and Sentiment; Birds, Weeping, Poetics, and Song in Kaluli Expression*.
    Philadelphia: University of Pennsylvania Press
    1984. Sound structure as social structure. *Ethnomusicology* 27: 383–409
Ferraz, Iara 1983. Os Parkatêjê das matas do Tocantins: A epopéia de um lider Timbira. M.A.
    dissertation, Department of Social Sciences, University of São Paulo
Franchetto, Bruna, 1986. Falar Kuikuro. Ph.D. Thesis, Museu Nacional/Federal University of Rio de
    Janeiro
Frisbie, Charlotte (ed.) 1980. *Southwestern Ritual Drama*. Albuquerque: University of New Mexico
    Press
Giddens, Anthony 1979. *Central Problems in Social Theory*. Berkeley and Los Angeles: University of
    California Press
Goffman, Erving 1973 [1959]. *The Presentation of Self in Everyday Life*. Woodstock N.Y.: Overlook
    Press
Gregor, Thomas 1977. *Mehinaku, The Drama of Everyday Life in a Brazilian Indian Village*. Chicago:
    University of Chicago Press
Gross, Daniel 1979. A new approach to central Brazilian social organization. In Margolis, M. and W.
    Carter (eds.) *Brazil, Anthropological Perspectives*. New York: Columbia University Press
Herndon, Marcia 1974. Analysis: the herding of sacred cows? *Ethnomusicology* 18: 219–262
Herndon, Marcia and Roger Brunyate (eds.) 1976. *Proceedings from the Symposium on Form in Perform-
    ance, Hard-Core Ethnography*. Austin: Office of the College of Fine Arts, the University of Texas
Herndon, Marcia and Norma McLeod (eds.) 1980. *The Ethnography of Musical Performance*. Norwood:
    Norwood Editions
Herzfeld, Michael 1979. Exploring a metaphor. In *Journal of American Folklore* 92: 285–302
    1985. *Poetics of Manhood; Contest and Identity in a Cretan Mountain Village*. Laurenceville: Princeton
    University Press
Hubert, Henri, and Marcel Mauss 1964 [1898]: *Sacrifice, its Nature and Function*. Chicago: University
    of Chicago Press
Hugh-Jones, Christine 1980. *From the Milk River: Spatial and Temporal Processes in Northwest Amazo-
    nia*. Cambridge: Cambridge University Press
Hugh-Jones, Stephen 1980. *The Palm and the Pleiades: Initiation and Cosmology in Northwest Amazonia*.
    Cambridge: Cambridge University Press
Izikowitz, Karl G. 1935. *Musical and Other Sound Instruments of the South American Indians*. Goteborg:
    Kungl. Vetenskaps-och Vitterhets-Samhalles Handlingar
Keil, Charles 1979. *Tiv Song*. Chicago: University of Chicago Press
Kensinger, Kenneth 1973. *Banisteriopsis* usage among the Peruvian Cashinahua. In Harner, Michael
    (ed.) *Hallucinogens and Shamanism*. Oxford: Oxford University Press. Pp. 1–9
Kingsbury, Henry 1984. Music as a cultural system. Ph.D. Dissertation, Department of Anthro-
    pology, Indiana University
Koetting, James 1984. Africa/Ghana. In Titon, Jeff (ed.) *Worlds of Music*. New York: Shirmer Books
Ladeira, Maria Elise 1982. A troca de nomes e a troca de cônjuges: uma contribuição ao estudo de
    parentesco timbira. M.A. thesis, Department of Anthropology, University of São Paulo
Lanna, Amadeu D. 1967. La division sexuelle du travail chez les Suyá du Brésil Central. *L'Homme* 8:
    67–72
Lave, Jean C. 1979. Cycles and trends in Krĩkati naming cycles. In Maybury-Lewis, D. (ed.) *Dialectical
    Societies*. Cambridge: Harvard University Press. Pp. 16–46
Lea, Vanessa R. 1986. Nomes e Nekrets Kayapó, Uma Concepção de Riqueza. Ph.D. Thesis, Museu
    Nacional/Federal University of Rio de Janeiro
Lévi-Strauss, Claude 1963a. *Totemism*. Translated by Rodney Needham. Boston: Beacon Press
    1963b. *Structural Anthropology*. New York: Basic Books
    1969. *The Raw and the Cooked; Introduction to a Science of Mythology*. Translated by John and Doreen
    Weightman. New York: Harper and Row, Inc.

Lins, Elizabeth Travassos 1984. A Música dos Caiabi. M.A. Dissertation, Museu Nacional/Federal University of Rio de Janeiro

Lomax, Alan 1968. *Folk Song Style and Culture*. Washington D.C.: American Association for the Advancement of Science, publication no. 8

McAllester, David P. 1954. *Enemy Way Music*. Cambridge: Peabody Museum Papers, vol. 41 no. 13

Maybury-Lewis, David, ms. n.d. Dual organization as will-o'-the-wisp. Paper presented at a conference on dualism, Jerusalem, 1983

Melatti, Julio C. 1970. O Sistema Social Krahó. Ph.D. Dissertation, University of São Paulo

    1974. Myth and shaman. In Lyon, Patricia J. (ed.) *Native South Americans; Ethnology of the Least Known Continent*. Boston: Little, Brown & Co.

    1976. Nominadores e Genitores: um Aspecto do Dualismo Krahó. In Egon Schaden (ed.) *Leituras da Etnologia Brasileira*. São Paulo: Companhia Editora Nacional

Merriam, Alan P. 1960. Ethnomusicology: discussion and definition of the field. *Ethnomusicology* 4: 107–114

    1964. *The Anthropology of Music*. Evanston Illinois: Northwestern University Press

Nimuendaju, Curt 1942. *The Serente*. Publications of the Frederick Webb Hodge Anniversary Publications Fund, vol. 4. Los Angeles: The Southwest Museum Administrator of the Fund

    1946. *The Eastern Timbira*. University of California Publications in American Archaeology and Ethnology, volume 41. Berkeley and Los Angeles: The University of California Press

Ortner, Sherry 1984. Theory in anthropology since the sixties. *History and Society*: 126–166

Rabinow, P. 1977. *Reflections on Fieldwork in Morocco*. Berkeley: University of California Press

Rappaport, Roy A. 1979. *Ecology, Meaning, and Religion*. Richmond: North Atlantic Books

Rivière, Peter 1984. *Individual and Society in Guiana*. Cambridge Studies in Anthropology 51. Cambridge: Cambridge University Press

Roseman, Marina 1977. To try and catch the wind: notation of shifting pitch in a Suyá example. Course paper. Xerox

Rowell, Lewis 1983. *Thinking About Music; An Introduction to the Philosophy of Music*. Amherst: The University of Massachusetts Press

Sá, Christina 1982. Aldéia de São Marcos: Transformações na habitação de uma comunidade Xavante. M.A. thesis in History and Archaeology, University of São Paulo

Sahlins, Marshall 1981. *Historical Metaphors and Mythical Realities, Structure in the Early History of the Sandwich Islands Kingdom*. Ann Arbor: University of Michigan Press

Schneider, David M. 1968. *American Kinship: A Cultural Account*. Englewood Cliffs: Prentice Hall

Seeger, Anthony 1973–1986. Deposit of Suyá Materials in the Indiana University Archives of Traditional Music. Accession numbers: 73-097-F; 80-081-F; 85-341-F; 86-316-F

    1979. What can we learn when they sing? Vocal genres of the Suyá Indians of central Brazil. *Ethnomusicology* 23: 373–394

    1980a. Sing for your sister; the structure and performance of Suyá akia. In Herndon, Marcia, and Norma McLeod 1980, pp. 7–43

    1980b. Os Índios e Nós, Estudos sobre Sociedades Tribais Brasileiras. Rio de Janeiro: Editora Campus

    1981. *Nature and Society in Central Brazil: The Suyá Indians of Mato Grosso*. Cambridge: Harvard University Press

    1984. Ten Suyá myths. In Wilbert, Johannes and Karin Simoneau, *Folk Literature of the Gê Indians Volume Two*. Los Angeles: UCLA Latin American Center Publications

    1986. Novos horizontes na classificação dos instrumentos musicais. In Berta G. Ribeiro (ed.) *Suma Etnológica Brasileira: Artesenato e Tecnologia, volume III*. Rio de Janeiro: FINEP e Editora Vozes

Seeger, Anthony and A Comunidade Suyá, 1982. *Música Indígena: A Arte Vocal dos Suyá*. 12-inch long play record and notes. São João del Rei: Tacape (007)

Sherzer, Joel 1979. Strategies in text and context: Cuna *kaa kwento*. In *Journal of American Folklore* 92: 145–164

    1983. *Kuna Ways of Speaking: An Ethnographic Perspective*. Austin: University of Texas Press

Steinen, Karl von den 1942. *O Brasil Central*. São Paulo: Companhia Editora Nacional

Stone, Ruth M. 1982. *Let the Inside Be Sweet: The Interpretation of Music Event among the Kpelle of Liberia*. Bloomington: Indiana University Press

Turner, Terence S. 1966. Social Structure and Political Organization among the Northern Kayapo. Ph.D. Dissertation, Harvard University

1969.Tchikrin: a central Brazilian tribe and its symbolic language of body adornment. *Natural History Magazine* 78 (October 1969): 50–59, 70

1979a. The Gê and Bororo societies as dialectical systems: a general model. In David Maybury-Lewis (ed.), *Dialectical Societies*. Cambridge: Harvard University Press. Pp. 147–178

1979b. Kinship, household, and community structure among the Kayapo. In David Maybury-Lewis (ed.), *Dialectical Societies*. Cambridge: Harvard University Press. Pp. 179–214

Turner, Victor W. 1967. *The Forest of Symbols*. Ithaca: Cornell University Press

1968. *The Ritual Process, Structure and Anti-Structure*. Chicago: Aldine

Urban, Greg 1986. Semiotic Functions of Macro-Parallelism in the Shokleng Origin Myth. In Joel Sherzer and Greg Urban (eds.) *Native South American Discourse*. Berlin: Moulton de Gruyter. Pp. 15–59

Verswijver, Gustaaf 1985. Considerations on Mẽkrãngoti Warfare. Ph.D. Dissertation, Rijksuniversiteit, Gent

Viveiros de Castro, Eduardo B. 1977. Indivíduo e Sociedade no Alto Xingu: Os Yawalapíti. M.A. Dissertation, Museu Nacional/Federal University of Rio de Janeiro

1986. *Araweté: Uma Visão da Cosmologia e da Pessoa Tupi-Guarani*. Rio de Janeiro: Editora Zahar

Index

ANTHONY SEEGER is Professor of Ethnomusicology at UCLA; Director Emeritus of Smithsonian Folkways Recordings; past president of the Society for Ethnomusicology; past president and current secretary general of the International Council for Traditional Music; Fellow of the American Academy of Arts and Sciences; author or editor of four other books and more than fifty articles on anthropological, ethnomusicological, archival, and Indian rights issues.

The University of Illinois Press
is a founding member of the
Association of American University Presses.

University of Illinois Press
1325 South Oak Street
Champaign, IL 61820-6903
www.press.uillinois.edu